Using All the Colors
Life Stories from Monte Vista Grove Homes

Compiled and (slightly) edited by
Anna Walker

To Anna, our facilitator who has encouraged us and has kept us writing the stories we kept telling ourselves we should write someday.

The Writing Class

Foreword

"Detail makes the difference between boring and terrific writing. It's the difference between a pencil sketch and a lush oil painting. As a writer, words are your paint. Use all the colors."

Rhys Alexander

I lead a very happy life: I am married to a wonderfully loving man (who cooks no less!), I have an angel of a little girl, and I live very close to my two incredibly supportive parents and my sister, who is my best friend. But every Thursday my life gets a little bit better, a little bit richer, a little bit fuller.

For every Thursday I drive to Monte Vista Grove Homes in Pasadena, California to "facilitate" a Life Journaling class through the local city college. I say "facilitate", but actually, I am fortunate enough to spend most of the time listening to some of the most incredible stories I have ever heard.

Monte Vista Grove Homes is a community for "retired" Presbyterian ministers and missionaries and their spouses, however, they are anything but retiring: they are vibrant personalities, full of energy and spirit. They travel the world, bike to the beach, volunteer their time in their community, and altogether put me to shame for my idleness.

The stories you will find here are as varied as the people who write them: dogsledding through Alaska; living through an internment camp experience in the Philippines; marching with Martin Luther King Jr. We always said "Wouldn't it be great to put some of these stories together in a book?"

Whether they are writing about their childhoods, relating work adventures, or reflecting on the impact of society, they are taking to heart Alexander's reminder and using all their colors! I feel so blessed to have had this experience and to have met these incredible people... Anna Walker

Table of Contents

Childhood and Early Adulthood

Early Days Before School by Howard Den Hartog	11
Country School Days by Howard Den Hartog	15
Chinese Aspirin by Sherman Fung	20
The Year 1931 by Sherman Fung	23
Newport by Kenneth Grant	27
Yikes, I'm a Seagoing Cowboy! by Robert Lodwick	31
Climbing Mt. St. Helens by Jim Symons	35
The Summer of My Awakening by Gene Terpstra	39
"Don't Bet on It!" by Gene Terpstra	48
Our First Car by K. Roberta Woodberry	51

Occupational Adventures

Memorable Preaching Experiences by Robert Bos	59
Making Visible the Invisible by Jessie Coates	63
A Brush with Death by Dick Dosker	68
Honeymoon on the Bering Sea by Carolyn French	71
Arctic Christmas by Carolyn French	75
The Manse by Mary Froede	77
Off to Corumba by Rosemary Pierson	80
Daily Life in Corumba by Rosemary Pierson	85
Going Into the Mato by Rosemary Pierson	90
Where is Your Home? by Norman E. Thomas	94
What is Your Name? by Norman E. Thomas	97
Going to Egypt by Dorothy Turnbull	100
It's the Taliban! by K. Roberta Woodberry	106

Interesting People and Places

My Friend Jonathan by Carole Bos	113
Celebrity Encounters by Annabelle Dirks	115
You Must Have a Good Mantra by Dick Dosker	117
Met on the Metro by Dick Dosker	120

On Stage at Carnegie Hall NYC by Art French	123
Seasons in Tucumcari by Mary Froede	127
Gastronomic Goodies by Mary Froede	131
Unexpected Visitors by Bill Hansen	133
What Would You Have Expected by Bill Hansen	137
Broken Wings and Lonely Hearts by Hedy Lodwick	139
The Intruder by Robert Lodwick	143
The Kubota Garden by Jim Symons	147
Once is Enough by Gene Terpstra	151
Paulus by K. Roberta Woodberry	153

World War II Memories

Sayings by Thomas Bousman	159
Aboard the Escambia by Kenneth Grant	162
The War Years by Hedy Lodwick	168
The War Years: 1941 -1945 by Robert Lodwick	172
Rosie Reunion by Jacquie Terpstra	175
Minnie's Story by Jacquie Terpstra	178

Noteworthy Events

The King's Visit by Don Hawthorne	185
A Night I Won't Forget by Robert Lodwick	186
The 500 Year Flood Plain by Hedy Lodwick	188
Martin Luther King's Finest Hour by Jim Symons	193
That September Day by Jacquie Terpstra	195

Family Matters

Dreams by Carole Hoffs Bos	207
Two Family Reunions by Bruce Calkins	210
The Lord is My Sheep Herder? by Bruce Calkins	214
Pregnancy and Child Rearing by Carolyn French	216
Chee Gah by Sherman Fung	231
Talking with Mom by Sherman Fung	234
Coffee and Sympathy by Laura Berthold Monteros	237

The Wild Side
    Meeting a Bear on the Trail by Bruce Calkins   241
    Noel by Charles Castles   244
    Arctic Travel: St. Lawrence Island by Art French   246
    Lady of the Night or the Great Escape by Art French   252
    Wildlife in Tucumcari by Mary Froede   256
    The Kindergartener by Bill Hansen   261
    The Gift Horse by Kenneth Grant   263
    Racing Days by Kenneth Grant   266

Remembrances and Musings
    Early Morning Musings by Carole Hoffs Bos   273
    Traffic Tickets by Robert Bos   275
    Walking with My Shadow by Bruce Calkins   279
    Recipes Through Time by Annabelle Dirks   282
    Chinese Rugs by Annabelle Dirks   284
    Laundry in the Arctic by Art French   285
    Operating on Autopilot by Don Hawthorne   288
    Do You Journal? by Laura Berthold Monteros   290
    Swooper or Basher? by Laura Berthold Monteros   293
    Lured of the Rings by Gene Terpstra   296
    News of the Day by Jacquie Terpstra   300
    The Art of the Pie by Jacquie Terpstra   303
    Pasin by Dorothy Turnbull   308

The Next Step
    Old Fiddle by Robert Bos   313
    Never Give Up! by Jim Symons   317

About the Authors

Childhood and Early Adulthood

Using All the Colors

Early Days Before School
Howard Den Hartog

I had a very humble beginning. I was born in a one-story, four room house. The house was first built as a home, then later used as a chicken house. Before my folks could move into it, they had to scrub it down with lye, soap, and water before making it livable. Our home was located approximately one half mile off the main road in Columbia Township, Wapello County, Iowa. Iowa has ninety-nine counties with Ottumwa being the county seat. Many of Iowa's counties and cities have Indian names such as Winnebago, Winneshick, Pottawattamie, Mahaska, and Tama.

We had no running water, electricity, or inside toilet. To get water we had a hand pump located by the kitchen sink. That water was used for washing the dishes and floors, and also for bathing. Bathing was done in a big wash pan. The water was heated in large pans sitting on top of a wood burning stove. Pans with water left in them overnight in the winter would be frozen the next morning. We had no refrigerator, but we had a large root cellar dug out of the ground. It had a large door which you had to lift to open and then walk down four or five steps to the entrance. Things were stored on shelves. This is where were kept our meat, butter, vegetables from the garden, and canned goods (we canned fruits, vegetables, and also meat). Because the cellar was underground, things did not freeze in the winter.

One of my earliest memories was being afraid of the steam engine freight train as it went by our home. The tracks were probably no more than seventy-five to eighty yards away. I was only around three years old at the time. I would be playing in a sand box and when I heard the train coming I would quickly run into the house. I was particularly scared of the loud whistle the engineer blew when he came to the nearby railroad crossing. Every day, besides the freight train going back and forth through the middle of our farm, another train we called a "Doodle Bug" went by twice a day. The Doodle Bug was a one car passenger train. I regret that I never had the experience of riding it. Not only did it haul passengers but also mail and freight. The Doodle Bugs were in existence from the 1920's until World War II or the early 1950's.

Another early memory was having Vicks rubbed on my chest if I had a cold, and then a soft cloth was laid over it so it would not stick to my pajamas. When I had a sore throat or cough, whisky was mixed with honey and used as a cough syrup. Our family doctor was Dr. Traister. When making house calls he use to carry the typical doctor's bag like what you might see in western movies. He also carried medicine with him so you did not need to go to the pharmacy like you do today.

Dr. Traister delivered both my sister, Alta Mae, and me. Alta Mae is almost exactly four years older than I am. My birthday is April 17 and her's is April 19. She and I use to deliver clothes that my mother laundered to a bachelor, Lum Deshield, who lived down the road and over the railroad tracks about a quarter mile away. Every time we crossed the railroad tracks we would put rocks on the rails. We put rocks on one too many times because one time it caused a section car to go off the tracks! I also remember trying to follow her to school one day. It made her cry so I probably only tried it once... I do not remember.

There were several buildings around the house where I was born: an outhouse, a wash house where the washing machine was kept, barn, corn crib, and a chicken house. I was too young to remember, but my mother told me that she and dad use to take me out to the cow barn and sit me in a high chair while they milked the cows. During the winter, when days were short, a kerosene lantern was used for light.

When I was three years old, things changed for the better. Wow... what a change! Our landlord, George Gaass, built for us a new two-story modern house. Downstairs we had a dining room, living room, bedroom, and a good size kitchen with running water, a refrigerator, and an electric stove. Good-bye to the wood burning stove for heat, cooking, and hot water! Now we also had electric lights. The upstairs had three bedrooms and a bathroom with a sink and bathtub. No more baths using a wash tub. We had a full basement with a furnace which provided central heat. It used coal for fuel. We also had a hot water heater with a small stove connected to it. In the summer we had to fire it up in order to take a hot bath. We usually used corn cobs to get the fire going. Water pipes ran through the regular furnace used for heat so in the fall, winter, and spring we always had hot water.

Me standing in front of the old wash house

I have faint memories of when our new home was built. In order to dig out the basement one or two horses were used to pull a tumbling bug. The tumbling bug had two handles on the back like a wheelbarrow. A person who walked behind would tilt it so dirt could be scooped out of the ground and hauled away. Today backhoes are used to do the same thing, only a back-hoe can do the job much more quickly and easily.

I also remember the plastering of the walls. Wall board was not used like we have today. Instead, plaster laths were nailed on first over the 2 X 4's. The plaster laths were around four feet long, one and a half inch wide, and a quarter inch thick. There was a half inch space between each lath. The plaster was mixed in a large wooden trough approximately seven feet long and three feet wide. The plaster was applied on the walls with wooden trowels. The walls were so slick and smooth. The men who did the work were marvelous skilled craftsmen.

We only lived in this new home a couple of years and then we moved to what was called the "Main Place" about a mile away. Our hired man then moved into our new home. Near our second home is where all the main farm buildings were located. This is where I lived for the next sixteen years until I graduated from college and got married, and where I really called "Home."

Country School Days
Howard Den Hartog

One of my cherished childhood memories growing up was attending a country school called the Brown School. I don't know why it was called that because it was always painted white! A small meandering creek ran past the school called Brown Creek. The name probably stems from an early settler named Brown, who knows.

Brown School was located in Columbia Township, Wapello County, Iowa. Wapello County has fourteen townships. Each township was the base of support for the county schools. Brown School operated from 1902-1949. According to the Historical Society, at one time there were 106 schools in Wapello County.

My first morning going to school was actually not a happy experience. We lived approximately one and a half to two miles from school. My mother drove me to school the first two days. When it was time to get out of the car, I began to cry and cry. The teacher, La Rue Long, told my mother, "Alice, he will be okay," and my mom drove off. The same episode happened the second day, but by the third day I walked with my sister, Alta Mae, who was four years older, and from then on everything was fine. I attended the Brown School from kindergarden through seventh grade. Then the school was closed. I attended eighth grade in our home town of Eddyville, Iowa which was three miles away. This time a school bus picked us up.

I was five years old in 1942 when I began attending school. At the time we were in the mist of World War II. Not only was Miss Long our teacher, she was also the janitor. When it became cold she had to fire up the large heating stove in the back of the room and then carry out the ashes every morning before firing it up again.

Using All the Colors

The first agenda of the day was the Pledge of Alliance. In the spring and fall of the year we would gather in a circle outside the school house and repeat the Pledge of Alliance. If it began to rain during the day someone would always rush outside and bring the flag in so it would not get wet.

The kids in my class-I am on the right

After the pledge, we would all go inside, line up in a long line, and then march to our desks. Our desks were wood with a cast-iron frame. Music was the first thing we did in the morning. We had no piano; we use a hand-cranked phonograph which played 78 RPM records. We had a record for every song in our music book so we sang along with with the music.

If my memory serves me correctly, we had reading and phonics, penmanship, science, and arithmetic in the mornings, and history, geography, language, and spelling in the afternoons.

We had a long wooden bench in front of the student desks where we would sit for our classes. Each class was approximately five to ten minutes long. We would discuss and correct our assignments from the previous day and then go back to our desks and work on our assignments for the next day. We never had any homework to take home. It was all done at school.

Our school day was from 9:00-4:00. We had recess from 10:15-10:30 in the mornings and from 3:00-3:15 in the afternoons. Noon hour was 12:00-1:00. Everyone brought their own lunch to school except the last couple of years when the parents would take turns bringing a hot meal for everyone two to three times per week. These meals were usually some kind of casserole. I do not recall how we washed the dishes as we had no running water. The students took turns carrying the drinking water to school from a neighbor approximately 150 to 200 yards away. I also remember we had outdoor toilets, one for the boys and one for the girls.

The most fun parts of the school day were recesses and the noon hour. In the fall and spring we would play Annie, Annie, Over, Hopscotch, Softball, or Kick the Wicket. In the winter, Fox & Geese was fun when there was snow on the ground or we might go sledding on a good hill just across the creek from the school house. The hill was in a pasture on the farm where I lived. If it was raining or really cold (zero or below) we would stay inside and play games. Button, Button, Where's the Button was always fun. We also played Hangman or Tic-Tac-Toe on the blackboard made of slate. Another fun game was similar to bowling with wooden balls. We would roll the balls to a round tin tray which had indentations in it. To win you had to have the highest score. I made one of these for my grandson, Romero when he was four or five years old.

Another great memory of the country school was either a Thanksgiving or Christmas program. These programs were held in the evenings. We learned parts for plays or memorized poems (we called them "pieces"). As we had no electricity, I believe we had four two-mantle kerosene lamps hanging from the ceiling for light.

Using All the Colors

Parents, as well as people from the community, would attend. After the program we played bingo, had refreshments the parents had brought, and then went home. For a few years, Lawrence and Mary Van Zante, the parents of four of my classmates, donated a live turkey as a fundraiser. We sold raffle tickets for something like 25 cents each. Money raised was used to buy program plays, library books, school materials, etc.

Before the school year began, we went to the county court house in Ottumwa to get our school books for the coming year. This was an exciting time of the year as I always looked forward to the beginning of a new school year. School usually began the week before Labor Day. We had Labor Day and Thanksgiving off. We went to school the Friday after Thanksgiving. We had only a week off for Christmas and New Years Day off and no spring break. Around March 15th we had an afternoon off. That's when the farmers, usually parents of the students, got together to decide if they would hire the teacher for the next year.

In my seven years of attending country school I had three teachers; La Rue Long, Rosemary Johnson, and Alice Lambert. I liked all of my teachers, but probably my favorite was Rosemary Johnson. She was very nice and pleasant and always had a sweet smile. She also happened to be my Sunday School teacher. She had five brothers who served in World War II and returned home safely.

In my second year of school I had a first cousin, Wilma, as a practice teacher for six weeks. In those days a senior in high school who desired to be a teacher would practice teaching in the spring, take a "normal course", pass a state test, and then begin teaching in the fall. After three years of teaching, they were required to take a six-week summer course in college to continue teaching. In 1943 Wilma began teaching in a country school for $125.00 per month.

In the southwest corner of the school yard stood a small grove of trees. Underneath the trees Kentucky blue grass grew and scattered among the grass you could find beautiful clumps of wild violets. When I was around five or six years old I picked my first bouquet of violets and gave them to my mother on Mother's Day. I continued this tradition of giving my mother a bouquet of violets every year until I got married.

Chinese "Aspirin"
Sherman Fung

As far back as I can remember our family used aspirin. Whether the brand was Bayer or something else, we believed that the whitish pill would give us almost instant relief from headaches. We also believed that it would ease, if not remove altogether, minor body pain. While our family acted on such beliefs, we would also resort to Chinese herbs for such common ailments as colds, sore throats, indigestion, and hives. To cure an ailment my father or mother would take us to an herb shop in the heart of San Francisco Chinatown.

The front part of the shop was a large, longish room whose walls were lined with built-in wooden drawers that were stacked high. Some of them were higher than the ordinary reach of the clerks and required a stool or ladder to reach. In these drawers were stored all sorts of ingredients for boiling the medicinal tea or soup. Most were roots, seeds, leaves and other parts of plants. Some were insects or their discarded shells, dried parts of animals, powder of various kinds, and who knows what. The clerks knew where each ingredient was stored.

The back portion of the shop was an alcove type of space where the customer would consult a Chinese "doctor". First, my father or mother described the condition to be treated. Then the "doctor" would inspect my tongue and my eyes. Putting his two forefingers across the underside of my wrist, he would carefully take my pulse. This might be followed with some questions. Then, using the brush and ink pad laid out on the table where he was sitting, he would write out a prescription, that is, a list of herbal substances and the amount of each. The handwriting looked as undecipherable to the lay person as modern day prescriptions written by some western doctors. Only this was in Chinese calligraphy, a script called "grass pen".

I don't remember that we ever paid the "doctor". What we paid for the herbs must have covered his consultation. He was the proprietor of the shop. We knew some of his children who went to the same Chinese school where we kids went. I often wonder what happened to that shop and whether or not it was taken over by one of his sons.

While we waited for a clerk to finish assembling all the items in the prescription, I sometimes would watch another clerk working a chopper or slicer. The "machine" consisted of a wooden frame base, on top of which was mounted a huge cleaver shaped metal blade. The clerk would place a thick root or plant stem or hold a bunch of material under the up-raised blade. Then he would pull down the wooden handle that stuck out from one end of the blade, cutting his material in much the same way an office worker today operates a manual paper cutter. I often thought to myself: *If his finger gets in the way, there will be a very nasty cut. What will they do with the herbs spotted with his blood?* Another instrument the clerks regularly used was a scale to measure the amounts of the ingredients. It was a hand held balance type of device. A smooth wooden stick hung from the clerk's grasp. A small shallow pan hung from one end of the stick and a small weight hung further down the stick. The pan held the ingredient to be measured. The clerk would move the weight back and forth along the stick to determine the amount he wanted. If the pan dipped, the clerk would remove a bit of the substance. If the stick favored the weight side, he would sprinkle a little more in the pan until a balance was achieved. I admired the skill of the clerk. This instrument depended on the "touch" of the clerk, in contrast to the modern sensitive scale with its fine calibration.

Sometimes we did not need a consultation or a prescription. The herb shop had already made up remedies for common ailments. All we needed to do was to ask the clerk for the "tea" that is good for, for example, a sore throat. Such "off the shelf" items were a convenience for the shop as well as for the customer. For us

Using All the Colors

American-born Chinese, herbal aspirin stood on a par with Bayer from the drugstore shelves. Now as much as the years have led us to greater assimilation into the majority culture of America, Chinese herbs are still even with Bayer on the balance scale.

The Year 1931
Sherman Fung

In 1931, I was five years old, turning six in August. I must confess that I do not remember much from those early days. Moreover, regarding what I will say that I remember, I must qualify it with the caveat that it is not with much accuracy I pinpoint the events to a particular time.

Last week I came across an issue of "Reminisce". Some of its pages helped jog my memory of my early years, so it is against their content that I now relate what I do remember of 1931.

I don't remember people being forced to sell apples on the streets of San Francisco nor do I remember the adverse effects of the Great Depression. Certainly at home we always had something to eat. At that early age rice was the main staple of our family. Bread was incidental though milk was considered a necessity in our household. Mother must have gone along with the prevailing American practice in regard to feeding infants and youngsters.

When we ate rice—that is, Chinese food—sometimes mother would put an inch of water in the rice pot after all the cooked rice was eaten up and then boil it. This was to soften up the hard crust at the bottom, to make it easier to eat. Usually we did not do this out of frugality; we did this when we had miscalculated the appetite of the people around the meal table. Making more rice would have involved too long a wait. It was much easier to soften the crust at the bottom of the pot and offer that to those who wanted more. Mother, however, used to say condescendingly, "The Fourth Dialect people habitually do this. We Third Dialect people don't." I can understand why she thought so. In China, she grew up in a relatively well-off home where servants looked after the comfort of the master's family. Of course, at meal times the family ate first. The servants ate afterwards and most likely the leftovers,

Using All the Colors

including the softened crust from the bottom of the cooking pot if the situation required.

In those early years we were too young to be given pocket money. Even if we weren't, I doubt the times would have permitted such a practice. My father had a job that apparently provided for our basic needs, not much beyond.

This did not mean we were without entertainment. We heard Bing Crosby croon, "Where the Blues of the Night Meet the Gold of the Day," on the radio. I remember other popular songs sung and played on the receiver set: "Between the Devil and the Deep Blue Sea," and "Lady of Spain." Those who understood English enjoyed weekly programs such as "The Eddie Cantor Show", and we kids eagerly followed episode after episode of "Little Orphan Annie".

If we went out, "The March of Times" was a regular filler at Acme Theater, just on the western edge of Chinatown. This movie house, near the corner of Stockton and Broadway, had a reputation of being a "flea house". In spite of this, we kids regularly patronized it, perhaps not when I was five and six but certainly by eight years old. Of course I went with my older brother, Bob. The attraction of this place was the habitual showing of serial movies such as the Flash Gordon adventure fantasies, the Tom Mix westerns, and various bad-guy vs. good-guy conflicts. Sometime or other the antics of Charlie Chaplain in the now classic "City Lights" entertained us innocent children. Another thing in the flea house's favor was the price: five or ten cents. Either here or in another movie theater named Verdi we passed many Saturdays looking at the black and white screen figures: Wallace Berry, Jackie Cooper, Boris Karloff, James Cagney and Jean Harlow playing various roles, or the Marx Brothers fooling around.

In the area of sports we youngsters could not escape the exploits of baseball figures such as Babe Ruth and Lou Gerig or the changing boxing championship of people such as Max Schmeling.

Football was also a popular sport, but none of the prominent figures in that sport made an impression on my memory.

My brother, Bob, and I playing cowboy and Indian

As for what we kids did for fun, our toys were simple, at least more simple than those of today. Instead of texting our friends, we punched holes in tin cans, connected them with lengths of string and pretended that we were communicating with whoever was on the other end of the contraption. An iPod or MP3 player makes it possible for today's youth to carry around their music wherever they go. In earlier days, listening to music was done through the home-bound radio and the stationary Victrola. One portable toy that "trained" our young eye/muscle coordination then was the paddle ball—a small rubber ball attached to a wooden paddle that resembled a ping-pong paddle. The long attaching rubber string allowed us to aim our upward and outward strokes so as to hit the ball, let the string jerk it back toward the paddle. Then we could hit the ball again and again to rack up a competitive score. Nowadays, a kid plays video games on a laptop, a notebook or a Netbook, honing his reflects by hitting humanoid images flittering around on the small electronic screen.

Though it was not a tradition in our family to buy books, we kids went to the public library a lot. We enjoyed browsing the shelves of children materials. We thought carrying home all those books in our arms, without having to pay for them, was a great thing. Books helped us pretend and we certainly did a lot of that. Dad saw the potential of a cowboy/Indian outfit. There is a photo of this on the previous page. I am on the left wearing a crown of feathers. My older brother Bob is wearing the cowboy part of the costume package.

Newport

Kenneth Grant

He was ten, with a healthy scattering of freckles across a face that featured a button nose and green eyes that hinted at the boyish imagination that lay behind them. This was topped by a tassel of red hair that refused to stay combed the majority of the time. And today he was excited... Grandmother Grant was visiting! While that was not unusual in itself, today was different. Any minute now, friends were coming by to pick her up and take her with them to the beach. And this was exciting. I remember well, for the boy was me.

I was on the front porch of our house, the one on Ard Evin in Glendale, and I was waiting... waiting for the Howells, old friends of Grandma's from her years in Leadville, Colorado. They were due any minute!

Then, it happened. Two aging autos pulled up, square and box-like as old cars were, their color a dull black, or maybe it was a green or grey (time has a way of blurring things). On top of the lead car was a large mattress and every indication suggested a maximum load of all sorts of useful things. I was fascinated, and stared as Mr. Howell approached the porch, paused, and smiled down at me. Mom and Grandma came to the door and warm greetings were exchanged. "Ready to go Margaret?" Mr. Howell asked. And then, the amazing, the unthinkable happened. Looking down at me and smiling from his adult height he ruffled my already ruffled hair and said, "Would you like to come too, Kenneth?"

It took only a split second for the realization to set in before I began jumping for incredible joy! The prospect! The adventure! The whole world had suddenly opened before my eyes and I was near delirious with joy. Looking at my mother only a bit anxiously I saw the look of approval in her eyes and was reassured. It took only a few minutes to get some things together (for the stay was to last for

Using All the Colors

several days) and I was somehow squeezed into one of the ancient cars with the rest of the Howell family... we were off.

It was long before freeways which would not come for decades. Our route took us along Telegraph Road and other arteries, many of them two lane, and as I look back now we must have traveled through a good deal of farm land, long since transformed into the sprawling suburbs and stylish businesses districts of Orange County. The journey continued at comfortable speeds that would seem like a crawl to me now until we at last approached the ocean. I was no stranger to the beach, for my father had often taken us to Santa Monica where I had played in the sand and splashed in the edge of the Pacific. Yet there was no end to the magic for me. The sight of the sea, the scent of salt air, the cry of circling gulls and the crash of the surf, all were pure wonder and joy. And now, we were approaching it all again, and I was to spend several days at someplace called Newport Bay... a place at the beach!

We arrived, at last, at the "Nineteenth Street Camp Ground" which bordered the bay. Mr. Howell pulled up beside a bay front lot and began to unload, Mrs. Howell helping, as did the older Howell boys. Gordon, my age, and I assisted in whatever way we were asked. And while I cannot begin to recall all that must have been involved, I do remember one detail.

Before erecting the large, homemade tent, the sand must be prepared. Using a garden rake, the sand was leveled and smoothed. Then, flattened cardboard boxes (part of the cargo of the cars) were spread over the sand to the dimensions of the tent. Over this, now relatively smooth, surface were laid some ancient rugs which, I soon learned, were to be kept swept and free from sand! To insure this detail, a bucket of fresh salt water was kept at the entrance to the then-erected tent so that bare feet could be dunked and sand removed before entering! The "foot bucket" was a detail not to be overlooked!

The warm sun shown, and I was as close to Heaven as a small boy could possibly be. Bare footed, fancy free, my friend Gordon

Childhood and Early Adulthood

for companionship, I was given free range... not only of the rather extensive camp ground and its many other tents, but the "little dock" nearby. Here the live bait boats discharged their daily cargo of sport fishermen, their bulging burlap bags full of fish caught during the day somewhere far out at sea. It was from these boats that Gordon and I scavenged live bait, which we used on our fishing adventures around the bay, all done from the "Nellie S".

Mr. Howell was an old hand at camping at Newport where, I am told, he reserved a bay front lot each year and took the family down to stay for extended periods as circumstances allowed. He was a carpenter by trade, though he and Mrs. Howell managed the aging court where they lived, on shaded Acacia Street in Glendale. His trade allowed him to build a small boat for use in the Bay. The "Nellie S", which he named after his wife, was about ten feet long and pointed at each end. About a foot at bow and stern was given over to a built-in air chamber which kept the boat from sinking even when full of water...and two small boys! Gordon and I explored every nook and cranny of the bay in the Nellie S and our adventures would take more than this brief report to describe.

The little burg that was then the town of Newport Beach was just a block away, situated on the ocean side of the peninsula and baking in the hot California sun. Its sturdy pier of weather beaten planks was the clear focus of the town and was usually lined with fishermen and women, patiently baiting hooks, intently watching lines, and waiting for a sign that a fish was toying with their bait somewhere down in the crystal blue-green sea.

One detail I will relate about that aging pier has to do with patches. Some of the thick planks which formed the surface of the pier had large knots in them. These dried out and shrank over years of exposure to the blazing Southern California sun. Eventually, they simply fell out into the ocean beneath and a sheet metal patch was nailed over the hole. That was well and good. However, when a barefoot boy with white zinc oxide on his freckled nose and a celluloid visor on his tasseled red hair carelessly stepped on one of those sun heated patches, there was a loud yelp and a quick leap off the spot! Nevertheless, nothing could rob the pier of its magic. The circling gulls and their cries, and the blue shadows of fish far below in the constantly surging blue water beneath, all were part of the magic of the Newport Pier to a small boy, many years ago.

There are countless other things I remember about what was undoubtedly my childhood's most magical place. I recall the dory men, who kept their boats pulled up on the sand beside the pier, as they do today, selling the fish they caught on set-lines left over night in the ocean. On the bay side, there was the going and coming of the live bait boats that we came to know by name (the "Maude" and the "Tillicum" were two I recall). We also knew the hours at which to expect to see them coming up the bay from their trips out at sea with a deck load of sport fishermen. I remember seeing the occasional yacht (the bay is full of them now) and the mysterious "mud flats" with their coating of green sea grass rising above the water in the middle of the bay at low tide, disappearing when the tide came in. Only we "old folks" remember them for they were dredged away many years ago. Of course there was the other side of the bay which, as we looked across from our tent, revealed Lido Isle, now an up-scale neighborhood of tightly clustered beach homes but then, only a long stretch of low sand with a lonely house or two along a single road that ran the length.

The memories abound, and will go with me to the grave. I shall forever be grateful for the day the Howells came by to pick up Grandma to take her with them for a stay at Newport Bay, and invited one, ecstatic little boy to go along!

Yikes, I'm a Seagoing Cowboy!
Robert Lodwick

In 1945, as the war was ending, I turned 17 just before graduating from Hughes High School in Cincinnati. The following week, I simply crossed the street and enrolled at the University of Cincinnati.

During my freshman year, I became active in the University YMCA. There I saw a notice that the Church of the Brethren Service Committee was looking for a record number of cattle handlers to care for the heifers they were sending to war-torn Europe. It sounded interesting, but that certainly was not my cup of tea.

Just after the spring term ended, my father told me that he read in the Cincinnati Enquirer that the Church of the Brethren was looking for "cattle handlers" or in the vernacular, "seagoing cowboys" to work on the UNRRA relief ships. I told my father that I knew of the program, but didn't bother to even broach the subject "Since I knew you wouldn't let me go."

That was the wrong thing to say! A telegram went the next morning to the Brethren in Norfolk, VA saying in effect, "Here am I, use me!" I was sure it was too late so thought no more about it. Twelve days later I received a telegram to be in Norfolk by Friday to get shots and on Monday board the SS Mount Whitney. "Uh oh" I didn't have the courage to back out. It was a whirlwind to get a train ticket and other things I might need on this adventure which really hadn't been my idea. When I got on the train, the full impact of what I was about to do began to hit me. As I listened to the click, clack of the wheels on the train, I kept rhythm with them, asking myself, "What are you doing? Why are you doing this?" I didn't sleep a wink sitting up on the train that night and frankly I was scared because I knew I was the furthest thing from a cowboy as one could be.

Using All the Colors

I was shocked when I reached the Brethren headquarters to learn that there were no heifers being loaded on our ship. Rather our cargo was 1502 horses on their way to Poland. Well horses were better than cows, I guess. At least I knew how to shovel manure since my father raised Arabian horses as a hobby but that was never a preferred task. I'm really not an "animal person." Nevertheless, when I saw the horses, I was taken aback. They were no Arabians, but what we would call "old nags" who had long passed their prime and should be put out to pasture. I was ashamed that these were our gifts to war-torn Europe!

My Merchant Mariner's card

The SS Mount Whitney was a giant transport ship, the largest of any of the ships leased by UNRRA. Our duties were to feed, water, and care for approximately 25 animals per attendant. We didn't have enough "cowboys" so we each had some 30 horses in our charge. The 438 tons of hay was at the very bottom of the ship along with 45 tons of oats and 1600 pounds of salt. We had a pulley system to pull up the bales of hay each day.

Our day started at 5:30 in the morning. For 30 horses that meant pulling up many bales which meant many sore muscles the first few days. Sometimes a horse would try to bite one's shoulder

Childhood and Early Adulthood

so after a couple of "ouches", I learned to be very careful. We each had to carry 30 buckets of water as well. Try that when the ship is sailing in rough seas. No Thanks. Of the 1502 horses, 7 died aboard ship and were unceremoniously thrown overboard to feed the fish. We also had to keep the horses standing at all times. On a ship, cows can lie down but horses can not.

Our ship was too large to go through the Kiel Canal so we went north around Scotland and through the North Sea. Our list of duties hadn't told us that in the North Sea, we also had to take turns to stand watch on the deck, looking for floating mines left by the German submarines. Now that was more scary, especially if you had a night watch. Luckily, we didn't encounter any mines.

Arriving in Gdynia, the port for Danzig, Polish workers came aboard to unload our horsy cargo. We had about four days of shore leave to wander the ruins of these two cities. Our sailing papers from the Church of the Brethren said, "We cannot approve of unchristian practices in port such as drinking, black market, etc." Well, the Communists had already taken over the Polish government and Moscow was calling the shots. No one seemed willing or wanted to take dollars. The currency was American cigarettes. A simple pack was enough to purchase a meal, two packs to purchase something in the flea market. We wondered how people lived when so much in the two cities had been bombed, with rubble still most everywhere. I saw, and felt, the devastation of war first-hand, and it left an indelible impression on my mind.

Another surprise... near the end of our shore leave, we learned that our ship was not returning to Newport Beach, VA, but was ordered to go to Iceland to pick up 2000 Icelandic ponies to work in the Polish coal mines. OHHHHHHH! So I might not be back in time for the coming semester at the University. I panicked until one of my new friends on the SS Mount Whitney said, "Bob, relax. As Mark Twain said, 'Never let your schooling interfere with your education.'"

Using All the Colors

Wow! What great wisdom. I relaxed as Icelandic ponies brought closure to this unique experience for this city boy's first real adventure away from home.

Childhood and Early Adulthood

Climbing Mt. St. Helens
Jim Symons

Every human being is called by God into life. For some of us, that calling leads to Christian ministry in the church. But prior to that particular call to ministry is a sense that we are chosen by God for life. Here is one of my key experiences of that calling.

The Cascade Mountains divide the State of Washington from north to south, and include some of the nation's most spectacular peaks—Mt. Baker, just south of Canada; Glacier Peak; Mt. Rainier, with the largest glacier system in the lower 48; and, north of the Oregon border, Mt. Adams and Mt. St. Helens. In 1980 Mt. St. Helens blew its top off, leaving a volcanic stump that was a mere shadow of its former self, fully 1300 feet lower than its previous height of 9665 feet above sea level. My story is about the mountain long before the eruption, a time when it thrust its symmetrical peak high into the atmosphere above the coastal plain, reminiscent of the dramatic contours of Mt Fujiyama in Japan.

I had just celebrated my sixteenth birthday, and I wanted to do something special. I approached two of my best friends, Tom Winter and Bill Douglas, and suggested that we climb a mountain. Most of our previous hiking and climbing had been in the Olympic National Park across Puget Sound, west of our homes in Seattle. The mountains there are lower than those in the Cascades, so I suggested we climb what I considered the most beautiful of Washington's peaks, Mt. St. Helens.

We left Seattle after school late on a Friday afternoon in June of 1950, driving two hours south on U.S. Highway 99 toward Portland. The three of us had grown up together in the Boy Scouts and had learned how to carry the minimum of clothing and food so our packs would not be too heavy. While Mt. St. Helens was not particularly challenging in terms of technical difficulty, it did require that we carry first aid and other supplies for emergencies in alpine conditions, a climbing rope, and ice axes. I always liked hiking with Bill, because he had the best trail mix I had ever eaten, and it would taste specially good on the summit. We drove into the Spirit Lake parking lot on the northern slope of the mountain an hour before dark, and we could see the towering peak hovering over us.

Mt. St. Helens, before she blew her top

Our plan was to camp at the edge of the tree line at 4800 feet. We had four miles to hike, carrying packs that were relatively heavy because of our climbing gear, going up a trail that would climb over a thousand vertical feet above the lake. We made it in less than an hour, the fastest four miles I have ever walked in my life. Our camp was in the last grove of trees before emerging on the open mountainside. I threw my pack down and felt a sudden weightlessness, as if my body was floating in air. The view of the mountain was hidden by a low ridge a short distance from our camp. I wanted to view the peak before the sun settled below the western horizon, so I scrambled up the ridge and emerged at the top to see... to <u>really</u> see in a way that I had not seen before.

The top of Mt. St. Helens was now shrouded in clouds that filled me with a sense of mystery. What were they hiding? Creeping out from under those mysterious clouds were five long fingers of snow, stretching down into the deep basin that opened below me. The sun was low on the horizon, beneath the clouds, and the snow reflected the orange and pink of the sunset. The vastness of the huge basin seemed to draw me in so that I was not Jim, watching this magnificent scene from my perch on the ridge, but I became one with the clouds, the sun, and the fingers of snow drawing me into the basin How long did I experience this epiphany? It could have been seconds, or several minutes, but time could not measure or hold this experience, because I was in touch with something timeless. I knew that my life was changed. At Westminster Presbyterian Church in Seattle I had learned about God in the Bible, studied Christian beliefs, and read about the Holy Spirit. Now, for the first time, I knew God—I experienced the spirit connecting me to the *All*.

When I came down from the ridge, Tom and Bill were already preparing dinner. I could not find words to describe what had happened to me. We ate our meal and climbed into our sleeping bags because we would be up at 4:00 AM to begin our climb. At 2:00 AM we were awakened by the sound of over 50 climbers from Portland whose flashlights were guiding them up the mountain track. They had left Spirit Lake at midnight, and we thought it a strange way to climb a mountain.

We got up at 4:00 AM, ate breakfast in the dark, and began climbing as the first rays of sunlight crept over the eastern horizon. We caught up with the climbers from Portland before 7:00 AM— they seemed to be bogged down at the edge of a giant snow field. We roped up and began our long climb in the snow, zig-zagging our way toward the top. By 9:00 AM we were on the summit on a crisp, cloudless day. Mt. Adams seemed a stone's throw away, and Rainier, Glacier Peak, Oregon's Mt. Hood—all were crystal clear in the morning sunshine. We signed the register on the summit, enjoyed some of Bill's trail mix, and prepared to descend.

Using All the Colors

Each of us had brought a piece of plastic we could sit on. Below us stretched a smooth and steep snow field that dropped almost 2000 feet, and we could see nothing that would stop us. Sitting on our plastic and holding our ice axes in case we needed an emergency stop, we began our glacade down the mountain. Faster and faster we went until the wind was whistling past our ears. Talk about pure FUN! What had taken us over two hours to climb that morning was covered in a matter of seconds. It was the most exhilarating experience of my life!

We were back in our camp shortly after noon. We packed our gear and hiked out to Spirit Lake in a leisurely fashion compared to the previous day when we pushed ourselves so hard in the opposite direction. The drive home seemed to take no time at all as we shared stories, laughs, and plans for future adventures.

Later I reflected on those moments on the ridge above the vast basin, when time stood still and I discovered a new dimension of myself in the presence of God. I knew that I had reached a turning point in my life. Something had awakened in me, and I would spend the rest of my life discerning what it was and where it would lead.

The Summer of My Awakening
Gene Terpstra

When I was nine years old, our family spent the summer camping at Lake Michigan. It was 1943, the height of World War II. The camping was not a vacation, but a three-month relocation from our home in Grand Rapids.

My father, a barber by trade, had taken a job at Continental Motors in Muskegon, what we called then a "defense plant." Continental Motors normally made truck engines, but after the United States entered the war the plant converted to making engines for army tanks. For 1942 and 1943 alone, President Roosevelt set a production goal of 120,000 new tanks. Continental Motors played a significant role in this production, with full employment around the clock. The factory work paid well, and frequent overtime hours gave our family a significant increase in income over my father's meager earnings as a barber through the years of the Great Depression.

The downside of my father's new job was commuting between Grand Rapids and Muskegon, a 40-mile trip on a two-lane road, often made in early morning or late at night.

He was always home on Sundays and occasionally on a weekday, but he rented a room in Muskegon so he wouldn't have to make the round trip every day. To ameliorate his spartan and lonely circumstances, my father arranged for the family to spend the summer months with him in Muskegon. We did move for the summer of 1943: my mother, two sisters, two brothers and me, ranging in ages from seven to sixteen, joined later by a sixteen year-old cousin. We lived in two tents at Pere Marquette Park, along with many other families in tents and trailers.

Our immediate neighbors were a Polish couple with a new baby. Spending the summer next door to people who were Polish and Catholic was a new experience for me. In Grand Rapids, our neighborhood and church were almost exclusively Dutch and

Using All the Colors

Protestant. I don't remember the name of our summer neighbors, but they had a friendly Chow dog named "Machiko". My mother was not an animal lover, so having Machiko living only a few feet away for three months was as close as I ever got to having my own dog. That's probably why I remember his name instead of the neighbor's. The mother was a plump woman, smiling and friendly. One time she gave me a whole navel orange, a rare treat for me. In our family, we had navel oranges only as dessert after Sunday dinner, along with half of a Mound bar. Being given a whole orange by this new neighbor surprised and pleased me, and I thanked her with genuine appreciation. She replied, "You're welcome, I'm sure." Her adding "I'm sure" to the usual "You're welcome" was new to me, and it impressed me as both elegant and gracious.

Soon after we set up our tents I met Scottie, a boy whose family lived in a nearby trailer. We were inseparable that summer, Tom Sawyer and Huckleberry Finn roaming the park and beach all day and experiencing numerous adventures and misadventures. We went barefoot, wearing nothing but our bathing suits, the rest of our bodies turning an ever deeper tan as the weeks went by. At the same time, the constant sun bleached our hair and eyebrows. Our normally white skin and brown hair became brown skin and white hair, so that we would have been virtually unrecognizable to the school friends we had left in June.

One spot we visited periodically was the channel for ships traveling back and forth between Lake Michigan and the port. We stood on the concrete wall of the channel and waved to the men on the decks of the huge cargo ships. Almost invariably they waved back, cementing our silent bond with these romantic strangers.

Backing the channel walls for several yards were chunks of broken concrete. Anyone wanting to reach the channel wall itself—which we always did—had to cross this challenging terrain. One day we got the idea of dropping pieces of this concrete in the channel. The only thing in our mind was the anticipation of hearing the kuh-sploosh and seeing the water shoot into the air—much the same motive that makes teenage boys do "cannonballs" in crowded swimming pools. Scottie and I had each dropped in one or two chunks of concrete when we were transfixed by a thunderous voice from heaven. Instead of asking, "Why are you persecuting me?", it said, "Boys, stop that!" The voice actually came from the attendant of the lighthouse on the channel, shouting through a megaphone. But whether it was God or man, there was no doubt about the authority in the voice. Scottie was holding a chunk of concrete, ready to drop it in the channel. He dropped it immediately, but not in the channel. It fell right on my big toe. Blood spurted and I screamed. In fear and trembling we scrambled over the broken concrete and ran home, with me wailing at the top of my voice and hobbling on the heel of my right foot to spare my wounded toe. It was smashed but apparently not broken; I don't remember ever going to the doctor about it. My mother cleaned and bandaged it, and for weeks I ran around with dirty bandages on my toe.

The park was crowded with tents and trailers that summer. More than just vacationers, I think many of the campers—like my father—had come to Muskegon to work in the defense plants. In addition to the parents-with-children families of our home neighborhoods, the campers included a variety of households new to us: individuals living alone, men living together, young women living together, and, especially fascinating to Scottie and me, young men and women of dubious marital status living together.

One day we saw two young men setting up a tent, their motorcycles parked nearby. Their bikes and their independent existence were exciting to us, and we hung around to talk with them. A couple days later there were two young women with them, dressed in jeans and shirts rather than the skirts and blouses my sisters wore. More striking than their clothes, though, were their fingernails: they were painted bright green. My sisters weren't allowed to wear any fingernail polish (which church folk disparagingly called "barn paint"), let alone such an outlandish color. Scottie and I were amazed—and amused. We stood around

Using All the Colors

and said things to each other like, "greenhouse", and then we would laugh. Then the other would say something like "green grass", and we'd laugh again. After a minute or two of this, one of the girls said, "I bet you boys have never seen green nail polish before, have you?" I said, "Sure we have, lots of times." And Scottie added, "We weren't talking about you." My transparent youthful lie would be as unconvincing today. I can count on the fingers of one hand the times in my life I have seen someone wearing green nail polish.

Movies were not acceptable entertainment in my family or church. The only films we could see were "Christian" films, like those made by Billy Graham, or the science films ("God of Creation" and "God of the Atom") made by Moody Bible Institute. Travelogs were acceptable, too. But I saw my first real Hollywood movie that summer. The park would show a film for campers one evening a week. It was shown outside after dark. I don't know how I happened to see it. Maybe my mother and siblings didn't know I was there. I saw it with Scottie, but I don't remember anyone else in my family being there.

The movie was a comedy about someone on a ship. The star was Joe E. Brown, a Jerry Lewis type of pratfall comedian. I can recall only one scene from the movie: Joe E. Brown's character was in a room on a ship that ran into rough seas. The room had two portholes that burst open alternately, letting water pour in. Joe E. Brown rushed frantically back and forth between the portholes, slamming the covers shut, only to have each burst open again as soon as he ran to the other one. Of course, through all this the water kept rising in the room. Scottie was terrified by this scene. He put his hands over his face and said pleadingly to me, "Let's not watch!" I obligingly put my hands over my face, too, but I kept looking, peeking between my fingers while Scottie whimpered next to me. I don't know why I didn't share Scottie's fear. Maybe I realized it was a comedy. More likely, I knew this was a real movie —the first one of my life—and I didn't want to miss any of it (by the way, Joe E. Brown and Scottie both survived the ordeal).

Childhood and Early Adulthood

Just before our summer of camping I was given a copy of *Little Men* for my birthday. It was one of the few personal possessions I had that summer and I showed it to Scottie soon after meeting him. He wanted to read it and I let him borrow it. I don't think he ever did read it (nor did I) and he never returned it, but the title was an apt description of our pretensions in the summer's most memorable misadventure. Scottie and I took up—literally—smoking. We couldn't buy cigarettes, of course (and had no money to do so anyway), but we picked up butts from the ground and smoked them. The hygienic risk occurred to us no more than a connection with cancer did to regular smokers in 1943. The attraction was in the image: we felt very grown up to be smoking, like "little men," though not the kind Louisa May Alcott wrote about.

Our tobacco habit proved to be short-lived. One day we were smoking about fifty yards from the bus stop where people waited to go into town. That day my mother and thirteen year-old sister were waiting at the bus stop. My sister saw us and pointed us out to my mother. We quickly discarded our lighted butts, but not before she saw us. My mother called us and I ran—ran!—to her. (For being a nine year–old smoker, I was still an obedient son.) When we reached her she asked, "Were you smoking?" I didn't know yet what a rhetorical question was, so I answered her. "No," I said. (I was a liar, too, but an obedient one.) "Go straight home," she said; "I'll take care of you when I get back." Obediently, I went straight home and waited anxiously to learn my fate.

My mother did take care of me that night. When she was bathing me in the bathhouse wash tub, she told me she was going to tell my father when he got home from work that night (which she did), and said she was going to tell the park police (which she had no intention of doing) the next day when they were making their rounds. That was a lie, too, but a far more effective one than mine had been. I was terrified. I imagined being taken away and spending the rest of my life in jail. I cried and pleaded with her not

Using All the Colors

to tell the police. I promised fervently "I'll never do it again!" (a refrain I used with my parents whenever I was punished for some misbehavior). But that time it was a promise I kept: in the sixty-three years since that summer, I never again smoked cigarette butts I picked up from the street.

The summer of '43 also provided my first experiences of religious awe, and introduced me to new dimensions of art and music. All the time I spent in church services and Sunday school brought familiarity with the Bible and hymns, but it never occasioned a sense of mystery or wonder. We didn't have "art" in our home or church. Pictures or paintings were primarily utilitarian: the flowers or figures on a religious wall plaque, Sunday school pictures of people or stories from the Bible, pictures of family or grandparents. Music on the radio and on our records was hymns ands gospel songs. Our church didn't have a choir, though we often would have "special music" in the services. Of the various singers and musicians who provided such music, three have left particularly vivid memories.

One was Al Koenes, who imitated bird whistles. He would bird-whistle his way through a hymn, twisting his hands by his mouth to vary and modulate the sounds, his face growing redder as he went along. His imitation of bird songs was really remarkable. If you listened with eyes closed, you could imagine real birds singing—birds well versed in Christian hymns, that is. But watching Al whistle a hymn was not a devotional experience.

Other periodic special music was Ed McCarthy and his uncle, Andy Visser, who sang duets. Ed had a rich, resonant baritone voice, and Andy had a strong though plaintive tenor voice. They blended well, and they made fine music together. But here again, what I saw interfered with what I heard. Andy probably didn't read music, because he would sing with his eyes closed, harmonizing with Ed, who sang the melody. Andy would lean slightly towards Ed, often raising his face and tilting his head back slightly, as though picturing something in his mind. Ed, who was somewhat taller, looked down at Andy from time to time with the hint of a frown on his face. I wondered what sin of omission or commission Andy might have done to cause that look. I was always distracted by their mannerisms, and I felt a little guilty that I was distracted.

Someone playing a musical saw was another occasional special music performance at church. A "musical saw" was really just an ordinary carpenter's saw. The player would play it sitting down, the handle held firmly between his knees. (The player was always a "he." A woman might play a saw as well as a man—but not in church. The reason was not musical or theological, but stylistic. In those days women always wore skirts or dresses; women's slacks and pant suits were still many years in the future. For a woman in a skirt or dress to hold a saw firmly between her knees would have been a wardrobe miscalculation at least, if not actually a "wardrobe malfunction.")

Once the player secured the saw handle between his knees, one hand held the small end of the blade out to the side, and the other hand drew a violin bow against the back of the blade to produce the sound—rich sounds quite unlike any traditional musical instrument. Different parts of the saw blade produced different sounds or musical notes. A player could make a sound linger, like the reverberating sound of a bell after it is rung, just by letting the blade vibrate before touching it again with the bow. And he could make the sound rise or fall by bending the saw blade from the free end. The music from the saw was beautiful and peaceful, somewhat harplike. I was fascinated with the ingenuity of making music with a saw, and impressed with the skill of someone who could actually produce beautiful music with it. However, as this description indicates, my experience was an intellectual engagement with the mechanics of sound production rather than a devotional connection with the music.

Al's whistling, Ed and Andy's duets, and music from a saw were the religious musical experiences I remembered particularly by the time I was nine years old, along with experiencing visual art as practical or didactic. Saturday evening services at Maranatha, a Bible Conference grounds near Muskegon, changed all that for me. Cornelia and Otis Skinner, directors of Maranatha, were fine musicians themselves, and they also brought in vocalists and instrumentalists from near and far.

One who impressed me was Gene Jordan, who played the marimba—an instrument almost as unusual to me as the saw. Playing the marimba requires a degree of dexterity and nimbleness needed for few other instruments, but that was not what impressed me. Rather, I was impressed—moved—by the expressiveness of the music. The bold, triumphant sound was there, of course, but also discord, and joy, and passages of delicacy and tenderness. Despite the strange mechanics of producing music by hitting bars of wood with small hammers, Jordan's playing engaged not my mind but my heart. I was one with the crowd in the breathless hush that followed the last note of music he played.

A frequent Saturday night guest was Carl Steele, an artist. Late in the program he would draw in colored chalk on a large easel some scene from a biblical story. While he drew, the auditorium was dark, the only light coming from the easel and the two pianos where the Skinners sat. He worked quickly, and it was fascinating to watch a story become a picture. While he was drawing, the Skinners played the pianos or sang, the music picking up the theme or story of the drawing. They were virtuoso pianists; far from mere "background music," their twin pianos resonated to the emotions of the scene we were watching unfold on the easel. And they sang—oh, how they sang! At times it was Cornelia in her glorious mezzo-soprano. At times it was Otis in his rich baritone. And at times they sang together in magnificent harmony or dialogue. I was in awe, transfixed by the overwhelming experience of sight and sound. Finally—too soon—Carl Steele stood aside and let the audience view without obstruction what he had drawn. The moment was the sensual and emotional climax of what had been building for 20 minutes. And then he turned on a black light over the easel, the ultraviolet light waves revealing some shading or detail or figure that was invisible before. The black light transformed the scene we had watched being drawn, deepening its impact and adding mystery to its previously representational quality.

Experiences like these at Maranatha were both exhilarating and awe inspiring. More than providing mere entertainment or aesthetic enjoyment, they caught me up into something mysterious and wonderful, something I could not have named then but that I know now to be worship. Worship that was an epiphany, meaningful in a way that didn't come just from words and cannot be adequately expressed just with words. It was a nine year-old's initiation into that world so often described by the psalmists, a world where they and all about them are "lost in wonder, love, and praise."

"Don't Bet On It!"

Gene Terpstra

"How much you wanna bet?" was a challenge I threw out—and received—countless times while I was growing up. It was more a metaphor than an actual invitation to put money, or something of value, at risk regarding the truth or reality of some disputed situation. Sometimes we said it in absolute certainty, as if someone had said, "The grass is blue," and all that was needed to prove him wrong was simply to point at the grass we were standing on. Sometimes we said it with bravado to save face when someone questioned a boastful statement, or doubted an excuse we had made, like "I missed the ball because the sun was in my eyes."

But we never made it with real money in hand or even in mind. Money was too scarce to take a chance of losing it, and even a sure bet had its danger. If we did win money by betting, it was likely our parents would learn of it, and then we'd have to explain it to them—and probably to the parents of the losing bettor, too. At best, we bet some action that would be embarrassing to the loser, like "If you lose, you have to kiss my sister" or ". . . eat this candy bar wrapper"—or something even more gross and disgusting. We didn't actually enforce these conditions. They were a tactic to protect our adolescent egos, a juvenile "Don't mess with me!" manifesto.

There was also a moral constraint on betting. Betting was gambling, and gambling was wrong. Taking someone's money by a bet was money we didn't earn; it was like stealing from the other person. I never reflected on this at the time, but it seems curious to me now that this attitude assumed that we would *win* any bet we made, not lose. The possibility, and the morality, of *losing* a bet were never addressed.

Despite the economic and moral constraints on betting, I did make a real bet when I was 12. I worked that summer picking

Childhood and Early Adulthood

tomatoes in the Gorsline Brothers greenhouses. Some of the other guys from our neighborhood worked there also, and we rode our bikes 3-plus miles each way every day. Working in a greenhouse is hot, humid, and dirty work. The vines grew on wires to a height of 7 feet, with perhaps 2 feet between rows. However, the vines were as prolific as the tomatoes, so the tendrils and leaves encroached on that aisle as well as everywhere we reached to pick the ripe tomatoes. Before long, we were soaked with sweat, and our hair and faces and arms and clothes acquired an increasingly green patina as the day wore on. We worked 8 hours every day except Saturday, which was a half-day, making a 44-hour week.

The miserable conditions were made somewhat more tolerable by the camaraderie of our buddies, but the real incentive for keeping on with the work was the money. We made 50 cents an hour, which meant $22 a week. That was big money for us at our tender age. We were paid in cash on Saturday noon, and we celebrated our affluence—and cooled off—by stopping at a root beer stand on the way home to enjoy a couple mugs of ice-cold root beer, 10 cents each.

We took our mid-morning and mid-afternoon breaks at the sorting and packing area, away from the greenhouses. In addition to more tolerable temperature, the men working there could listen to the radio while they worked. The owners were Christians, so the radio was usually tuned to a Christian radio station, unless the Detroit Tigers were playing.

One day as we came in for a break I heard a familiar bass voice singing a hymn, a rich, resonant voice I had heard countless times while my mother listened to WMBI, the radio station of the Moody Bible Institute in Chicago. I said, "That's Beverly Shea." (Beverly Shea, or George Beverly Shea, later became famous singing for the Billy Graham evangelistic crusades.) John, who worked in the sorting and packing area, said, "No, it isn't." I said, "It is too!" Again John said, "No, it isn't." This was one of those situations of absolute certainty for me, so I said, "What do you bet?" I don't remember whether John or I proposed it, but we ended up betting the week's pay. He extended his hand and we shook on it. Everyone else was strangely quiet. Then he said, "That's Henry Bosch." Henry Bosch was a local singer with a voice much like Beverly Shea's. I was familiar with *his* voice also from his singing on the radio and in churches. I immediately regretted my foolhardy confidence and embarrassing myself in front of everyone. Before our break ended, I endured listening to the Beverly Shea sound-alike sing again. I didn't say anything, but one of the other guys said, "Hey, that's Beverly Shea!" Everyone snickered.

That day and the rest of the week I was subject to periodic moralizing and commiseration and teasing from my working buddies. "You shouldn't have bet him, Gene." "Do you think he'll really keep your money?" "What are you going to tell your parents?" "If you need money, I'll lend you some." I didn't think John really would keep my money, but I wasn't at all sure, and the thought was never far from my mind.

Saturday noon came and John passed out the pay envelopes with our $22 week's earnings inside. He bypassed me and gave envelopes to all the others. I said, "Where's mine?", afraid to hear his answer. "I've got it," he said, showing me the envelope and then putting it back in his shirt pocket. "That was the bet." Everyone stood around watching in silence. I said, "Give it to me!", but he just stood there with his arms folded. I started crying and repeating, "Give it to me!" After awhile he extended his hand with the envelope in it. "Here," he said. "I hope you've learned your lesson."

The root beer on the way home that day was the most glorious drink I've ever had.

Oh, and that was the last time I ever bet money on anything.

Our First Car
K. Roberta Woodberry

We had met in Lebanon. I had just returned to the States after graduating from Beirut College for Women. Dudley, after just finishing his divinity degree at Fuller Seminary, had driven across the country to St. Paul, Minnesota (my family home) for our wedding on September 9, 1960. We were on our way to graduate school.

I didn't even notice it when I first saw it, for standing beside it was my sweetheart, Dudley. He had just arrived, having driven all the way to Minnesota from California. We were to be married in two weeks.

With great delight he showed me our "new" car. It was a Studebaker—the kind you couldn't tell whether it was going backwards or forwards because the trunk stuck out as much as the engine. It was silver gray, with new brakes and tires—and No Rust! A friend had given it to Dudley after previously using it to haul sand and gravel. Sand and gravel? That seemed rather harsh to me, but who could complain. It was free! And we needed to get to Massachusetts!

The morning of our wedding dawned bright and early, and while Mother and I took care of minor details before our evening ceremony, Dudley and Ginny (my Matron of Honor) were outside washing and waxing our car.

After the service, as we were leaving the church, there was our Studebaker with streamers and tin cans and written all over the side was "Bert Married a Dud!" We all laughed.

Returning to St. Paul after our honeymoon, we started to pack up for that long drive. We were grateful for the big trunk. My dad gave us a homemade wooden roof rack and between that, the trunk and the back seat, we got almost all our lovely wedding gifts, plus lots of books in or on the car. We were quite a sight! The roof rack was too big (it had been made for a station wagon), so it stuck out over the windshield (providing a nice shade) and was tied with a rope to the bumper on the front and back. Even though the rack was forest green, it went well with our lovely gray Studebaker. Everyone always noticed (especially in Minnesota) that it had No Rust!

Mom had packed a lunch and sent along extra food. My family all gathered around to see us off. It wasn't easy; I was the first one to leave our close family unit. Dad prayed for us and we waved goodbye with tears to Dad, Mom, my brothers, Bob, Karl, and Mark, and my little sister Wibby.

Our Studebaker with No Rust

Things were going fine. The car was just humming along. We had left Minnesota and were in Wisconsin, when all of a sudden it sounded like an explosion. It was the most awful noise I have ever heard a car make. Dudley pulled over to the shoulder and said, "It sounds like we've blown a gasket. We need to get to the nearest garage." Since there was a farmhouse in sight, he left me in the car and walked there. They told him the closest garage was Humbird, just down the road. We drove about 10 miles an hour but finally

Childhood and EARLY ADULTHOOD

made it to the garage. We had travelled 150 miles from my home.

The mechanic was a jovial fellow. I guess it was easy to laugh when you looked at us. He checked out the engine; yes, we had blown a gasket, the piston rod had broken off. He could fix it in a day or two and it would cost $150.00. We gulped—that was how much money we had to get to Massachusetts and school was starting soon. What should we do?

Dudley told him we were going all the way to the East Coast and asked, "If something else happens, could we limp into the nearest gas station?" (He was thinking of the expense of being towed on the Pennsylvania Turnpike). The mechanic laughed. "Limp in?" he said, "Brother, you're limping right now!"

We decided to go for it. As we backed out onto the highway, the mechanic came running after us, waving something in his hand. It was a stamped, addressed postcard. "Hey!" he said, "Send this back to us and tell us if you made it!" And we were off.

It was quite a trip! When we pulled into a gas station, we realized I couldn't open my door. The car rack clamp had pushed the main gutter down over the door and it wouldn't open. To get out, I had to slide under the steering wheel and exit on Dudley's side.

Then the starter died. Since I hadn't yet learned to drive, Dudley would send me out to push. I was the decoy. As Dudley would try to jump start the car, I would always be joined by several men eager to help us on our way. When the car roared to life, Dudley would put several books on the gas pedal so it would roar and not stall. He'd get out, I'd slide in. He'd take the books off and put his foot on the gas. Then he'd take a screwdriver and screw the clamp down (over the door on his side) and we would wave to all our helpers standing with their mouths open. By then we were a little white cloud of smoke going down the highway.

We used over 20 quarts of oil coming across the country. We'd pull into a gas station, Dudley would unscrew the rack so he could get out and ask them to "Fill the oil and check the gas!"

Using All the Colors

We were only about 50 miles out of Zanesville, Ohio where my grandparents lived. My Grandpa was seriously ill and we were planning to get there in time for supper. We were doing just fine. We came into the town of Newark and were right in the middle of town when the light turned yellow. Dudley was afraid if he slammed on the brakes the roof rack would take off flying, so instead he gunned it. Well, in that town they had ditches to drain the rainwater right across the streets and, you guessed it, we hit the first one and the roof rack broke its struts and collapsed on the roof, buckling it. I called Grandma and Grandpa while Dudley raced to find a hardware store to buy new struts.

Then we had to unpack. Everything in the roof rack and the backseat came out and was lined up between the street and the sidewalk. Pushing with our feet in the backseat, we were able to straighten the roof. Then we had to put on the new braces, pack it all again, jump start the car, my pushing, helpers coming, books on the gas pedal, Dudley out, me in, screw driver, etc, and we were off! Grandma and Grandpa were delighted to see us, even if it was past their bedtime.

Yes, we made it to Massachusetts and yes, I sent the postcard back to Humbird, Wisconsin. That old Studebaker kept going for several months. We even got the starter fixed.

Unfortunately, we needed some groceries and drove to the market about three blocks away. Dudley forgot to put oil in the car to come home though, and there was that death rattle again. We were on Massachusetts Avenue, in Cambridge, and people were coming out of stores to see what was happening. I hid my head down under the dashboard while Dudley headed to our local gas station where we filled the oil and checked the gas. The owner came running out waving madly and blocking the driveway. "Don't bring it in here!" he shouted. So Dudley coasted to a parking spot on the street.

The next day he called a junk yard and told them about our California Studebaker with No Rust! "I'll give you 13 dollars if you can drive it here, and 10 dollars if you can't," the clerk said. Dudley answered, "I'll take 10!"

Using All the Colors

Occupational
Adventures

Using All the Colors

Memorable Preaching Experiences
Robert Bos

In my senior year of seminary one of my classes was homiletics, where the intent was to learn the art of preparing and delivering sermons. On occasional Sundays we, as students, were assigned to preach in churches in the nearby Holland, Michigan area that needed a pulpit supply. My first opportunity was to deliver a sermon in a large Reformed Church in Grand Rapids. I knew that this would be a little intimidating because the church broadcast its Sunday service. I had such feelings as awe, fear, humility, and pride in being given this assignment. Whatever pride I might have felt, it melted away when I saw the next list of assignments. Mine was to bring the Word to a small country church in Drenthe. It was a church that one might picture, white framed with steps leading to the front door, and a steeple, but it was hardly what one would call a tall steepled church. It seated about 100 souls. I still recall looking out the side windows and seeing cows grazing in a nearby field.

Another experience I haven't forgotten is when I was assigned to preach in Grand Haven. This, too, was a good sized church so I wanted to not only preach a good sermon but to conduct a proper, worshipful service. When I came to the place in the service to read the scripture lesson for the day, I approached the pulpit on which was a very large pulpit Bible. When I opened it I felt a great sense of panic because the chapters were divided by Roman numerals. The scripture I had chosen was in the higher numbers, beyond my understanding of the system. I kept flipping pages like I knew what I was doing. What was I going to do? Would I have to ask one of the Elders to come up and find the passage for me? How embarrassing that would be. I stopped turning pages like I had found the desired passage, looked down, and there were the very words I had selected to read. I could hardly believe what I saw.

Using All the Colors

It had to have been an act of God. Some guardian angel rescued me at the very last moment.

In the 1950s, while serving as associate pastor at 1st Presbyterian Church, Santa Ana, CA, I had an experience that has stayed with me, too. Robert H. Schuler was just beginning his ministry in nearby Garden Grove. He was conducting worship services out of the Orange Drive-In Theater. I knew him when we attended the same seminary in Holland. He was two years ahead of me and I heard him preach his senior sermon. Now, as neighbors in California, he invited me to preach for him one Sunday. This I did while standing on top of the concession stand to deliver the sermon, looking out on an audience of windshields on cars hooked up to listening posts. After that service I stood at the exit greeting people through the car windows, hoping not to get that rundown feeling. Following that I drove to a small nearby church where I conducted a second service. Later I was amazed to learn the guest preacher for the next Sunday was to be Norman Vincent Peale. As we know, Schuler had adopted Peale's message of Positive Thinking.

Observing the 200th birthday of our country was an occasion for me to remember. The year was July of 1996. I was pastor in Westlake Village at the time. What was unique was that our congregation celebrated the 1776 birth of this nation at the Old North Church, not in Boston, but in Burbank at Forest Lawn Cemetery. On a Sunday closest to the July 4th date, our parishioners assembled in colonial garb at the church. I wore my black robe, clerical collar with two white tabs, and delivered the sermon from an elevated pulpit. It was a fun and meaningful experience, imagining the place and the times of such a historic occasion.

Delivering a sermon in the German language during a Sunday worship service in Germany was certainly something to recall. When I was on staff at Bel Air Presbyterian Church in L.A., I organized a partnership with a congregation in former East Germany, one that had been under the rule of Communism. Early on, I had studied German so I was reasonably familiar with

Occupational Adventures

speaking the language. The pastor of the church had invited me to preach in his pulpit on a Sunday celebrating the 275th anniversary of the church. I accepted but it took much preparation on my part to get ready for such a daunting task. Ralph Hamburger, our resident German theologian, was helpful in tutoring me. Thankfully the experience was appreciated by the congregation. The applause was very affirming for me. I think that it expressed their appreciation for my effort in doing what was out of the ordinary for me.

Helping to lead worship at Bel Air Presbyterian Church in the presence of President and Mrs. Ronald Reagan was an experience that not every one has. He was retired at this point in his presidency so that the Reagans were regular attenders as members of the church. They always sat in the same place with a Secret Service agent sitting behind them; two were in the balcony, and two were standing in the back of the sanctuary. No special attention was given to them aside from the congregation singing Happy Birthday to him each year. The Reagans remained seated until after the benediction. They would then leave at the postlude as other parishioners did. As participating pastors we would greet the Reagans after the service as we did all others. People knew that they were not supposed to take pictures or try to delay them with any conversation. The Secret Service would lead them directly to the limousine and the party would leave. It was all done smoothly but for me, there was an added excitement to know that I was privileged to offer words of faith to a former president of our country, and who had been such a world leader.

These, then, are some of my most memorable preaching experiences in proclaiming God's Word. The times and places have varied but all are unique in the tablet of my memory. They take me from a large church in Grand Rapids to a country church in Drenthe; from a drive-in church to a chapel that led to a Crystal Cathedral; from a worship service similar to one of 1776 to today; from the presence of a president to an ordinary parishioner; and from a Bible divided by Roman numerals to one in Arabic

Using All the Colors

numbering. The important thing is to be faithful. I am grateful to God for calling, preparing, inspiring, and directing me to these and all times and places where I could serve. It has been a blessing for me when lives were changed and, over a course of time, to see people grow in the faith and continue in loving and faithful service.

Making Visible the Invisible
Jessie Coates

Most people have witnessed the baptism of a baby, and enjoyed the celebration that follows. Because the timing of the event happens to coincide with Sunday noon, the celebration needs to be much more than finger food. Usually it is a sit down dinner. Family and friends say nice things about the baby; grand parents treat their grown children with an unusual degree of respect, cousins and siblings who once quarreled greet each other peaceably and pass careful compliments. The whole thing is a rehearsal for world peace, and perhaps those who are able should produce babies more often so that we could have more opportunities to practice grace.

The baptism of an adult is slightly different. For years respectable citizens regarded baptism as equivalent to admission into civilized society. When the board of a certain old and stately church heard that an adult was asking for baptism they were shocked and suggested that the pastor baptize the person privately so as not embarrass her.

Someone once published a book entitled, *There is Algae Growing in the Baptism Font*. In older congregations this is sometimes true. The font is a stone or wooden pillar holding a bowl of water to sprinkle on the head of the infant or adult being baptized. After a long time with no new babies being born into the congregation the font gets forgotten. Sometimes it gets hidden behind the huge displays of flowers that relatives of deceased neighbors have donated to the church. Those flowers are the new relevance. The congregation knows which of their neighbors has died and remembers both their lives and their funerals. Some people even consider a funeral to be the most validating event in that person's life. On Sunday the assembled members don't really need a sermon;

sitting in the pews, looking at the flowers, thinking about death and what follows, they are busy composing their own sermons.

All such congregations eventually receive a new pastor; brash, hopeful, reforming and also disturbing. In the anticipation of both renewal and new members the pastor disturbs the accustomed front of the sanctuary by pulling out the font from behind the flowers and placing it prominently. In every church there is a lady who has, for many years, been 'in charge' of the flowers. She is usually extremely dedicated and fiercely opposed to anything she sees as an invasion of her territory. Sometimes she even worries about the possibility that the flowers on the table (which she persists in calling an alter) don't match.

One bold but experienced pastor believed that the baptism font needs to be visible so that everyone can see it and be reminded of what it symbolizes. This pastor attended the women's meeting and gave a brief impassioned explanation of the many things that the baptism font signifies. New life, cleansing, spiritual nurture and the river of grace that flows from God to all persons. This made an impression on the 'flower lady'. The next week, she helped lift the font from behind 'her' flowers and then compassionately reassured the pastor by saying "We shouldn't quarrel about this, after all it's only furniture."

Not all churches use furniture for baptizing adults, some of them use rivers. Jesus was baptized in a river so the desire to identify with Jesus is partly satisfied by being baptized in the same way that he was. One problem is that no one knows whether the river was in flood or in draught at the time, therefore opinions about whether Jesus was immersed in the water or sprinkled with water differ widely. It doesn't really matter you think, but if you ever get bored listening to a group of clergy people talking, you can liven things up considerably by asking whether adults should be sprinkled or immersed.

The church I grew up in believed that adults should be immersed when being baptized. This calls for structure: a pool with space enough for two people, one of whom is to be laid down in the water, and another to lay him down and quickly raise him up. Also the pool has to have steps down into the water. In my youth in England this was inelegantly called a baptismal tank and was built into the floor of the church usually at the front of the sanctuary. This kind of pool requires a lot of involvement from church members; it has to be scrubbed clean, filled with lots of water, and heated. There is usually a supper provided for the volunteers who do this and a lot of cheerful casual conversation. A friend of mine had a baptism pool that took a long time to heat; in the early hours of the morning he went into the church and bending down tested the water with his hand. The local policeman seeing a light on in what he thought was an empty church hammered violently on the door and my surprised friend fell into the pool.

Even the manner of baptizing can be interesting. Because Jesus immersed himself in the will of God when he was baptized my husband thought it important that the waters of baptism should completely cover the head of the person being baptized. After he had gently laid the young man down in the water he paused to make sure his face was completely covered. The splashing that followed had a wrong kind of significance.

Most people only get baptized once in their lives, I did however know a woman who had been baptized fourteen times. She told me that every time she sinned she got re-baptized. Imagine, only sinning fourteen times in your whole life.

Clothing is important although it doesn't have to be. Early Christians left their old clothes on one side of the river and dressed in new clothes on the other side. I really like this idea but what should the new clothes look like? The Bible calls the close relationship between Jesus and his believers a marriage and refers to the Church as the bride of Christ. One young lady, fourteen, slim and pretty, asked if she could make her own gown instead of wearing the shapeless ones the church issued. She presented herself for baptism wearing a long white, fitted bridal gown. Because she did not know how to sew a zip fastener in, she had fastened the back of the gown with twenty small buttons and corresponding loops. The cheap white sateen shriveled up in the water and the tiny buttons were too slippery for wet hands to grasp. After the ceremony it took a long time to get her undressed and dry again. She shivered a lot but she had made and worn a visible symbol of her new identity.

In Japan in 1956 a great many young men were opening small congregations, these student pastors did not baptize until they were licensed or ordained, so my husband was asked to do the baptizing. Japan was still recovering from the war, fuel was expensive so the water was not heated. Only one person was being baptized so nobody would be in the cold water for very long. Eight years before these young men and my husband had been on opposite sides of a vicious war, they had no animosity, but were still young enough to want to prove something. After my husband was in the pool, in cold water up to his waist, they began to sing a hymn, it was a very long hymn. David did not shiver but he became rigid. So rigid that I wondered if we would need to defrost him before we could take him home. Afterwards I asked him if he'd like to hear what I had heard whispered just before he got into the pool. He looked interested and I repeated, "Watch the white man turn blue."

There is one baptism I have only seen on television; I would like to travel to Ethiopia to witness it. Because the bishop only baptizes once a year and because there are so many young men wanting to be baptized, they use a small lake. During the service the young men sit around the pool with their feet in the water. When the signal is given they all leap into the pool at the same time and swim vigorously and freely. Like the holy river flowing with grace and mercy, deep enough and wide enough for everyone. Many people, individually and corporately being re-born by the will of God. Human beings being embraced by God in the same way that the water embraces their bodies. They come up from the water exuberant and expectant ready to walk in the light until the time when they return to the Source Of All Life and share with him the wonder of a whole new era.

The secular equivalent of baptism is a wedding ring, which symbolizing the union of two people into one new relationship. Sometimes the partners divorce and the promises are made null and void. The ring is thrown away and forgotten. Occasionally a person who has made baptism promises wishes to forget their baptism and negate their vows. It can only be a one sided divorce because God does not break the promises he has made. As long as the baptized person lives, God will neither forget nor ignore that person.

Every so often a person or a congregation says, 'Let's renew our baptism vows' and then they remember why they made their vows the first time, repeat them again and place their hands in the baptismal water. Whenever that happens, God rejoices and the angels sing.

A Brush with Death
Dick Dosker

It was the summer of 1953. It was also the end of my middle year at Princeton Theological Seminary. Having worked a fully secular money-saving job the previous summers, it was time to hopefully combine Christian service with some income. Fellow student, Bob Blade, and I heard of the summer ministries available in Alaska through arrangements with Presbyterian missionary, Bert Bingle. We would be working jobs in one of the many communities Bingle tried to cover during the year and helping to maintain and advance the cause of Christ in those far-flung places. Bob was to have the rail head at Healy Junction. I had the soft coal mine at Suntranna, where we both would live in the back of the school house and I would preach and teach the families of the miners. I would also try to minister to the miners in their shower house and dining halls and wherever possible. A daunting task, to say the least.

Suntranna, by the way, meant something like "always smokes." Some of the exposed veins of coal in the cliffs above the mine had been set afire by lightening strikes and had smoldered away, smoking for years. Some of the main mine buildings had burned a short time before I arrived. They had been rebuilt on a different location, but the underlying embers were still hot enough to burn through the boots of one young man of my acquaintance. When he was flown to a Fairbanks hospital and administered sulfa drugs, he had died. They didn't realize that he was allergic to sulfa. We had hiked together into the tundra. His death was a loss and a reminder that a mine could be—was—a dangerous place.

My work was as an outside laborer. Every time it rained the mud would cascade down the hillside and cover the tracks for the mine cars. I learned well the use of a "muck-stick" shovel. The entrance to the mine shaft passed through considerable depth of scree on the slopes. I learned to drive a 4-wheeled drive power

Occupational Adventures

wagon and to empty flat cars full of various dimensions of timbers, then drive them to the mine train to be taken into the mine to support the entrance. Exhausting, to say the least.

Soon, however, I was moved to the job of car dumper. Each car in the mine train had to be successfully dumped as it passed over the chute leading to the crusher. The crusher very efficiently processed the irregular chunks to be passed by conveyor belt to the tipple and loaded into waiting rail cars.

My job was to break up chunks of coal too big to pass through the two doors at the bottom of each car as it passed over the dump zone. I used a pick axe or a long, heavy iron bar to strike the oversized chucks, causing them to fracture and fall through into the crusher. This particular day my engine operator was a feisty, impatient man. He would move the train ahead at my signal, visible to him only as a silhouette in the opening of the dump shed. If I wasn't quick enough to signal, he would move ahead anyway! The bottom doors of the cars were rigged to be tripped open as they centered over the crusher. They were snapped shut as they left the chute area. The problem was that if a chunk of coal was still hanging below, it would prevent the door from closing, the whole car would derail, the unloading would stop, men would have to be summoned. Backbreaking work with bars and cursing galore would be the result. Of course, the dumper (me) would be the goat.

With this consequence in mind, I would work furiously, using the heavy bar, striking the reluctant lump over and over. Usually, even large chunks would surrender and fall through. This time, however, the pieces refused to fall. I jumped into the car to attack them. Using both feet and the weight of my body, I jumped mightily on the fractured lump. The next thing I knew the load fell away with my legs left dangling below the car above the crusher, my hands having grabbed the sides of the car on the way down. I could expect no help from the irritable engineer. Somehow, with desperate effort and adrenaline pumping, I pulled myself out, jumped to the platform, and shot up my hand to signal the driver,

Using All the Colors

just before the doors clanged shut and the train moved farther out on the slag heap.

I had a few minutes to compose my shaking nerves and slow my beating heart while the empty train returned into the mine for another load. I thanked God for his protecting care, and went on earning tuition money and experience for ministry—and having further adventures in the "Great Land"—Alaska.

Honeymoon on the Riviera of the Bering Sea

Carolyn French

Two weeks of travel in the summer of 1957, carrying our winter coats and visiting supporting churches in Illinois, Oklahoma, and Seattle, Washington, this newlywed couple in their 20's finally arrived "home" to a place never before seen—Gambell, St. Lawrence Island, Alaska, 40 miles from Siberia!

On this chilly, very gray overcast windy day, the coats felt good. Many of the Eskimos came to meet us and some of them said, "Oh, you're just babies!" We were escorted by several of the villagers to our home in what we came to call the Sheldon Jackson museum, the first frame home in Gambell that Sheldon Jackson had built in 1892. The house was all clean and two fresh loaves of bread were on the kitchen counter to welcome us.

The apartment part of the building had the kitchen with an oil stove for cooking—built like the old wood burning stoves. There was also a kerosene refrigerator, cupboards and a sink with no faucet, and instead a large 50 gallon aluminum painted former oil barrel containing water. Off the kitchen was the living room which ended up serving us as music room, office, and library and off the living room was the bedroom where the old coal bin had been. There was a second floor which was primarily a storage room for a year's supply of groceries that came from Seattle via the North Star freighter each summer. The bathroom was like a little closet on the first floor where the honey bucket was—the chemical toilet, that is, which was anything but "sweet!"

The elder from the church who took us into the building to show us around told us where to dump the contents of the honey bucket and then also instructed us regarding the process to get drinkable water. It needed to be hauled up in garbage cans from the lake a mile from the village. Then it was to be filtered through the sheet that was clipped across the 50 gallon aluminum drum in the kitchen, which enabled filtering out of any fish or gunk that might be floating in the water. Then it was ready to be drawn out of the spigot on the side of the drum. Then, after boiling it for twenty minutes and cooling, it would be all set to drink! He surprised us later saying something that I don't recall, but preceding it with, "Just keep this under your Stetson!" Oh yes, these Eskimos do know English!

Two days into residency was the anniversary of our first month as a married couple, so I thought it would be special to bake an angel food cake in celebration. Well, I learned quickly how different an oil stove with the heat on one side greater than heat on the far side can affect baking!! It came out blackened on the top and very sticky on the inside, but bless my dear husband who remarked that it looked like the shape of the Island and tasted like roasted marshmallows which made our new "camping experience" most memorable, to say the least!

Further initiation for me was immediately trying to learn all I could from the Public Health nurse currently on the Island. She would be leaving in two weeks and I was to take over her job! I followed her around like a puppy dog learning everything I possibly could. On top of that, we were to have a planeload of church visitors coming to the Island and were to provide lunch, so we were making up lots of jello for salad in preparation. Much to my relief, they didn't make it and decided to go somewhere else in Alaska instead!

In late summer I was introduced to the first but smaller epidemic among the villagers—viral hepatitis. However, I was amazed how quickly the Eskimos seemed to recover from it, after just a week or two. I had been used to it taking a six-week or more toll on its victims.

In September the army contingent that had been based out nearer the mountain in Gambell, was totally pulling out and the medics left me a number of useful items for the clinic including

Occupational Adventures

dental filling material. They also gave us some heavy parkas for the winter, which we used until we could get the better ones made by the Eskimos. That month the nursing supervisor from Fairbanks came out to orient me more completely to all that the job of an itinerant public health nurse required since I was to take care of Savoonga, the village 60 miles east, as well as Gambell. Along with her came a social worker, the x-ray technician to do chest x-rays on all the villagers, and the new doctor from Kotzebue with whom I would be consulting via short wave radio when needed. They were housed between us and the school teachers but all ate at our place. God in mercy doth provide, I was quickly learning, when the woman missionary from Savoonga willingly jumped right in and took over the cooking for me. What I would have done without her I do not know as I was responsible to be with the medical people all day they were there. I remember we had sourdough pancakes almost every morning because someone had given me sourdough starter that could be kept going!

Well, after that whirlwind of activity the blessedly good news was that for the first time in years no one turned up with active TB on the x-rays! The use of the drugs INH and PASA were clearing TB quite successfully and a lot of sanitariums in Alaska were closing down, much to everyone's relief.

Then in October—the last time this was attempted in the fall—the North Star Freighter arrived with our year's order of groceries and a piano the church in Seattle had shipped to us. Well, it turned out that the ship had water in the bottom of the hold due to a big storm at sea before arrival in Gambell and since we were the last stop for the ship before return to Seattle, our stuff got wet and all the cartons were broken open—canned goods rolling all over the beach and oven fresh crackers looking anything but fresh! The teachers, Art and me, and the local native store owners had to sort the mess out, by checking it with the order manifests. The piano couldn't be unloaded, as the Bering Sea was too rough, so it was returned to Seattle to be reshipped the following July.

Using All the Colors

The next big initiation that year for me was the Asian Flu epidemic. Both the doctor in Kotzebue and some Arctic Health Research doctors had told me to alert them when it hit the Island and they would come right out! I had begged the health department to send me vaccine before our contingent of National Guardsmen returned from Ft. Ord in California, which was a hot bed of Asian Flu, but they kept saying they could only send to the villages where the flu was present. Well, the day after the Guardsmen arrived in Gambell, Asian Flu broke out and spread like wildfire in the village. Were the doctors now available? No, since the one in Kotzebue had his hands full there, and the Arctic Health Researchers were already dealing with it in the Pribilof Islands. THEN the vaccine was sent and we immunized the pregnant women, the teachers, me, and all in the village who had not contracted it. Art had a raging case of it so I was treating him, too, as the vaccine was too late to do him any good. I kept telling the villagers to notify me if any cases were getting sicker despite the early treatments and I gave out lots of symptomatic medical items to the homes. The village was like a sleeping village as hardly anyone was about. Miraculously, there were only two pneumonia cases and both survived. One of those was a man who rejected all "white man's medicine" but whose cousin took me to him when he was really quite ill. I started him on what was supposed to be a 10-day course of penicillin injections, but on day three I couldn't locate him, and I was informed he'd taken off with his dog team to go to his trapping cabin... and that was THAT.

The Arctic Health Researchers did come after it was over, read my record keeping and wrote an article about the spread of an epidemic in a remote village. They also added my name as 4th author! Most of all I praised God for no deaths in the village!

Arctic Christmas
Carolyn French

It was a bitterly cold December day—about 20 degrees below zero—in Nome, Alaska, only four days before Christmas. I was alone, awaiting transportation to the village of Gambell on St. Lawrence Island. The plane's engine was being warmed up with a heater and the pilot had just informed me that if it didn't heat enough to start by noon, the flight would need to be cancelled. If I couldn't leave that day it would be two weeks until the next flight to Gambell.

Why was I in this predicament? I had been hired as the itinerant Public Health Nurse for the two villages of Gambell and Savoonga on St. Lawrence Island, and was the *only* resident medical person. Art and I had arrived in July, one month after our marriage! I had had an emergency call the previous Saturday night from the Eskimo midwife. An Eskimo woman, with a baby in abnormal transverse position, and who was scheduled to travel to the hospital on the coming Thursday's flight, was in labor now.

70 mph winds, and blowing, wet, snow made visibility zilch! I literally clung to the midwife as she led me through the blinding snowstorm and over many accumulating snowdrifts. At the home, I found the woman in labor and the baby still in the crosswise position. However, the infant's heart tones were strong and regular and the mother was in no undue distress. We prayed about the situation and decided we needed to keep close observation of both the mother and the baby and hope that if labor progressed, the baby's position would somehow change. Both remained stable and the mother's contractions eventually stopped later that night. I was able to contact the doctor in Kotzebue, on Sunday, via the school's short wave radio. He said he'd arrange for a flight on Monday and instructed me to escort the patient into Anchorage, getting her checked over at the hospital in Nome while awaiting the flight

connection to Anchorage to the Alaska Native Service Hospital. Thankfully, she and the baby did well on the trip and the infant was born safely by Caesarian section.

So here I was, back in Nome, praying the plane would start so I wouldn't miss Art's and my first Christmas together. The call came to board quickly—the engine was running—Hallelujah!

When I got to Gambell, Art showed me the Christmas decorations that the youth had put up in the church. He pointed out the artificial fir trees especially, and asked "Do you notice anything different?" I looked and replied "Oh yes, the needles are all turned upside down." Art explained he hadn't been paying close attention when they were inserting the individual branches into the trunk, forgetting that these youth had all grown up in a treeless environment! The custom among the Eskimos in the village is to decorate the church and school because their crowded, one-room homes don't have extra space to spare. After the school Christmas program and also after the church worship program there would always be an extensive exchange of gifts—whole mail bags full of presents for their families as well as friends. The Deacons of the church wrapped and gave each person a new outfit, as well as distributing toys and games that had come to the mission from the supporting churches.

Here we were, newly marrieds, on a remote island—nearer to Siberia than to the mainland of Alaska—in sub-zero weather, but the warmth of celebrating Christmas with the whole village of families kept us from feeling overly homesick for all our relatives in California and Pennsylvania. No problem having a white Christmas here even if no real trees.

To top it all off, the new year began with our walking out of the house in 20-30 below, crystal clear air to see the most spectacular beauty of the aurora borealis—wavy and concentric circles of light—reds, yellows, greenish blues in a dance across the sky. We were filled with the same awe of God's powerful presence just like we imagined the shepherds felt on that very first Christmas!

The Manse
Mary Froede

Our car coasted into the driveway. The front door opened and my husband, Jim, danced into the room singing "I've just applied for the position as pastor of the church in Tucumcari, New Mexico". I cried out "Where the hell is Tucumcari, New Mexico?" We both dashed for the atlas maps and a magnifying glass to find a tiny dot in Northern New Mexico, halfway between Albuquerque, New Mexico and Amarillo, Texas... Thus began our great adventure.

When we first moved to Tucumcari, New Mexico, we were "put up" in what had been a tarpaper shack formerly used for storage by the church. It was called "The Manse". Ah, yes, the manse—the dictionary description is "the house and land occupied by a minister or parson—root word MANSION). Parts had been added periodically and it became a HOUSE.

Admittedly, there were three bedrooms, but unfortunately, in order to get to the bathroom, we had to go through my daughter, Ruth Ann's, lean-to bedroom. Her roof slanted to the point that she had to use caution when sitting up in bed. The heater provided was a massive furnace under the floor between the living and dining room. When it belched forth its contents, the metal grate was so hot, many of us sustained blisters if walking over it. Of course, covering the grate with a rug defeated the original purpose of dispensing heat. In summer, you can bet I kept a rug over it to prevent varmints from coming to visit. The immediate area around the large grate was overly warm while the outer edges of the house remained frigid all winter. We spent a lot of wintertime huddled in the living/dining room.

When we first arrived with all our belongings not too far behind, inside the house we found various scattered pieces of furniture here and there that been donated. Our guides to the home were not very pleased with the fact that we had been married for

Using All the Colors

many years and had a house full of furniture as a result. They rather grudgingly removed the items but I did manage to keep the old round oak dining table and mirrored sideboard (which incidentally, I hated leaving behind when we left as it was a true relic, eligible for Antiques Roadshow). When various people came to help us settle in, a few helpers were astonished and very vocal about all the sturdy packing boxes I had garnered from the local liquor store before packing up. I assured them, emptying all those bottles had been very difficult for us!!!

One of our most loyal families were ranchers. Mr. B., at one point, decided that the existing manse was not befitting the status of our church in this town and went forward to see about building a new house. He finally found a vacant piece of property in the newer and more genteel area of town, wangled the owner into selling it to the church and proceeded to hit up everyone in town for some commitment to this new venture of his. Sure enough, he was able to raise enough money to build a lovely, three bedroom house, which we were the first to occupy. (Incidentally, it still stands and is occupied by the current pastor).

One of the things that was not taken care of was "thought about the yard". Neither Jim nor I have a green thumb, so it remained an area scattered only with scrubby orphan trees, ankle high weeds and lots of dirt. I casually mentioned it to Mr. B. and he immediately responded that what that lawn needed was fertilizer.

Jim had gone that week to be a counselor at one of our church camps and would be gone for about ten days. I figured we would wait until he returned to face the problem. Unfortunately, Mr. B. had other plans. At four o'clock the following bleary morning, the phone rang and I was greeted with Mr. B's boisterous voice saying "Aren't you up yet?" I groaned and said "What can I do to help you?" He informed me that his workers were on their way with the fertilizer he had promised—would I please meet them outside in the front yard.

I threw on a robe and dashed out the front door, in the

dark, to find a huge dump truck, backing up to the curb and gradually raising the truck bed to deposit a full load of steaming manure (freshly obtained, I am sure). It lay in a mountain shaped pile with fumes exuding from all sides. The driver said we just needed to spread it out over the lawn and we would enjoy beautiful grass. I went back into the house, crashed into bed, and prayed for Jim's quick return.

    Well, that didn't happen and the massive mountain remained where it had been dumped. Summer was in full bloom and the full day's sun shone down on the pile. It got to the point where I had to keep the windows closed 24/7 to survive. My neighbors started bugging me about it, but I didn't know what to do. The die was cast when my next door neighbor called to exclaim "THERE'S SOMETHING DEAD IN THERE!!" Well, I would have been a fool not to acknowledge that fact and so I started with a shovel and mask to spread as much as I could handle. Jim got home in a few days and it took us at least one week to spread the reeking mass over the yard.

THE GRASS NEVER GREW IN THAT SPOT AGAIN.

Off to Corumba
Rosemary Pierson

In 1956 my husband, Paul, and I, with our two-year old son, Steve, traveled by ship to Brazil. We were to begin work as Presbyterian missionaries with the Central Brazil Mission. On our arrival, we were taken to the lovely city of Campinas where we studied Portuguese for a year. We were challenged to learn the language and culture quickly. Six weeks after our arrival, our daughter, Kathy, was born. The doctor did not speak English, and I did not speak Portuguese, but that is another story.

Our continual question concerned our first place of service. That was answered at our annual mission meeting at Belo Horizonte. After discussion the mission decided to send us to Corumba, Mato Grosso. Corumba was located on the western edge of Brazil, bordered by Bolivia on the west, and the Paraguay River and the pantanal, the world's largest wetland, on the east. The town was isolated from the rest of Brazil by the pantanal and was accessible only by train or plane from the east or riverboat from the north.

When we finished language study, Paul and Art Lindsay, a missionary friend, began their trip by jeep station wagon to Mato Grosso. Our mission was adamant that the children and I not go with them but travel later by plane. There were no adequate places for lodging or food for us on the route. Road conditions were precarious, bumpy, dusty, and full of ruts. Rain made them worse. Shortly after they left Campinas, paved roads ended. Paul and Art looked on it as a great adventure, which it turned out to be.

Three year-old Steve, one year-old Kathy, and I moved to the mission home in Sao Paulo. We were there for several days. At last I had a phone call from the mission executive saying that Art had flown back to Campinas and that Paul was on the last lap of the trip, the train ride from Campo Grande to Corumba. I later learned more details about their trip.

Occupational Adventures

When they arrived at the border between the states of Sao Paulo and Mato Grosso, they faced the broad, swiftly flowing Parana River. On that river they saw a rustic, simple raft that held, at most, three vehicles. With trepidation they eased the jeep down the steep bank over planks onto the raft. With two other cars they crossed the river. Carefully driving off they went a short distance, then watched in amazement as the jeep ahead of them stopped. The men exited the car, took their guns out of the glove compartment, and strapped them on. Welcome to Mato Grosso, the wild west!!

After traveling several hours, needing gas and a place to stay, they arrived at a place marked on the map as 'Porto Feliz' (Happy Port). They found it consisted of a building or two and a few men around a camp fire, each with guns strapped around their waists. They seemed to be watching them menacingly. There were a few barrels of gasoline. One of the men siphoned what they needed into the jeep. They paid an exorbitant price and left as quickly as they could. Paul and Art remarked that it was neither a port nor was it very 'feliz'. They do not remember where they stayed that night. There were just glad to get out of 'Porto Feliz'.

The next day they continued on the road until it ended in a cow pasture. They turned back to a nearby farm where a boy volunteered to guide them to the new road being cut through the wilderness some distance away. Sitting on the fender, he told them to "turn left at that tree and right at that bush," and so on until they arrived at the road under construction. They appreciated driving on the smoother road. Eventually they reached the city of Campo Grande. After eating better than they had for several days and getting a night's rest, Art took the plane back to Sao Paulo and then on to Campinas. Since there was no road across the pantanal, the train was the only land-based way to get to Corumba. Paul drove to the train station and put the jeep on the wood burning train and made the trip to Corumba. It was extremely hot and humid and sparks from the engine often blew through the open windows; one

81

Using All the Colors

had to be careful with clothing and reading material.

The children and I were eager to join Paul. We all missed him. The mission office bought tickets for our travel to Corumba. When the day arrived, the children and I, with our luggage, went to the airport. The plane was a DC3, the workhorse of air travel in the interior of many countries after World War II. It was not a luxury flight. We had frequent stops along the way and the flight was often bumpy. The meal of sandwiches of stale cheese and ham made my stomach feel as bumpy as the ride. Steve eagerly watched every aspect of our trip. As the time approached for our arrival in Corumba, I looked out and was completely startled by what I saw. My first thought was that I could understand the ancient mariners who thought they were arriving at the end of the world, and said, "Here be demons." What caused this reaction? I saw a vast unending nothingness of silver, blues, pinks, greens, and browns stretching ahead, with water vapor rising from the many lakes and streams below. That was my first impression of the Brazilian pantanal, the largest wetland in the world and now a national park. It is half as large as France and full of remarkable wild life. It included millions of caiman, a smaller relative of the crocodile, along with jaguars, anacondas, and many other exotic creatures.

Our plane made a bumpy landing on a dirt airstrip but we were safely in Corumba. The terminal had burned down the year before and there was only one small building left to shelter people from the hot tropical sun. When we disembarked I felt like we had walked into a sauna. The air was so hot and muggy it was hard to breathe. Simmering heat waves bounced up from the ground, but we had arrived. Of course Paul was not there to meet us. If the mission office had sent a telegram, he had not received it and there was no telephone service. I later heard the common saying that if you sent a letter and telegram at the same time, you said in the letter, "telegram follows."

So what next? We were at the airport surrounded by the forest. A few men stood around and there were two or three cars nearby. We were in Corumba but where was Paul? How would I find him? With Kathy in my arms and Steve by my side, I went up to a man who looked more official than the others, and with my far from fluent Portuguese, I asked, "Is there a taxi here? We want to go to Corumba." In rapid fire Portuguese he asked at length if I wanted to go to Corumba. I really did not know of any other place around so the answer was easy." Sim, yes." "And a taxi?" he asked." "Yes," I replied.

The man yelled at someone lounging by the building. He went to an old blue car and drove over to us. "Is this a taxi?" I asked. There were no obvious signs on the outside or inside of the car to mark it as a taxi. "Sim, yes. Let's go," He said impatiently. We agreed on a price. I thanked the man at the airport and off we went. As we bumped along on the dirt road he asked, "Where do you want to go?" "Please take us to the home of Senhor Getulio, the riverboat pilot." "Don't know him," he replied. "Do you know Senhor Sebastiao, the foreman at the flour mill?" "No." "Do you know where the Presbyterian church is?" "No." Almost running out of the names of leaders in the small congregation, I asked, "Do you know Senhor Paulo Paiva, he owns a jewelry store?" "Yes, yes, I know Paulo Paiva. I will take you there."

We continued our trip past isolated mud and wattle houses with small gardens around them. The car stirred up clouds of white dust along the road. Finally we arrived in Corumba!! The dusty main street was very wide with small one story commercial buildings built of brick. There were cobblestone streets for a few blocks around the center. The rest of the streets were not paved. On one of the streets we saw a sign that said jewelry store. The driver got out of the car and said, "Wait here." He entered the store. A man walked in behind the counter. They talked a while. Then the driver came to the car, opened the door, and said, "Get out. Get out." So we did. I paid him and wondered, what next?

About that time, Paul came rushing out of the store. He was completely amazed to see us, but also overjoyed. "How did you get

Using All the Colors

here? Are you all right," he asked over and over. It turned out that Paul had gone to visit Paulo Paiva shortly before we arrived. They were talking in the living quarters behind the store when the driver came in. Paulo then returned to Paul and said, "I think you have people here." Thoroughly confused, Paul went out and found us. It was some time later that I remembered I had rushed off to Corumba even though the plan was that we would wait until Paul found a place for us to live before sending for us. Hence the confusion. He had been looking unsuccessfully for suitable housing.

We spent the next few days at the 'Hotel Grande de Corumba.' It was the only hotel in town. It was the highest building in town, with four stories, located on the main square. It had no elevator and we were on the fourth floor. It was there that I first began to hear the night music of the town. It started that first night with the street sounds of donkeys clomping along, the occasional car driving by, children shouting, church bells ringing, and men yelling, either for the joy of it or because of arguments—often because of too much 'pinga,' the cheap sugar cane rum. There were always loud fireworks. Or were they gunshots? The dogs barked and the roosters crowed all night. In my keyed up state, I heard it all during the night while Paul slept soundly.

Now I was in Corumba and wondered what the future would bring. God had led us this far and we knew He would continue to do so.

Dedicated to my dear husband, Paul, who literally took me to "the end of the earth."

Daily Life in Corumba
Rosemary Pierson

After Paul's adventures driving our jeep across Brazil, the children and I followed, arriving in Corumba, Mato Grosso, Brazil, in 1957. As Presbyterian missionaries, we were the only Americans in town at that time. After a search of several days we found a small two bedroom house to rent. It was a duplex.

Our first morning in the house I heard clanking and clapping from the street and someone calling out, "Milk! Milk!" Steve and I rushed to the window. We saw a donkey loaded on each side with metal milk cans. The maid from next door went out with a pitcher and the milkman ladled milk into her pitcher. I gasped! It wasn't white. It was blue! After all, if you add enough water to milk it will look blue in the sunlight. At times we read in the Sao Paulo paper (which we rarely received) that the milk sold was around twice the amount that actually came into the city. Apparently that was also true of the milk brought into Corumba. Because of the dilution of the milk plus its long trip by donkey under the hot tropical sun, we used canned powdered milk.

At 5:00 or 5:30 in the morning people flung open their shutters and hurried to the bakery. They returned with long loaves of crusty crunchy bread, partially wrapped in a small piece of paper. The bread was delicious but I did not buy ours at that hour. All day long someone passed by, calling out their wares. Sometimes it was fish, dangling at each end of a long pole, held across the fisherman's shoulder. The fish were usually 'pintado' (like a large catfish), 'pacu' (a fatty fruit eating fish), 'dourado' (golden colored), and piranha. I would never eat a piranha, I didn't know who it might have been nibbling on! Not knowing how fresh the fish was, we did not eat fish sold on the street. We could buy it fresh down at the harbor. Paul turned out to be our fisherman. Other items we bought were bananas, field corn, and some fruit. Because of the limestone soil, very little fruit or vegetables grew there.

Using All the Colors

Buying food consumed a lot of time. The meat market, where they sold 'well aged' beef, was some distance away. The tough and stringy zebu cattle were driven into town at the end of the day. The next morning I could buy a chunk of meat from the freshly killed animal at the butcher's shop. The meat was tasty after it had been beaten, ground, or cooked in a pressure cooker. A tiny grocery store had a few canned goods along with potatoes and large, tough carrots that had come by train from Sao Paulo. The store also sold flour, rice, beans, sugar, and coffee. If we had wanted to, we could have purchased dried cod that had been caught off the grand banks of Newfoundland, taken to Portugal, and from there, across the Atlantic, finally made its way across Brazil to Corumba. That was a delicacy we did not care to try. Later, when we lived in Portugal, we found that dried cod was considered a treat.

Rosemary's access to curbside shopping

We soon became involved in the church and community. Paul was calling in homes every afternoon, while conducting evening services twice a week in the chapel. Church members asked Paul to conduct services in homes or the streets of various neighborhoods

Occupational Adventures

in Corumba or the neighboring town of Ladario. He was soon doing so six evenings a week.

Wanting to visit isolated people along the river, Paul had a boat, six meters long, built. However, he needed an outboard motor. Tariffs on imported goods like a motor were astoundingly high. But the amount seemed to be quite arbitrary. He went to the customs house, requesting an interview with the chief customs agent. The appointment was made for early the next morning. But when he arrived, Paul had a shock. The man had been assassinated the night before. They said it was a professional job. While he had five bullets in him, the man next to him was not injured. The word around town was that the man was involved in smuggling. Contraband coming across the river from Bolivia included American cars and electrical items. It was a lucrative business and probably the customs agent was involved in some kind of conflict. I recently read a section on Corumba in a current travel book on Brazil. It noted that Corumba is a major center of smuggling today, especially for drugs and firearms. After that incident Paul decided to ask our New York board to send the motor with a new missionary who would arrive by ship. That was usually the best way to bring things into the country. After some months the motor arrived and served Paul well, both for evangelistic trips up and down the river, and for fishing. Our family, and many others, enjoyed the fish.

We came to know many interesting people. One day when Paul was visiting a family his hostess said, "Come with me." Paul followed her down the street until they stopped at a tiny ramshackle mud and wattle hut, with a dirt floor. It leaned at a precarious angle. Stooping to enter, Paul had to become accustomed to the darkness inside. There he saw, sitting in a chair, a tiny woman who appeared to be very ill. She was coughing constantly. She was alone with no family to care for her. After prayer and a short visit, Paul and the neighbor left. When they returned to her house, she explained that the woman was being kept alive by the 'believers," (church members) on that block. Daily they took her some rice and beans, bread, and coffee, and on rare occasions, a bit of meat also. Paul visited Maria several times. When he began to tell her about Jesus, her face lit up and she smiled. "Oh pastor, I know about Jesus. I'm just waiting to go and be with Him." The care of the neighbors had showed her the love of Christ. Shortly after that, Paul and the elder, Sebastiao, went to her house and baptized her. Two weeks after that she died and went to be with the Lord she had come to know through a bit of rice and beans, coffee, and bread.

At one point we met a German man at an outdoor service. Franz had been a merchant seaman during the war, had deserted and remained in Brazil and found his way to the far west. He was living with his common law wife. They had three children. At first he seemed to be strongly opposed to any Christian faith. Then he was dramatically converted. So in an evening service in our little church, Paul married the couple, baptized the parents, and then the children. Franz eventually became the leader of a small congregation that met at a manganese mine where he worked thirty kilometers from town.

Our first Sunday in Corumba, Senhor Sebastiao, the lay leader of our little congregation, spoke to Paul. "Pastor, shall we give a turn this afternoon." Not having any idea what this idiomatic expression meant, Paul agreed. So after lunch, Sebastiao appeared and off they went. On his return, Paul explained what the expression meant. They spent the afternoon visiting Sebastiao's friends and neighbors sharing the Good News of Christ. They continued to do that nearly every Sunday during our stay in Corumba, and Paul baptized a number of people as a result. While Sebastiao faithfully visited his friends, he was bothered by a recurring thought. "Go and visit Rafael." Rafael was a relatively well to do cattleman who lived nearby. When he saw Sebastiao going out on Sunday, he watched him and scoffed, saying, "Look at the man! He works long hours each day at the flour mill and what does he do on Sunday, he goes to people's houses with that big black book under his arm. Doesn't he have anything better to do?" Rafael's family was well known in the community. His father had lost much of the family fortune through gambling and alcohol.

Sebastiao was aware of his attitude and, thoroughly intimidated, avoided going to his home. But the message persisted in his mind. "You must invite Rafael to church." So one day he did. To his amazement Rafael agreed to go the following Sunday. That night Paul saw a well dressed man standing at the back of the church, close to the door. Paul was not sure if Rafael would stay but he did. When he heard the announcement that there was to be an outdoor service at a certain location that week, surprisingly, Rafael asked if he could go along. Of course he was welcomed. He went to the outdoor service and returned to church the following Sunday, where he amazed Paul by stating that he wanted to commit his life to Christ and become a 'believer'.

After that he attended church when he was not leading cattle drives across the pantanal. That involved driving herds of a thousand or more zebu cattle to the next town to be loaded on the railroad and shipped to Sao Paulo. The zebu were a very hardy breed, with a large hump on the back, long ears, and strong enough to survive in that difficult environment. Rafael and his father in law were both baptized and became faithful members of our growing church.

Rafael told interesting stories of encounters with jaguars on the cattle drives. On one occasion, he told us, one of his cowboys shot a jaguar that was in a tree. The animal fell to the ground and the cowboy decided to try to lasso it from his horse. However as he rode by, the wounded jaguar jumped up from the ground and killed the man. Tragic. The moral of the story… Don't fool around with jaguars.

Going Into the 'Mato' (Jungle)

Rosemary Pierson

While the work was progressing in Corumba and the neighboring town of Ladario, an interesting new work developed in the 'mato,' as the jungle was called. One night Paul and the elders were asked to go to an outlying area in Corumba to hold a service and preach. There, a man named Ze accepted Christ. He became very enthusiastic about his faith. After awhile he told Paul about his background. He had lived in the drought stricken Northeast. During a brawl in a bar one night his friend was shot and killed. Then Ze killed the assailant. He served a short prison sentence, was freed, and made his way to Corumba, around twenty five hundred miles distant.

He asked Paul to go to an area in the mato where he had friends so he could share his faith. Paul was anxious to go, wanting to see this impenetrable jungle. The trees were so densely entwined with vines and other vegetation that if you were put into the midst of them a few feet from the road you would be completely lost. It was a long, hot, humid, and dusty trip. The road was narrow and rough. And one often had to dodge the Zebu cattle who roamed freely. The mato was home to countless animals, including birds, reptiles, and insects. In the evening, colorful parakeets, parrots, macaws, and other birds flew in from the pantanal. Furry tarantulas, as large as kittens, hopped across the road. Jaguars, anacondas (up to thirty feet long), monkeys, wild pigs, and capybaras (the world's largest rodent, the size of a pig), lived there.

Leaving one morning, the men finally arrived at a clearing. There, Ze's friend, Anesio, and others, worked cutting wood for charcoal. Anesio was the foreman. Ze went to invite his friends while Paul prepared for the service. He connected a record player to the car's battery and began to play hymns. As the music wafted through the trees the people came. After all, there was no other entertainment. A sizeable group of men, women, children, and dogs gathered. Again utilizing the car battery, Paul showed a filmstrip of a Bible story, closing with a short message explaining the story and sharing the Gospel. Ze told the story of his conversion. That night Anesio and his wife, Berenice, and a few others accepted Christ. Although Anesio could not read, Berenice could, and between the two of them they led the local group in worship twice each week.

The home of Anesio in the Mato (Jungle)

It was only later that Paul heard the rest of the story. Anesio and Berenice had two children and were struggling in a rocky marriage. Anesio learned that another man had been courting his wife, wanting her to run away with him. She was apparently interested. Anesio was furious and had resolved to kill the man the next time he appeared. He had his revolver ready, as all the men there did. At that point Paul and Ze arrived and Anesio and Berenice were converted. The next time the would-be lover appeared, they began to share the Gospel with him, telling of the change Christ had made in their lives. He was definitely not interested and made a hasty retreat and was not seen again. But he never knew the Gospel had saved his life!!

A little later, Anesio asked Paul if he thought he should get rid of his gun. Paul agreed that it was a good idea. That was very unusual in that area. Life was cheap and guns were not infrequently used. One time Anesio and Paul invited a neighbor to come to the service. But he refused. A few days later Anesio came to our door in Corumba. He had come to town to see what he could do to help that neighbor who had killed a man in an argument over a suckling pig. In that context, guilt or innocence was not the most important factor in a man's fate, rather it was whether or not he had money to pay a lawyer.

On one occasion, most of the people in the Corumba church went by truck to the mato to hold a larger service where there were baptisms and Communion. That was a memorable time.

The children and I made many trips to the mato. They liked to play with the children who lived there. The mosquitoes and other insects were a constant problem. The Brazilians always carried a cloth, constantly waving it in front of their faces or swatting themselves to keep the mosquitoes away. Occasionally one flew in Paul's mouth when he preached. Not a good feeling!! Sometimes at the close of the service, a new group appeared out of the darkness. They had heard the music and walked a long distance so then the service was repeated. There was great openness to the Gospel message. Life was very difficult. Most had never had any contact with a priest or pastor, had never been in a church, had never heard anything of the Word of God. They often responded to the incredible message that God loved them and would help in their lives. Often, when Ze was present, after Paul had preached in his best language school Portuguese, Ze got up and said, "What the pastor wanted to say is this." Then in his local 'caipira,' or hillbilly speech, he would repeat the sermon. But one day Ze suddenly disappeared. We never knew what happened to him.

One day a man came to our front door and clapped loudly. That was the Brazilian doorbell at the time. He had come on a truck from the mato to find Paul and tell him that Anesio was critically ill. It was summer, and we had two students, Eurycles and Pedro, interning at the church. So Paul and the two young men immediately went out to visit Anesio. When they arrived at the clearing, Paul backed the jeep off the road, preparing to park it. But some shrubs had just been cut, leaving sharp ends. When they got out of the jeep they saw that the gasoline was pouring out of the gas tank. The two students ran to a nearby house and borrowed a pan to catch the gasoline. Obviously there was no more gas nor did there seem to be any way to repair the gas tank there in the mato. Concerned about Anesio, Paul told the young men to do what they could to resolve the problem and rushed to Anesio's house. He was greatly relieved to find his friend much better. After a visit and prayer, he walked back to the car, wondering what to do. It would soon be dark and no one could survive a night in the mato without shelter and mosquito netting. It was bad enough to have a mosquito fly into his mouth when he was preaching, but it would be impossible to spend the night there.

As he approached the car he found that the two students and a neighbor had been very ingenious. They had cut a piece from a tin can and flattened it to make a patch for the gas tank. But how would they attach it? The neighbor remembered that he had recently gone hunting for wild bees' wax. He found the ball of wax, melted some with a candle, and used it to secure the tin patch to the bottom of the gas tank. Then they put the remaining gas back into the tank… It seemed to be holding!!! Relieved and grateful, the three started the long journey home, driving very carefully. Their thoughts centered on the bees' wax. Would the patch hold? Would gasoline dissolve bees' wax? If it did, what would they do? They drove and drove and finally arrived in Corumba. The patch held!! In fact Paul was so busy the next three days, he did not take the car for repairs until the fourth day. Brazilian ingenuity and wild bees' wax had saved the day!!

Where is Your Home?

Norman E. Thomas

I shall never forget my first Sunday worship in Africa. It was in February 1962 at the Nyakatsapa Methodist Church near the Shona Language School in Southern Rhodesia. Near the simple brick church was the Methodist primary school to which children came each week day in their uniforms from the surrounding villages. Some of the homes nearby were made of red bricks with corrugated tin or asbestos roofs. Others were constructed with sundried bricks and grass thatched roofs. Every homestead included small round storage bins for grain that the family harvested from their fields. All looked out on a broad valley with wooded hills and with rock outcroppings behind.

This was my first time to be segregated in worship—men and boys sitting on the left; women and girls on the right! After worship we stayed separated to greet each other.

"*Kwaziwai*," (Hello) the men said greeting me as they clapped their hands together rather than shaking my hand. They taught me to cup my hands together with fingers together as men do. Women cross their hands as they clap. They also taught me my response: "*Kwaziwai.*"

"*Muriwadi here?*" was their next greeting to me. One translated the Shona words for me, "How are you?" and taught me my response—"*Ndiriwadi kuti muriwadiwo.*" It was translated as "I am well **if** you are well." Later I grew to appreciate the profound meaning behind this simple greeting—that I can be my true self only in community—that I am who I am only because we are.

Next the men asked me: "*Musha wenyu uripi?*" which one translated as "Where is your home?" That was a more difficult question for me to answer. "What do you mean?" I asked. One answered that they were asking not where I was living but rather where my parents lived. They felt that "home" was where family members and friends formed a community of caring and support.

How was I to respond? Five months earlier I had said a tearful "Goodbye" to my parents and boarded the Stavangerfiord in New York to begin our family's adventure as Africa missionaries. During the next four months my parents had moved from their home in Nashville, Tennessee to Birmingham, Michigan, a Detroit suburb where my father pastored a Methodist church. There was only one honest response to give, so I replied: "My home is in Birmingham, Michigan, in the United States, but I have never been there."

I shall never forget the looks of utter astonishment of the men that day. After a long pause that seemed full of suspended silence, an old man called Ishe Chimbadwa spoke up. Although short in stature, just five feet high, he was both a lay leader of the church and a sub-chief (*ishe*) of the Manyika people of the area. "We are sorry you have no home," the old man said to me. "But from today my home shall be your home. You will be of the Manyika tribe and one of us."

Norm greeting men after church

Using All the Colors

Had I been a homeless person? Outwardly I presented myself as self-confident, healthy, thirty-years old, well-educated, father of two, and missionary. Despite those assets, however, I was in fact a nomad.

Perhaps Ishe Chimbadzwa intuitively had empathized with me and with other new missionaries whom he had come to know. He gave me that day a gift far more precious and lasting than the live rooster or hen traditionally brought to welcome a newcomer. He gave me the security of a new home, African-style—not a building, but a caring extended family of love and support.

When did I emotionally arrive in my new home? It did not take place the day I disembarked from an ocean liner in Capetown, South Africa, and set foot on the soil of Africa. Instead, it happened as a Christian and community elder said to me: "My home is your home."

What is Your Name?

Norman E. Thomas

"What's in a name?" is what Shakespeare's Juliet asked her lover Romeo. Knowing that they were from clans at war with each other, she asked: "What's in a name? That which we call a rose by any other name would smell as sweet."

I thought I knew my name until one morning when a man asked me, a new missionary, "What is your name?" We were both dressed for church with suit coats and ties as was the custom then. The church yard had been swept clean by the women before worship. We were fortunate that the sun was shining but could expect afternoon showers so essential for the growth of the *maize* (corn) in this the rainy season as that was the staple food of the diet.

For thirty years when asked my name I had answered "Norman Ernest Thomas." I was proud to be called "Norman" after my uncle, "Ernest" after my father, and "Thomas," my family name. And "Norman Ernest Thomas" was enough for the immigration officer who admitted me to the country two weeks earlier to begin work as a missionary in Southern Rhodesia (now called Zimbabwe).

But that answer was not enough at my welcome that day. *Zita renyu uripi?* was the question asked—what is your name? What we want to know is **not** the name given at your baptism, **nor** your family name, the Zimbabwean continued. We want to know your **clan** name, your *mutupo*—you know . . . that animal or bird or fish that tells us what clan you're a member of. Often men would meet and greet one another using just their clan names. One might say, while clapping his hands in greeting, *Kwaziwai shumba* [Hello lion]. The other might respond with a handclap *Kwaziwai soko* [Hello monkey].

Using All the Colors

What was I to respond? I chose to be truthful and replied: "I'm sorry, but I have no such name." The looks of surprise on the faces of the men around me soon turned to frowns. Then their leader, sub-chief Chimbadzwa, responded: "Young man, we're glad that you have come to live and work among us, and we're sorry that you have no [clan] name. But from today my name shall be your name. Your name will be *shumba* [lion] of the royal clan of Chief Mutasa of Manicaland."

Norm teaching class leaders

In the months to come I experienced what a great gift had been given to me that day. For the next five years I travelled to many African villages and townships in my work as Director of Christian Education and Youth Work for the Methodist Church in that country. Always upon arrival I was greeted warmly by persons who were for me total strangers. We exchanged formal greetings with hand claps. Then they asked: "Where is your home?" I replied, "In the land of Chief Mutasa of Manicaland". "And what is your name?" they continued. "*Shumba*," I replied. Their response invariably was smiles of pleasure. Sometimes they voiced an audible

"Hmm" that meant that they felt "he's one of us". Once one added: "He may have a white skin, but he has a black heart," and this before the "black is beautiful" movement in North America!

Missionaries when they return from "the field" are expected to speak in churches about their missionary work. My favorite topic was "What Africa gave to me." I shared about the precious gift given to me on that first Sunday as a missionary in Africa. With my new name—*shumba*—I was no longer a stranger from a foreign land. I had been adopted as a "family" member of an extended clan of thousands in the land now called Zimbabwe.

Later other church people would add their deep words of acceptance, saying: "We want you to lay down your bones here in our land, among ours, when our lives on earth are over."

Going to Egypt

Dot Turnbull

My husband, Bob, and I started our fifteen years of missionary service in Egypt by taking Jersey cattle, three bred heifers and a six month old bull, to the dairy project in Assiut Egypt where we would be working.

The call came, the end of September 1950... a ship had been found that would take the cattle, Bob, and me to Egypt. We planned to drive our car from Stone Valley, PA., as far as Philadelphia where Bob's brother, David, lived. We left our car there for David to sell, and went on to New York where we stayed two nights in the Prince George Hotel in lower Manhattan. Dr. Hugh Kelsey, the Foreign Mission Secretary of the United Presbyterian Church of North America, was to take us to the ship on Monday. Our freight and the cattle were to be on the ship Friday, because the freighter was being moved to a restricted security area to load some military equipment.

As we were driving to Philadelphia I suggested to Bob that we needed to get a pitchfork to use on the ship to feed hay to the cattle and to clean the stalls. We really needed two forks but Bob thought that the ship would have something we could use. I had never been on a ship before, but I had grown up on a dairy farm, and I couldn't think of anything that the ship might have that would be useful. I finally just insisted that we get a fork, so he agreed, but said, 'We'll get it, if you'll carry it." I carried the pitchfork into the hotel, through the lobby, up the elevator, and repeated the action in reverse when we went to the ship. I did attract attention. At least, I didn't have to carry it when we did some last minute shopping in New York nor when we went to hear Dr. Norman Vincent Peale preach in Marble Collegiate Reformed Church on Fifth Avenue.

Occupational Adventures

In order to get to our freighter, *The Flying Clipper*, all eight passengers were taken by a small launch across the harbor and had to walk some distance across some floating docks to reach the ship. The crew was hanging over the rail and when they saw me with the pitchfork... they guessed we belonged to the cattle and called out a welcome. The cattle were still well after three days on the ship before we arrived. The pickled pigs feet someone had tried to feed them were still in the stall...

The fork was used everyday and for years in Egypt.

Excitement was high as we sailed out of New York Harbor past the Statue of Liberty and then headed up north along the east coast on October 2, 1950. Soon we discovered that we were heading for Portland, Maine, where we would be for three days loading large rolls of newsprint. We went ashore and made another last call home before we left the USA.

I had raved about the wonderful lobsters in Maine and how I loved to eat in some of the old seafood restaurants near the harbor. Bob went ashore one day and came back with a paper bag of lobsters. He had found a bargain and had bought three. I had forgotten to tell him that I liked boiled butter with my lobster and a little atmosphere! We were about to sail and since I am prone to seasickness I wasn't very hungry for lobster. We did eat some as we were on the fantail watching the beautiful fall colors of the trees fade away and again said goodbye to the USA.

What a surprise the next morning to find we were in a very small port further north where we were loading dynamite caps which they told us were too dangerous to load in a densely populated area. That made us all feel safe and secure. Finally, later that day, we sailed out of that port and headed across the Atlantic. I took dramamine but the first day out when I went to help Bob with the cattle I had to return to the cabin. He finished brushing and

Using All the Colors

feeding and was sympathetic but didn't tell me until much later that he had been sick too.

The other passengers were also missionaries: one family of three and two single women—all Lutheran, and an Indian woman, headmistress of a Methodist Christian School in India who had just gotten her master's degree. We passed the time reading, playing games, visiting, and planning the Sunday services at the request of the Captain. I learned to cut Bob's hair on that trip and I've been doing it ever since.

Although the ocean was never very rough, the Rock of Gibraltar was an encouraging sight and the Mediterranean was smooth sailing. About October 18th we made our first stop in Alexandretta, Turkey. I remember clearly my feelings of bewilderment—being surrounded by people communicating with each other and I couldn't understand. It took three days to unload cargo there. It was a small port and the only space available was the end of the pier but we didn't stay there long because the waves were pushing our ship against the pier and then pulling us away so much that we anchored in the harbor and unloaded on a floating barge. We watched with great interest the unloading of many jeeps onto the barge with no sides. The men unloading were having a wonderful time taking turns driving and parking the jeeps on the barge with no sides as it bounced up and down in the water. Several times I held my breath as we watched the jeeps racing for the side of the galloping dock.

The following day no one came to unload the ship and we were told that this was census day, taken every 10 years, and everyone had to stay home to be counted until the whistle blew. On land nothing was moving, but late in the afternoon a little boat came out into the harbor and stopped at all the ships. Officials from the cruiser came aboard and we all were counted in the census of 1950 in Turkey. A short time later the siren went off and everyone started going about their business again.

Occupational Adventures

At the last minute, the Captain told us that we might be going to Beirut first and then Alexandria. This was a big concern because we were almost out of feed for the cattle. Bob decided to try and get some before we sailed. He went ashore in a small boat and after what seemed like an eternity (because we were about to sail), Bob appeared in a very small boat with a big bundle of straw, the only thing he could find. What a sight; the little boat was bobbing up and down, the ladder over the side of the ship did not quite reach the boat. It looked like a long way down from where I was looking over the rail. Finally the sailors took pity on him and went down the ladder and helped him up with the straw. After all that effort we went directly to Alexandria. The Captain explained that he received his orders after we were at sea so couldn't tell us our destination.

The sights, sounds and smells of the port in Alexandria were more than we could take in. The dock was full of people wanting to help us or sell us trinkets or food, and the "gule gule men" (magicians) wanted to entertain us with a magic show. In the midst of the crowd we saw two foreign looking men. They had gray hair and Egyptians don't let their hair turn gray. They turned out to be Mr. Milo McFeeters, and Dr. Harold McGeogh, from the American Mission in Egypt that we were joining. Dr. McGeogh was the treasurer stationed in Alexandria and Mr McFeeters was from Assiut, the man who had started the dairy project thirty years ago and who would be retiring in two years—the man Bob was to replace. We were overjoyed to meet them.

All the other passengers said goodbye to us as they went off on a tour to Cairo and we were left to watch our trunks, barrels, and crates being unloaded, all twenty-three pieces. We watched in amazement, as one man would carry a very large and heavy trunk or crate on his shoulder. With the help of one or two other men the crate was hoisted to his shoulder and balanced against his head he would walk off to the customs shed. We never ceased to be amazed at the strength of these poor, underfed men. One we'll never forget

Using All the Colors

was KatKute (which means little chicken), one of our dairy workers, who carried a piano on his back up the stairs to the third floor flat with just one man balancing it on either side.

All our personal effects were cleared through customs except the refrigerator. It was decided that the cattle should stay on board until the following day and we also would stay until they were unloaded. The following morning we gave thanks to see the cattle successfully unloaded and in the hands of, Iyad, the head headsman from Assiut who had come to take the cattle to Assiut by truck.

Dot, Bob, and Mr. McFeeters

We were entertained in our first mission home by Dr. and Mrs. Charles Russell in Alexandria. They were to retire in one year and asked if we would be interested in their furniture. As it turned out we did buy their bedroom suite (bed, dresser, and chest of drawers) all made from Sudan Mahogany that Mrs. Russell's father had sent from the Sudan. The furniture was made in Egypt. It was sturdy and beautifully finished.

Our plan was to take an early train from Alexandria to Cairo where we would spend a few hours with my father's cousins, Mary Francis and Margaret Dawson, and see how Bob's sister, Jean, was getting along at the American College for Girls in Cairo and then take the train on to Assiut and arrive before the cattle. The plan had to be changed because of technicalities and the Cairo stop was abandoned. We just had time to change trains and go on. Mr. McFeeters was with us or we would never have made it. We arrived at 2:00 in the morning and were met by two missionaries, Paul McClanahan and Gordon Parkinson. Ordinarily there would have been fifty to one hundred people, Americans and Egyptians. We soon learned that meeting and sending people on the train was a very important social activity (a must!) in Egyptian Culture.

We spent our first night in Assiut with the McFeeters, and met most of the other foreigners in the city at a Halloween party the second night—which made them difficult to recognize the next time we met. Our first Arabic service was at the Prep School. Dr. Skellie was very helpful by preparing a summary of the service in English for us. After the service, we visited Rena and May Hogg, daughters of the pioneer missionary in Assiut, who lived on the second floor of the Prep School where the service was held. During our visit, word came that our cattle had arrived at the college. We made a hasty exit to go and welcome our cattle to their new home!

It's the Taliban!
K. Roberta Woodberry

After retiring in 1999 from teaching in San Marino, I went to Peshawar, Pakistan to teach in a small school there. My grandson would be in my class along with children of many nationalities. Dudley commuted about every six weeks while still teaching at Fuller Seminary. Our son John was the manager and a pilot of PACTEC, a small Christian airline that flew all over Afghanistan bringing humanitarian relief and personnel. During the Taliban times the airline was based in Peshawar. He lived there with his wife, Corinne, and our two grandchildren, Katharine and Daniel. It was during that time that we were invited back to Kabul where we had lived and served previously in a pastoral role for the Christian international community.

The shouting reverberated through the building. What was happening? My daughter-in-law Corinne and I looked questioningly at each other but continued to look at the beautiful Afghan embroidery—tablecloths, caftans, blouses, scarves, and purses—in the gift shop. It was the only means of work for the Afghan women and we wanted to buy as much as we could to take home for gifts.

The door opened quietly and the director's ashen-faced assistant, Miriam, told us "It's the Taliban. They've arrived to search the building for any illegal items." We were to stay quiet and they would let us know when it was OK to leave.

We quickly pulled up some chairs. Corinne, Katharine, my granddaughter, Daniel, my grandson, and I formed a circle and began to quietly pray. Almost instantly the door was opened and there stood the International Assistance Mission Director, surrounded by soldiers in tattered clothes carrying AK-47s. They stood beside the Taliban Commander. The sense of evil around him filled the room as he started to yell at Corinne. "What are you doing out in public as an Afghan woman? You know the rules! You must not leave your home!" His black beady eyes and black turban seemed to match his personality.

Corinne answered very politely in her best Dari. "Sir, I am sorry, but I am not an Afghan woman. I am an American and I came here to help your people."

His head jerked and he turned to me. Katharine, at this point, was sitting in my lap. He started yelling at her. "What is a young Afghan girl doing here with these women? You should not be in this building!"

I yelled right back and English came out. "She's not an Afghan girl, she's my granddaughter!" He jerked his head again, muttering something under his breath and the door slammed.

The four of us—alone in the gift shop—were shaken. Corinne and I again began to pray but I'm sure our calm was easy for the children to see through.

It wasn't long before Miriam again opened the door and said we should leave quickly and go back to the guest house. As we gathered our things, she pulled me aside. "Roberta," she said, "Would you be willing to take a couple of Dari Bibles out of the office. I know if they're found here, our Afghan staff will all go to prison." We ducked back into the gift shop and she handed them to me. I squeezed them under my arm, wrapped my shawl tightly around them and we were out the door—heads lowered, eyes to the ground—holding the hand of my grandson.

The guard at the compound gate opened it with a squeaking sound and we stepped out into the street. Right in front of us was a white Toyota pick up truck, the kind used by the Taliban. I thought they had gone. As I shifted my eyes to look, there in the back was our son, John, in his pilot's uniform, surrounded by Taliban soldiers carrying AK-47s. My heart went to my toes. Had Corinne noticed? Did the children know? I said nothing, but in my heart, my prayers were intense.

We walked quickly with our heads covered and bowed trying to be as inconspicuous and possible. About a block away, a gate creaked open and we heard our names. Inside there was Dudley and several others gathered to pray. We shared what had happened and heard that several homes had been searched as well. But they knew of no other foreigners taken—just our John. Why? We didn't know.

The guest house was next door, so I quietly went to my room, put the Bibles in my suitcase, and came back through the back door gate in the wall. It was hard to comprehend what was happening.

Slowly, we began to realize we all would be leaving Afghanistan. Our presence endangered the lives of our Afghan colleagues as well as our own. While we were discussing how we should proceed, the gate bell rang. There stood John. What a joy to see him! What had happened? How had he gotten away? How did they treat him?

He had spent the morning going from office to office getting visas and permissions for pilots and planes to continue their humanitarian flights into the remote regions of Afghanistan. Najibullah, his friend, had been with him—helping with all the forms and procedures. They were processing it all in Najibullah's office when the Taliban barged in to search the premises. In one of the drawers they had found an order blank for a Bible correspondence course and so Najibullah was arrested, even though the form had not been filled out and he was a Muslim. As they took him away, John stood up and said, "If you're taking my friend, you'll take me too. I know you will treat him better if I am along." And so John had climbed into the back of the truck with his friend.

They had driven a couple of miles down Darulaman Rd. when the commander realized he also had an American in the back. They stopped immediately and John was ordered out. He had walked back, but Najibullah was taken to prison.

We had come from Pakistan for a conference and since we were all there, they decided to go ahead and meet that evening. They could also discuss the latest developments and what the next steps would be. Evacuation was the obvious answer, especially when we returned to the guest house and the Taliban had been there too, putting a strip of paper around the front door with a wax seal—saying we could not enter—under penalty of who knows what.

It was a hard night for all of us. Our grandchildren couldn't understand why they couldn't have their teddy bear and treasured Samantha doll—locked back in the guest house. We slept in the director's home—some of us on the floor. Many didn't sleep at all that night as fires throughout the city burned constantly, erasing any evidence that might endanger lives.

The next morning, the Taliban gave us a half hour to pack our things while they searched the guest house. Fortunately, Dudley had taken the Bibles from my suitcase and hidden them on the floor behind the blank space at the bottom of a bookcase. A Taliban man squatted six inches from them looking at the other books, but never found the ones in Dari.

That afternoon, Corinne, Katharine, Daniel and I were flown out of Kabul with two other women. Dudley and Bob, our middle son, went overland through the Khyber Pass to Pakistan. John stayed behind to help with evacuations.

As our little plane took off, I couldn't stop weeping. Those beautiful mountains surrounding the city seemed to be the Lord's embrace—but the hatred and desolation of Kabul, along with all the blown up airplanes beside the runway told a different story. As I looked down we flew directly over the notorious prison built by the Russians. It was shaped like a wagon wheel with spokes coming from a hub. Would Najibullah be taken there?

When we landed in Peshawar, one of the women knelt down and kissed the ground. We were safe and free—less than 1 month before 9/11!

* *Some names have been changed*

Using All the Colors

Interesting People and Places

Using All the Colors

Interesting People and Places

My Friend Jonathan
Carole Hoffs Bos

Seeing him enter the classroom, I smiled inwardly. I had met Jonathan several times in various classes during my substituting years at our local middle school. He had a ready smile for me as he entered the eighth grade English classroom. Secretly I called him Jolly Jonathan because of his good-natured presence. Often when middle school students see that their regular teacher is absent, chaos reigns within the classroom. At least that is what the students TRY to achieve. Some are glum, uncooperative and even rude. Not so with Jonathan. He nearly always greeted me by name, chatting about school in general, biology in particular, but never much about sports. Jonathan's eyes danced from object to object as he talked but they would return to rivet mine as he made an important emphasis. I imagined Jonathan was on the receiving end of many jokes from his fellow middle school classmates: he was overweight and not much of an athlete. This never seemed to disturb him; he had enough self confidence to know who he was. That is a miracle in itself for an eighth grader. His dark curly hair and winning smile made him a stand-out in any class.

During a long-term substitute teaching position for fifteen weeks, I was delighted that Jonathan turned up in one of my classes. He was often excitable when called upon for his opinion as we discussed a piece of literature or a problematic grammar usage. I noticed that he would use "Oh, my God" or "Oh, God" this or that in his sentences without hesitation. After several days of listening to this, I asked him to stay a few minutes after class into our lunch hour. Gently I told him that he was using a word precious to me in a very careless, casual way. He seemed very concerned and very surprised at this, and when I told him it was the word "God" which was a concern to me, he was even more anxious. Jonathan knew a precious name when he heard one. He apologized and promised he would try to break his habit. And he did—I never heard those expressions from him again in my presence. We remained respectful of one another.

Later in the year when I was back to day-to-day substituting, the school office called at 5:30 a.m. in desperation. They begged me to take a PE class for a male teacher. At my request, I had signed up to substitute in music, English and social science classes only. This assignment from the district meant a boys' physical education class. I cowered as I let the voice on the other end of the phone talk me into helping her fill this substitute position. As I drove to school that morning, I began to doubt my sanity. What did I know about running a fifty-five member male class in basketball, soccer or even worse, football? I found my lesson plans and courageously made my way to the field to take roll for period 1. Much to my surprise and delight, I spied Jonathan who ran up to greet me—by name as usual.

"Jonathan," I began, "you can help me considerably today. I know virtually nothing about flag football and that's what the lesson plans entail. Tell me what I should know and how your teacher usually organizes the teams after roll call." He could have guffawed and planned a grand hoax on a naïve substitute teacher. I was at his mercy and I knew it. Instead, he retorted, "Leave it to me, Mrs. Bos. I'll take care of getting the teams on the field." Off he trotted to divide the class into groups. I anxiously stood on the sidelines thinking how much more flexible junior high boys seemed than girls at this age who argue over getting dressed into their PE clothes or borderline calls, and they often sulk when challenged with the house rules. The boys just play and accommodate all kinds of adjustments. Jonathan trotted back to me after several minutes of maneuvering huddle talks. "Don't worry, Mrs. Bos, we're organized and ready to go." He started to run back, then turned and added, "And, oh yes, I told them no swearing or dirty talk." I could hardly hide my smile, and not daring to hug this exceptional young man, I merely nodded my head and thanked him.

Celebrity Encounters
Annabelle Dirks

I have often pondered why we humans find such a thrill from meeting or having some personal contact with celebrities of one sort or another. Do we feel that there is a glamour that will reflect on us—or does the idea of name-dropping give us some vicarious importance—or is it just fun to see some of the people for real that we have heard of or that have reached certain levels of fame?

Usually, we choose the event or famous people we wish to see and hear. We pay our money for tickets to listen to speakers speak, musicians play, or watch movie stars act on the big screen. But then there are those chance encounters when it is merely the time and place that brings you face-to-face with a celebrity.

Because of my life in the academic world, I had the privilege of meeting some well-known people. Early on, for instance, I encountered Paul Tillich, Reinhold Neibuhr, and Bill Coffin. On another occasion, when WWII ended, there was a huge victory parade in New York City for General Dwight D. Eisenhower. I was in the crowd of thousands cheering for the war hero. A few years later, he became president of Columbia University. My husband, Ed Dirks, was also there, as the Counselor to Protestant Students. During a University reception held for Ed, Eisenhower was an attendee and we visited together. A few years later, he sent a personal note of congratulations when our twin sons were born. I still have the letter.

While my husband was at Columbia, I was at Good Housekeeping Magazine, then owned by the Hearst Corporation. William Randolph Hearst, Sr. showed up at the magazine about once a year, coming from his castle at San Simeon in California (where he lived with Marion Davies), to dispense bonus checks to "the help"—and I remember clearly all of us standing meekly in his office as he, behind a huge desk, performed his kingly duties.

Using All the Colors

On a night out at a dinner club in NYC with my husband celebrating our wedding anniversary, a young up-and-coming singer appeared at our table and sang to us. It was Frank Sinatra. A few years later, when I was living in Illinois, my family and I were in the same congregation with Adlai Stevenson at the local Presbyterian Church. He often sat in front of me while I tried to keep my brood of four quiet. We often spoke with each other after the service.

I've also met famous people on airplanes. On one trip, I sat one row in front of Eartha Kitt on a long propeller plane trip to Europe. We talked frequently during our many hours together. When we arrived in Paris 24 hours later, we were equally bedraggled. On another small DC-3 plane trip with my family from New Delhi to the Kashmir, we noticed holes in the floor of the aircraft with views of the ground and ever-so-close mountains below us. A fellow passenger on that trip was Ralph Bunche, a distinguished UN diplomat. My husband and I had an interesting conversation with him.

More recently, I've visited my son in NYC. One of his regular house guests (and nearby neighbor) is Salman Rushdie. Some of you may remember that he wrote the book *Satanic Verses*, condemned by the Ayatollah (Rushdie himself was condemned to death by a Fatwa—and spent many years in hiding). He is no longer under such threat, which allowed me the opportunity to sit next to him during a wonderful dinner party. I worried about what to say... but I needn't have worried, since he talked constantly and was happy to have an avid listener.

There have been many others... and I'm sure all of you have some similar stories about encounters with the famous—either by design or by chance.

You Must Have a Good Mantra!
Dick Dosker

Retiring as a camp director at Mount Hermon Christian Conference Center in 1989, I bicycled solo across the United States. My trip began in Whitefish, Montana, in honor of my grandfather, Rev. Edwin M. Ellis, who used a chainless Columbia bicycle to pursue his Sunday school missions work in Montana. My final destination was Washington, D. C. The incident recorded here happened after traversing Montana's Bitterroot Valley and entering the historic Big Hole battlefield.

It was an early September afternoon 1989. The wide open spaces of the Big Hole country of Montana surrounded me and my fully loaded Cannondale touring bike. Some wet lands to the south had just offered a glimpse of some beautiful white Sandhill Cranes. Behind me lay the strenuous climb of the Lost Trail Pass. I was making good progress. My arrival at the depot in Whitefish and the reassembling of my gear after the train trip from San Jose, California, had gone well. The prospects for my two-month solo bike trip across the country to Washington, D. C. looked promising. I had had a wonderful visit with Louisa LeFebrve, my former camp chef, including worshipping together at the Whitefish Presbyterian Church where my grandfather Ellis had been pioneering pastor. He had been my inspiration for this trip. On his chainless Columbia bicycle he had for years crisscrossed the state of Montana as Synodical Superintendent for Sabbath School Missions. It was at Victor in the Bitterroot Valley where in 1889 my mother had been born. A sod-roofed log cabin was her first home; she was rocked on the knee of an old Indian fighter, "Uncle Woodmancy." That same year the territory of Montana became a state. Now it was 1989. My mother at 100 had given her spirit into the hands of her Maker, and I had decided to honor both my grandfather and my mother by fulfilling a dream: crossing the United States by bicycle.

Using All the Colors

I retired from my career as a camp director and ordained Presbyterian minister, and, with my wife's blessing, set out for the East Coast, following the "bike centennial" route established in 1976.

My historical reverie suddenly turned to concern. A sharp snap and a wobbly sensation alerted me to the breaking of a spoke in my rear wheel. I coasted to the side of the road and contemplated my situation. I had never changed a spoke before. I had been too eager to start this adventure! Wisdom would have included a solid course in bike mechanics. Perhaps if I just loosened the brake cables in the rear, I could wobble until a bike shop came in view. (I was to find that next shop some 150 miles further!)

Few vehicles had passed—either way—on this road. Suddenly I was aware that a VW camper that had passed me going west had turned around and was slowing to a stop at my side. A bearded young man hopped out. "You could use some help?" It was both a question and a statement. He proceeded to tell me that he had been a bicycle mechanic for five years and had some tools with him in his van. He would help me! A brief examination of my broken spoke quickly revealed that: 1. He could fix it and true the wheel, but 2. He did not have a needed "free wheel extractor," and 3. None of the spokes he had with him were the right size.

While he was telling me this, along came Eric and Yolanda, also touring by bicycle. I had noticed them in a grocery store earlier that afternoon in a village at the foot of the pass. They were the only bicyclists I had seen that day. Could they help? Yes! Between them they found that one had the right extractor and the other a spare spoke my size! It was literally minutes later when my benefactors had disassembled and reassembled my rear wheel and I was fit to go. "You must have a good mantra," said my bearded friend. "Well, not exactly," I said. "You see, when I started on this trip, I consciously placed myself in God's hands, and I knew that He would care for my needs, and complete my inadequacies." He drove off, never to be seen again—but with my enduring gratitude.

"Praise God from whom all blessings flow!" I shouted to the heavens. I had no doubts that my mother and grandfather had interceded on my behalf to bring me help in a desolate place. My guardian angels were on duty! And, this was not to be their only work of intervention in time of need during my two months on the road to Washington, D. C.

Met on the Metro
Dick Dosker

The Los Angeles Metro has provided me a practical means to return home to Pasadena after 30 plus mile bike rides to the ocean at Long Beach along the area's rivers. Invariably I interact with one or more interesting characters.

By George, if it wasn't Juan in his painter whites plunking himself down across from me and busily peeling the fruit of his profession from his hands! As always, Juan had a friendly smile of recognition and his big mountain bike was stowed at my end of the car. This time he introduced me to his brother, the building engineer at the hospital where he worked. He had been the one to get his younger brother the job as staff painter. We chatted about his plans to take his children "trick or treating" that Halloween night, shepherding them on the mean streets.

I think it was the next stop when there was some commotion at loading: a loud "Is this the train to Los Angeles?" "Please stand clear! The doors are closing," came the voice of the engineer. A young African American, high school age I assume, jumped in and immediately began a loud and expletive-filled commentary about everything under the sun. Ironically, he inserted the words "my church" somewhere in the midst of his almost rap-like, blatantly obscene message for any and all to hear, if not appreciate. It seemed so ironic to me that he saw no conflict between his foul language and the mention of his church. He also said "I don't gamble" when challenged to bet on his height by a very tall, professional African American man with a degree in sociology who came aboard briefly. He was tall enough for his head to literally brush the ceiling. "Rap-man" had asked, "How tall <u>are</u> you?" As he exited, tall man revealed that he was six feet eight inches.

The train was much quieter after the young man left. I fell into conversation with a professional-looking African American man across the aisle. He wore a fabric lanyard around his neck with the name of the institution he worked for imprinted on it and a photo ID. Although he kept his modish sunglasses on, he opened up and shared about his work as a staff member of a Special Education Center in the Los Angeles area. For ten years he had been working hands-on with all kinds of special needs people. He loved being a teacher. He wouldn't want to be an administrator. His people needed him. I shared about my year after retirement as a substitute teacher's aid in special education classes, and some things I had learned from the students. And, I shared that my wife and I had been the parents of a special needs child during her short life.

At one station an older poorly dressed black African American man with deeply wrinkled and weathered face and eyes that appeared sightless entered our car talking loudly in a kind of mixed hard-to-understand tongue. His intent, however, was clear. He wanted money for food, a hamburger, I believe he said. To emphasize his need, he reached up and with one move snatched out his left eyeball, and displayed the white orb with lifeless pupil to all us fortunate passengers. Just as quickly, he popped it back in the socket. Looking around, it was a skit to see the wide eyes and dropped jaws of many of the folks aboard. Some others, of course, had seen it all and seemed indifferent. A Hispanic lady, who had been apparently studying or memorizing words held by a steel ring, passed him a dollar. "Another buck and I could get a soda with the hamburger," I believe he said. No word of thanks for the help, just looking for a bit more, but setting his sights low. My teacher friend told him, "You know, man, you qualify for SSI." As "eyeball man" passed by, he said quite clearly, "They threw me out." Then he was gone, I guess to try the next car, the next train. Man, I thought, how could this guy not contract terrible infections in his eye socket with his display tactics!

Using All the Colors

After the Blue Line came the Red Line, a short trip to Union Station. I stood with my bike, as usual in an open spot for a wheel chair in the last car. Over it a sign read, "Reserved for Senior or Handicapped Persons." I felt I qualified on the first count and hung on for dear life as we accelerated and then braked to a halt.

At Union Station I boarded the Gold Line for the last leg of the journey home. Fortunately, I was able to commandeer two single seats of the rear-most car. Here I would be able to sit down without being cramped and hold the bike securely between the upright rails. Hardly had I settled in when a young woman with display boards and a heavy bag asked if she could occupy the seat across from me. "Being hemmed in won't be a problem," she said. "I just need to get out at the Del Mar Station." We chatted about the restaurant plans for the restored train station at Del Mar. Then she began a series of calls that occupied her until her station. The very large book that she was initially reading, and the conversations on her several calls revealed that she was a student of the law, criminal law, and was excited about what she was learning. She talked at length with a friend about a woman who had been arrested by the border police on suspicion of smuggling drugs. It seemed they suspected that she had swallowed drugs in balloons. Although she denied everything, they determined to wait her out. Eventually it all came out! It's kind of amazing what you find out simply by listening to a person talking on their cell phone—openly.

"Last stop, Sierra Madre Villa Station. All please exit and be sure to take all your belongings with you." For me it was my bike, which would faithfully take me the last few blocks to The Grove and one of the famous buffet dinners. It had been great to experience another slice of life, but so good to be home again!

On Stage at Carnegie Hall NYC with Stabat Mater

Art French

Who or what is Stabat Mater and why were my wife, Carolyn, and I on a Jet Blue red-eye flight to New York City this past January?

It all began a year ago when the Kirk Choir of Pasadena Presbyterian Church (PPC) was rehearsing for our annual Good Friday Devotional Concert. The main piece was to be Karl Jenkins' Stabat Mater. This hour long work is based on a 13th-century Roman Catholic poem attributed to Jacopone da Todi. Its title is an abbreviation of the first line *Stabat Mater dolorosa* "the sorrowful mother was standing". This text, one of the most powerful and immediate of medieval poems, meditates on the suffering of Mary, Jesus Christ's mother, during his crucifixion.

In April of 2010 the Kirk Choir was offered the opportunity to perform with Distinguished Concerts International NY in January 2011. This was billed as a Concert for Peace—Celebrating the Spirit of Martin Luther King, Jr. What an opportunity! But the questions started—Should we? Could we afford it? NYC in January! ? Ok. We'll go.

S.O.S. to all family members: send money for all occasions! As we paid each installment there was the nagging suspicion in the back of our minds, "Is this the wisest thing to do at our age?" Fifteen decided to go from PPC. Our own rehearsals started again in November. We learned we needed to memorize two sections when "books would be down". More added pressure. The eastern weather was terrible in December and January. Hundreds of flights were cancelled and airports closed. This might not work after all. And it was really, really cold! Both of us bought boots on sale at Sears. Carolyn's were very stylish while all I could get would look good kick-starting a Harley!

Using All the Colors

Our flight was one of the smoothest we ever experienced. No problem with landing. The jet way tunnel was an icy welcome to what was ahead as we were wreathed in clouds of our own breath. At 5:00 am we were glad to get a taxi to our hotel in mid-town Manhattan directly across the street from Carnegie Hall. No rooms were available at such an early hour but Bob Thomas, bless him, was in the lobby to see that we got registered OK. We had breakfast at the hotel's breakfast room, then dozed in the lobby until a room became available. We rested and got acquainted with our new neighborhood. There were a number of restaurants within easy walking distance. We located the other hotel a couple of blocks away where our rehearsals were to take place.

Saturday afternoon we had our first rehearsal. There were about 250 singers altogether including a choir from England, University of Johannesburg Choir from South Africa, and a large high school choir from New Jersey. We had a good hard four hour work out under the direction of Jonathan Griffith. This added new understanding to our appreciation of what we were singing. Our second four hour rehearsal was Sunday morning. That afternoon several of us braved the cold—it never got above freezing—and walked a number of blocks to Saint Thomas Church Fifth Avenue (Episcopal) for the 4:00 p.m. Epiphany Procession with Carols sung by the Choir of Men and Boys. There were several hundred worshippers in attendance in the long Gothic sanctuary. Following worship we stayed for an organ concert. Upon exiting the church I was shocked to see a man in the bitterly cold weather with a very thin blanket around his shoulders and barefoot! One breathes a prayer while hurrying away clutching at a warm coat. We passed Fifth Avenue Presbyterian Church on our way. In between times we studied our music, read, ate and slept. Other Kirk Choir folk were much more adventurous.

Dress rehearsal call time was 1:15 p.m. on Monday. There was always a mass of performers pressed tightly together at the Artist Entrance to Carnegie Hall waiting to be let in while the cold wind sent the chill factor way down. We had another hour and a half rehearsal on stage with the orchestra. My position was second in the front row. I found myself squeezed by the timpani and right behind the bass horns! I figured some of my missed notes would not be too noticeable. Only my immediate partners would know and both of them were very good musicians thankfully. It was all coming together very well. Our rehearsal times were paying off, although Jonathan was not letting us get away with anything. "Hold your books up and look at me! You do not have to keep staring at the notes. They will not slide off the page!" Even the memorized sections were becoming a wall of sound. Hope springs eternal. It boded well for a good concert. After a quick bite to eat, we returned to the hotel to dress and then went back to the stage door for the 7:00 p.m. call time. This was a major poor planning glitch in the whole process. We were kept standing for over an hour until it was time for our part of the program. There was another choir of 180 voices which sang the premier of Karl Jenkins' "Gloria" first. We were a fine looking group with the ladies all in black and the men in tux or black suits, white shirts and black bow ties.

With the house lights up and sixty piece orchestra in place it was a thrill to walk out on stage at Carnegie Hall with its 2700 seat capacity nearly full! The principals came on stage, the conductor mounted the stand, the baton was raised and the opening orchestral notes sounded. I along with 250 others were performing on stage at Carnegie Hall NYC!

Stabat Mater dolorosa juxta crucem lacrimosa, dum pendebat Filius we began and sang until with the other choir of 180 voices joining us from the near balconies we rose in glorious crescendo for the final thrilling "Paradisi Gloria." Ending with a sudden shattering "AMEN" there was a haunting silence before the audience was on its feet thunderously proclaiming its enthusiastic appreciation for the night's performance, which I am not too modest to say, "We deserved." Afterwards Jonathan Griffith stood in the narrow hallway thanking us as he shook the hand of each performer as we came off stage. Also, our own Dr. Timothy Howard was there to greet those of us from the Kirk Choir. We ended the evening at Rosie O'Grady's for a wonderful buffet at which our conductor, Jonathan Griffith and the composer Karl Jenkins were present and most generous with their autographs and having their pictures taken.

Going out into the bitterly cold night to walk back to our hotel we were warmed by the thought of what we had accomplished over the space of three days with as mixed bag of people one could wish for—very young, very old, students, the employed, the retired, from different parts of the world. On stage at Carnegie Hall NYC. Who could have imagined such a possibility! Home to WARM California the next day.

Seasons in Tucumcari
Mary Froede

When my family lived in Tucumcari, New Mexico, the weather was probably the most IDEAL I have experienced. There were four distinct seasons. Coming from California, though having been raised in Wisconsin, I was enchanted by the fact that each season lasted just three months with an occasional "rogue" snowstorm in April that managed to kill the fruit that had just started to set.

Tucumcari Mountain

Summers were unbearably hot with each day becoming a blistering, dry 114 or so degrees on occasion. Life was only bearable indoors with a "swamp cooler" in the window. We had to wear gloves to touch the wheel of a car and were parboiled before the air conditioner (if you were lucky enough to have one) tuned up. At 5:00 or so, a breeze would come up to cool us off and we almost always slept under something, at least a sheet.

Fall was a glorious blaze of color and the balmy weather with the aspens in the local mountains turning yellow, the sage, purple and the sunsets like nothing I had ever seen before or since.

Using All the Colors

The first year I tried recording all this with a camera, but soon gave up as I ran out of room to keep the beautiful pictures. We raked the leaves, leaped in and out until we were exhausted. Steve loved to leap into the piles of leaves with our dog screaming "Banzai". How I miss the leaf burning time! No smog to worry about then and the smell was unforgettable. To this day, I wait anxiously to recapture that special change in the air and sky that precedes the coming of autumn.

Each year about Thanksgiving, we awoke to find that we had our first snow storm. Actually the snow was more like popcorn, dry and huge flakes. At the first sign of a flake or two, you turned on the radio to listen to all the announcements of events that were being cancelled. Immediately after the snow storm had hit in our first winter, I asked when the snow plows would come out to clear the streets (logical question from a midwesterner) and was told that the city owned no snow plows. Why bother to plow when you knew it would melt in a few days!! So the whole town, except for the milk trucks, took a vacation! No one went anywhere. Our houses were isolated cocoons of warmth within a white world. The milk truck came up and down the streets selling food supplies for those who were foolish enough not to have their freezers well stocked!! Neighbors all gathered and put sleds behind the four wheel vehicles so the parents and kids alike could ride the sleds up and down the empty streets. The first day or so the snow was too dry for snowball fights, but as it warmed up it got sticky and I remember my husband building a marvelous igloo for the kids. Actually, I think he and I enjoyed it more than they did!

My feet were freezing as I trudged down the hall on a particularly frigid, blustery morning at 2:00 A.M. My son Steve had awakened with, what I assumed was a nightmare. I finally got him settled back down to sleep, headed back down the hall to our bedroom. When I get up in the night, I have to take a trip to the bathroom, so as I staggered along, I gradually lowered my pajama bottoms, rounded the corner into the bathroom, backed up, and plunked down on the facility. I hadn't realized that my husband was already sitting there!!

Finally, with the coming of spring, all the trees budded out and the rainstorms arrived. When I saw the distinctive clouds begin to gather, I would call the kids and we lined up, sitting on our "lean to" porch with our backs up against the front wall of the house to watch the storm gather. What a display! The lightning shows were remarkable. When the rain finally came and we were getting wet, the weaker of us went inside, but mostly we would play in the rain, depending on the temperature. When the rain stopped and the usual rainbow formed, sometimes double, we hopped in the car and headed for the countryside to see the arroyos flooded. There was a genus of tree toad that hibernated deep in the soil and only came to "life" when it rained, so the desert floor was alive with little hoppy toads, the size of your thumbnail. Imagine the fun the kids had gathering these prizes to take home and keep for awhile.

One evening, as we had lost interest in the storm and were more interested in eating our dinner, lightning struck the meter box just a few feet from where we were enjoying our ham salad sandwiches and soup. It took quite a while to find Ruth Ann's sandwich, which she threw into the air as she screamed and headed for the base of the dining room table. The sandwich had landed on top of the refrigerator.

Storms like I had never seen before were commonplace. One summer day, we were invited to go on a picnic with our friends. We weren't able to go, but they did. Since it appeared to be a nice day, they proceeded to take their pickup truck down the dry arroyo with the back packed with food, drinks and kids. Suddenly, there was a flash flood with torrents of water coursing down the arroyo bed. The wall of water and debris smashed into the pickup, lifting it and carrying it down stream about two miles before it finally lodged in the side of the canyon. Everyone was okay, somewhat bruised and battered but all the food was gone and the truck destroyed. A lesson learned.

Using All the Colors

Jim had a similar experience after he had delivered me to be a counselor at a church camp in Taos. He brought our youngest child, Steve, with him for the trip. On the way home they came to an arroyo that was running with a small amount of water. Jim went ahead and entered the dip in the road when a wall of water surged down and hit the car. The car didn't move, but it rapidly filled with water as high as the seats. His camera, wallet etc., and he and Steve were all soaked. The flow of water slowed down and he opened the car doors to let the flood of water out. They finally limped back to Tucumcari to dry out.

Interesting People and Places

Gastronomic Goodies
Mary Froede

I have always been a lover of food. We used to joke that I was born "tired and hungry". With a Norwegian father and German mother, the food I had enjoyed growing up was really bland. However, food in New Mexico was so entirely different than any we had known that, to this day, I try to locate a restaurant that can equal its unique flavors. I finally have found a restaurant in Sierra Madre that makes enchiladas very similar to those I loved in Tucumcari.

My first exposure to the local food was a sunny day when Ricky and Ruth Ann were in school and Steven Paul was not yet two years old. I popped him into our buggy and took off for a walk up to Gaynell Avenue (Route 66). It was the commercial center of the county and solid on each side of the highway with restaurants, motels and curio shops. I headed for the restaurant that was owned by an older couple in our church. They also had a motel. When I reached the restaurant and was seated, I started examining the menu. I KNEW then, that I was in a foreign country. The one item that intrigued me the most was the "guacamole", which I of course mispronounced. The waiter described it. I may have eaten an avocado in something, at sometime in my life but certainly was not aware of it. Being from the meat and cheese eating state of Wisconsin contributed to my lack of awareness. The guacamole came with incredible chips, also new to me. Needless to say, I was hooked at first swallow and have been enamored ever since.

The next venture into this new gastronomic world was a trip to "La Cita" (which incidentally is still there, but was closed for repairs on our last trip). There I discovered the ethereal beauty of eating a sopapilla!! It sort of resembles a raised doughnut, but a slightly heavier texture, puffed up like a pillow (for which it gets it's name), hollow and warm. Tear off a corner and drizzle in the honey

Using All the Colors

and you know you have been transported to gastronomic heaven! Of course you end up with honey dripping down your chin but are delighted to lick it off. NO ONE in the outer civilized world makes sopapillas (other than a very poor imitation in which they fry up a tortilla). Needless to say, I got the recipe from someone and made them on many occasions. Our last trip was spent eating sopapillas at EVERY MEAL. The problem with filling up on their delicious food was that the owner, Maurice, made the most delicious PIES. I finally learned to hold back on the food I could take home in a doggie bag so that I could manage to cram in a piece of warm pie that had been made from whatever local fruit was fresh.

The Martinez family owned one of the really "native" restaurants close to downtown and walking distance from our first house. The front end was a small grocery store, the middle was a restaurant with picnic tables and oil cloth tablecloths. The back end of the house was their home. Mama M was the cook, Papa was the maitre d' and cashier and the kids all did the waitering and kitchen help. We inhaled the enchiladas and tacos, all prepared to include Mama. M's hand made tortillas. The beans were so delicious and I am sure they were cooked in lard. They served a dish which I called "colache". It was made with fresh chopped zucchini and hand cut corn from the cob all cooked by sauteing in butter. I make it to this day to the delight of my family. Yum! Yum!

If that didn't make your mouth water, I give up!

Unexpected Visitors
Bill Hansen

What could be worse than unexpected visitors at Christmas. But it was that way with the Innkeeper at Bethlehem wasn't it? Joseph and Mary and, of course, Jesus were unexpected arrivals at the door of the Inn at Bethlehem, but what if the Stable had not been available to the Holy Family? But then—that's how it is with unexpected visitors at Christmas!

It was not many weeks before Christmas one year that I became aware of a visitor at our 8 o'clock morning Worship service at the Church of the Valley in Apple Valley. He left the service quickly and darted out each Sunday morning during the last Hymn. I was curious, he was an Asian man and he seemed so very alone. The third Sunday I walked to the back of the Sanctuary before announcing the last hymn and I caught him while he was leaving during the first verse of the Hymn. He explained that he had just opened a small restaurant in Hesperia, and that he had to rush back to greet his first customers. He spoke broken English and told me that he was a refugee from Cambodia. His name was Pung.

The next week, one day, after the morning rush I went to see Pung in his little restaurant. We visited over a cup of coffee and talked about his escape from the Killing Fields of Cambodia. He had been a military officer in the royal army and he had been in grave danger. His family had spirited him out of Cambodia across the border into Thailand. Church World Service had sponsored him in his further escape to America. Pung had to leave his pregnant wife, his mother, his brother, extended family, and children behind. He had heard that their village had been attacked and that in all likelihood they had been killed.

Pung was faithful in worship every Advent Sunday. The Church was decorated with the garlands and symbols of Christmas. The next Sunday morning the lighting of the last Advent Candle was celebrated. Pung waited until after the last Hymn that Sunday...

his face was glowing and he was animated. "I SAW THEIR PICTURES" he stuttered breathlessly. I knew that he visited the Cambodian Center in Long Beach every week. He searched the bulletin board where they posted pictures and messages to establish contact with other refugees. But that week he announced that he had found their pictures... pictures of his entire family of TEN, posted on the Bulletin Board along with a message for Pung. Church World Service was sponsoring his family to come to America to join him. It was the first that he had heard of it—THEY WERE ALIVE! He wondered if we could help him. They were, he exclaimed, right now on the journey to America and they would arrive at LAX in six days—just two days before Christmas.

I was so thrilled for Pung. Then the reality hit me... Unexpected visitors two days before Christmas... TEN—T.E.N. unexpected visitors... And not just for a short visit—not even for a long visit but here to stay—for good! "Of course" I said (taking a deep breath), "We can help!"

The next Sunday would be Christmas Eve Sunday—that meant back to back services. Three in the morning and three that same evening! No, Christmas definitely was not the best time for unexpected visitors. But it was to be the time.

I was finally able to reach the Chairperson of the Mission Committee with the news. She said "You mean they'll be here on Friday, in five days after tomorrow, and did you say... TEN? Alright, I'll get the committee together as soon as I can."

None of Pung's family spoke a word of English. His mother and the baby that Pung had never seen were among them. It seemed unthinkable when they arrived that we might split them up even temporarily in different homes. We gave ourselves two days to spread out and come up with solutions. The Session met that night —we would need significant funds. It was agreed that the Lord had presented us with a great challenge. And there was heartfelt agreement that with His help we could meet the challenge... It was a short Session meeting followed by earnest prayer. After the other

Elders had left the meeting, one Elder remained—Oren Robertson stayed behind—he said to me. "Bill, remember the ranch in Sycamore Rocks that Reuben and Julia Osborne bequeathed to the Church? You know that I'm the executor for the estate and I can open the Ranch House up. With the out-buildings we can house the whole family!"

The ranch house would make an ample home but it had been closed up for a year. It was fully furnished. Some utilities would have to be turned on and it would take a small army to clean and wash windows... scrub floors... weed and paint... prepare the out-buildings.. and sweep and stock the cupboards and especially to make provision for a BABY!

Slowly it dawned on us... Christmas.... It really is a wonderful time for unexpected visitors. Especially when one of them is a BABY!!

It took six cars to drive folks to LAX that afternoon to meet Pung's family. We could have done with less, but there were quite a number who wanted to go along. And those who were there said that they could never forget the scene that transpired as Pung and his wife, mother, brother, and children poured out into the airport reception area and embraced in a mountain of love.

And then Pung stood apart, and for the first time held the baby he had never seen. He lifted the baby high into the air for everyone to see.

A group of us had remained at the church. Pung had helped us to know how to prepare a meal that the family would enjoy. The hall was decorated and the tables were set and there were candles and the sound of Carols. The family members were all shy as they entered the hall. Pung helped us to say words of greeting—we prayed and then we all sat down to eat.

The air around the tables was filled with two languages and interpretive gestures... and laughter. But the one language that everyone in the room that night understood was the language of love.

Using All the Colors

Pung's whole family attended worship together on Christmas Eve Sunday. And the whole Church felt involved with their story... especially because their story included a Baby. And everyone could agree that there is no better time than Christmas for unexpected visitors... Especially when one of them is a Baby.

The old carol tells it best in the story of the journey of Joseph and Mary as unexpected visitors to the Inn at Bethlehem and the birth of our Lord Jesus in the Stable behind the Inn.

THOU DIDS'T LEAVE THY THRONE AND THY KINGLY CROWN WHEN THOU CAMEST TO EARTH FOR ME. BUT IN BETHLEHEM'S INN THERE WAS FOUND NO ROOM FOR THY HOLY NATIVITY. O COME TO MY HEART LORD JESUS—THERE IS ROOM IN MY HEART FOR THEE!

What Would You Have Expected?
Bill Hansen

Michael was a Senior at Apple Valley High School. His parents were strict in ways that counted, but in non-essentials they were pretty relaxed. For instance, Michael was an all around young 17-year old. He was an excellent student and he excelled in most sports. He was liked by his teachers and fellow students alike. And he loved church... what more could you ask? Michael took out his search for individuality and identity in the manner of his dress. To be frank, Michael was sloppy. He wore old cut-offs, message tee shirts, and tennis shoes with holes... without socks. He wore them everywhere—every day—except to church.

Every year at Apple Valley High there was a Sports Award Banquet at which a trophy was presented to the ATHLETE OF THE YEAR. Unbeknownst to Michael, he had been chosen as the recipient that year! He was the uncontested favorite of his coaches.

The night of the awards banquet arrived... Michael's family, of course, was in on the secret. His grandfather who lived down below had driven up to Apple Valley for the occasion. They all did a good job of keeping the secret... MICHAEL DID NOT HAVE A CLUE!

The evening of the banquet, the family walked together up the stairs to the high school community building. There was Michael... wearing grubby cut-offs, a faded message tee shirt, scuffed tennis shoes with holes, and no socks. His grandfather had given some excuse for his rather dressy attire that evening. He was proud of his grandson. He wore dark blue slacks, a grey sport coat, a white shirt with cuff links and a matching tie, and highly polished black leather shoes. The contrast between the grandfather and grandson who stood together shoulder to shoulder could not have been more striking!

Using All the Colors

As the family walked together up the steps of the community building, Michael saw his friends dressed very differently than their normal attire at school... his friends were wearing slacks, neatly pressed sport shirts, and their Sunday shoes.

Reaching the top of the stairs, Michael had an uneasy feeling in the pit of his stomach. He was a minority of one—a stand out—he was beginning to feel self-conscious, which was an uncharacteristic feeling for him. As they hit the last step leading into the hallway, Michael suddenly turned and whispered to his grandfather. "GRANDPA...WOULD YOU CHANGE CLOTHES WITH ME?"

Without hesitation the two men ducked into the men's restroom and reappeared fifteen minutes later... Michael attired in dark blue slacks, a gray sport coat, a white shirt with gold cufflinks, a tasteful necktie and highly polished black leather shoes. THE ATHLETE OF THE YEAR. And then, on the other hand, Michael's grandfather appeared... dressed in a faded message tee shirt, grubby cut-offs with white hairy legs and knobby knees that had not seen the sunshine of day for many a moon. And he wore tennis shoes with holes and No Socks!

But then after all, and considering everything, WHAT WOULD YOU HAVE EXPECTED A GRANPA TO DO?

"Broken Wings and Lonely Hearts" And Operator 373

Hedy Lodwick

Going through some old letters last week, I found one from August, 1972. Our elder daughter, Margaret, was home for the summer, having finished her first year in college, and she was still in contact with many of her friends from high school. Among them were a number who were, or felt, somewhat marginalized in school. For some reason, they felt drawn to Margaret, who does indeed have a compassionate heart. Our preacher last Sunday spoke of those "with broken wings and lonely hearts" THAT, I felt, described Margaret's friend Audrey.

Audrey claimed her family did not understand or care about her. She was often at our home for meals or to spend the night. One night she phoned in distress because she was nauseated and her folks weren't home and she didn't know what to do. Margaret wasn't home so I drove over, helped her make Jello, cracked ice for her and prescribed coke with that. When it came time for the high school senior prom, she decided she would make her own dress, I think because Margaret was planning to make her own. The project was begun late because both girls had secured dates rather near to prom time. Audrey picked a very complicated pattern with large puffed sleeves and, not surprisingly, Margaret ended up practically making the dress for her, then had to scurry to complete her own, which, fortunately, was a simple but lovely design.

The girls went to different colleges. Audrey had decided to take some summer courses so was in school in August. From here on, I will describe what happened, using the draft of a letter I wrote to the manager of the New York Telephone company.

I quote: "Saturday evening operator 373 of your unit was most helpful to me and I want to write to commend her and to express my deep appreciation. One reads of the kind of help operators sometimes give. This is the first time I have needed help and I appreciate especially that it was given without me having to request it.

Around 7 p.m., our younger daughter answered the phone to receive a call from a friend of our older daughter who was away for the evening. The caller, away at college, was very depressed, said she was calling to say goodbye to our older daughter for she planned to kill herself in a few moments. She had made such threats in the past and while I felt she would not likely do anything this time either, I felt she did need help quickly. She had hung up on our daughter who then became quite frightened.

Quickly I tried to call our older daughter. I thought she might know who we should call at the college. I wasn't sure of the area code where she was and began to dial the operator for information. I couldn't get a dial tone. As I tried repeatedly, operator 373 came on the line to ask if I knew the number of the party who had just called us. I said I knew the name, not the number, and told her what had happened. She asked from where the party had called. I told her the name of the college. She quickly got the number of two pay phones there and tried one, with no answer. The second reached our troubled friend, still sobbing in the phone booth. I don't know why the operator tried to reach me about her in the first place, if it was a question of charges or if she had talked to the girl and realized her condition. This all happened so fast. As soon as I heard the girl's voice, I talked with her about everything and anything just to keep her talking. Our younger daughter went next door to try to reach her sister, to no avail. Finally I convinced our friend to go out to find someone there to talk with and to call me back in 20 minutes to report where she was. She said no one was around but I heard someone playing the piano in the background. I told her to go sit by the piano player.

When I hung up, I planned to try to get hold of someone at the college to go be with her, but, to my surprise, the operator came on the line and asked if all was o.k. I said not really and that I wanted to get hold of a responsible person at the college. 'I've the number of the security officer', she said and put me through right away. He was of little help at first. He did not know the number of the chaplain or the dean or anyone that might be around at that time. Finally he said there was a resident assistant and hunted, it seemed forever, for her number. As soon as we had it, my friend, the operator, was there to put it through. The resident assistant, fortunately, was in and responded immediately and promised help. Only after this call, after I had thanked her for standing by, did Operator 373 leave me. I was amazed to realize that I had hung up the phone only for 1 brief moment from the time I tried to reach our daughter and this operator had been there to help as long as I needed her.

Operator 373 may be happy to know that the depressed girl did what I told her to do and found someone to be with. She even called back shortly after I had finally hung up the phone. I called the resident assistant again to let her know where the girl was. As she was panicky at not having found her, she was especially relieved to hear with whom she was and promised to keep track of her.

Our daughter talked with her friend the next afternoon. She was still very depressed but she is to call again on Wednesday and come to visit this weekend. This may be enough to pull her together until she receives more professional help.

The above account is meant as a commendation and thank you to operator 373 and to let her know about what has happened to date. My family and I will cherish this incident as one that shows that in this increasingly depersonalized world there are those who are still willing and able to help."

Audrey continued to have a troubled life. For a time she lived with a man who played in a band. When that relationship broke up, she joined the army. She also changed her name to Amy. In the army she met a man she considered a kindred spirit. She brought him by to meet us. He seemed pleasant enough. After a time, they were married and Margaret was one of the bridesmaids.

Using All the Colors

Unfortunately, long after we had moved from Glen Rock, we learned they were divorced. Then we heard nothing more from Amy until we got news from another of her friends that she was dying from a brain tumor. When I phoned her mother with my sympathy, she told me that Amy had a man who was devoted to her and was with her regularly until she died. She was probably in her mid thirties then. My heart still aches for this girl with a "broken wing and a lonely heart" who we were never able to really help find meaning and peace in life. But we will always remember operator 373 who gave such significant help when we needed it.

After receiving a letter of acknowledgement from the Manager of the NY Telephone Co, we learned the operator's name was Nora McLaughlin and that her record would be noted for her fine service.

The Intruder
Robert Lodwick

On Monday morning, December 3, 2007, I awoke at 4:30AM to shower and have breakfast before leaving for Burbank Airport. Ellen Harkins, President of the House of Rest, was picking me up at 6:00 AM. I opened the curtains and turned on the lights in the living room, our den/guest room, and in the front hall so Ellen could find our house in the dark. El Nido Avenue is not very well lit. I brought in the newspapers and left the front door open. The screen door was shut. I kissed Hedy goodbye and she turned over and went back to sleep. I then went to my desk and was turning off my computer when a man came running through the front door, into the living room shouting "Mike", "Mike" with arms flailing. He was already near the back door when I began the chase; the back door was locked so he ran through our Pullman-like kitchen knocking over pots and pans and dishes as he dashed through the swinging doors, back into the living room, knocking over the floor lamp by Hedy's chair and out the front door into the dark. I was stunned! The clatter in the kitchen and the lamp hitting the floor woke Hedy up and she came into the living room. She couldn't believe what I told her but she saw the mess that had been made.

Just then, Ellen drove up. Being a gallant man, I kissed Hedy goodbye saying "Call the police." Then I was off to Burbank with rising disbelief knowing inwardly that I should be staying home rather than putting all this on Hedy's shoulders. All the way to the airport I kept telling myself to return home. As soon as we arrived at the Bob Hope Airport, Ellen handed me her cell phone and said, "Call Hedy!" Fortunately, Hedy is a strong women used to being in crisis situations when I have been overseas on extended trips.

Hedy answered the phone on the first ring. She said the police were there and they wanted to speak to me. But first she told me that the intruder must have grabbed her purse as he went past her

Using All the Colors

desk. I had not realized that or noticed it in his hands. Hedy passed the phone to one of the two policemen who answered her 911 call. He wanted my description of the man: 5 feet 8 inches, with kinky hair, an African American. His clothes indicated to me that he wasn't a street person but he certainly must have been high on drugs. I think he was wearing a brown jacket. He left his muddy footprints on the clean kitchen floor and so the police measured his footprints against their shoes to estimate his build. They also asked if the woman who then drove up might have been an accomplice and I was able to say "No! She is the President of the Trustees of the House of Rest. Ellen had not seen anyone on the street when she drove up.

Two police cars came and parked in our cul-de-sac with lights shining; their radios going full blast or enough to wake up our neighbors. When Hedy called the police she gave our address as 403 El Nido Monte Vista Grove. When the police heard Monte Vista Grove they called the Health Center to check the apartment number, D-69. The police then have a map of the Grove. Before they arrived, the Night Charge Nurse called Hedy to see if every thing was all right.

Hedy told me that the police dusted the door knobs in the kitchen with a purple powder looking for fingerprints and along the kitchen door where he pushed it open. The police then told Hedy to cancel her credit cards which she did immediately by calling the Hot Line. She then left a voicemail message on Debbie's phone. (one of our administrators.) When Debbie reached the Grove she tried to telephone Hedy but our line was busy. So she said to Ed and Jose, "we're going down to see Hedy."

Debbie was shocked to see the mess in the kitchen. She said she would call Housekeeping to come down. Hedy said, "No, I can do it." Debbie said "Sit down and eat your breakfast, I'm taking charge." And she did! She asked Ed and Jose to look through the dumpsters along El Nido, looking for Hedy's purse. They didn't find it. Before noon, Ed had the locks changed on all of our doors,

Interesting People and Places

screen doors included. Housekeeping came down and cleaned up the muddy footprints, and the purple powder on the locks for finger prints and picked up the things that had fallen on the floor.

We live in a community and the staff and community responded 100%. A neighbor took Hedy to the dentist for her appointment that fateful day and another colleague took her to the DMV for a new Driver's License which she received in record time. Every time I called from Louisville she would tell me of another item that was in her wallet such as her donor card to the USC Anatomical Gift program upon death, her Huntington cards, plus her Medicare and supplement card. It amazes me how much we carry in our wallets besides money. (She had only $15.00 in the purse at the time it was taken.)

By that evening, there were many stories going around campus regarding the "break-in". One was that I chased the man twice around the outside of the house. etc. Well Ellen and I had a good meeting with staff of World Mission in Louisville and Wednesday morning, we took the first plane to Phoenix and then ran to catch an earlier flight from Phoenix to Burbank which was loading passengers when we arrived at the gate. I was glad to get back home. I heard more stories from Hedy about people who helped her, one even offering to spend the night in our apartment (she declined as she was so tired and could double lock all the locks on all our doors and feel safe.)

Shortly after arriving home, I went to the Administration building to thank the staff. Debbie wasn't there but Helen was. I said to Helen, "You have a wonderful staff and I thank them all." and then I "lost it" and began to cry. I had held all my guilt feelings bundled up but released them all with these tears and thanks. It was a significant moment for me. Now I am trying to remember to lock all the doors when I go out, even for a short time or just next door. It is a pain to have to unlock the door but I guess it is essential.

As I was writing this story, the phone rang and it was the police asking if I saw the face of the intruder and could recognize

Using All the Colors

him in a line-up. I don't think I could because what I saw mainly was the back side of the intruder as I chased him through the house. I could tell them what he was wearing, but not much more as it all happened so fast. They had a suspect in custody along with the Arcadia police for robberies in that community.

I have been accosted on the streets of New York and stopped a man grabbing our suitcases as he was getting off of the subway but this was our first, and we hope last, invasion in our home.

The Kubota Garden
Jim Symons

The internment of Japanese-American citizens during World War II was one of the worst chapters in our nation's history. This story about my father's relationship to the Kubota family of Seattle during this stressful time is one more example of why he is my hero and model for life.

THE KUBOTA GARDEN. My wife, Marilyn, called my attention to the sign as we drove on an unfamiliar street in Southeast Seattle. Could that be the Kubota family I knew seventy years ago as a little kid before the War? I wanted to know more.

It was August 10th, 2008, in the early evening when shadows were lengthening. Marilyn and I drove to Seattle from Portland, where we had celebrated the sixtieth wedding anniversary of my sister, Margie, and her husband at Salty's Restaurant overlooking the Columbia River. My two brothers, Art and Tom, were there as well—the first time in ten years that the four Symons siblings were in the same place at the same time. My head was filled with childhood memories as we turned off Interstate 5 onto Martin Luther King and made our way toward the south end of Lake Washington. We were headed for the home of my childhood friend Tom Winter and his new wife Corinne McComber—they found each other at a Roosevelt High School reunion after each of their original spouses had died. I wondered if either of them would know anything about that Kubota Garden sign.

Tom and Corinne were gracious hosts, offering us a delicious bowl of homemade soup and a glass of wine as we sat on their deck overlooking Lake Washington, the early evening lights on the I-90 floating bridge, and the distant Cascade Mountains. I asked if they knew anything about the Kubota Garden sign—it was only a mile away from where we were sitting in the house that had been in Corinne's family for years. "Oh yes, we are quite familiar with The

Using All the Colors

Kubota Garden," she said. "Tom and I enjoy walking the many trails along the streams and through the beautiful flowers and trees. It is now a public park owned and operated by the City of Seattle, and many volunteers keep it looking beautiful." Then she asked, "Jim, why are you interested in a garden in South Seattle when you grew up miles away in the northeast part of the city?"

I answered by describing my childhood in the 1930s in Laurelhurst, west of the University of Washington on the northern part of the Lake. My parents moved to Seattle in 1926 when it was a frontier logging town. They built a large house in the new neighborhood of Laurelhurst, and hired an enterprising Japanese gardener to plant a spacious lawn, blue spruce and fir trees, a brilliant camellia bush, and a rich variety of flowers and shrubs. His name was Kubota. Dad was away on business much of the time, and Mom had four small children to care for, so Mr. Kubota came once a week from his South Seattle home to take care of our yard.

Our Kubota Garden

Interesting People and Places

He was a pleasant and reserved man who took time to talk with me—I was fascinated by his accent and he was the only Asian person I knew. Mr. Kubota seemed more like a family friend than an employee. Since we used the bushes and trees as hiding places for our incessant games of hide-and-seek, red light-green light, or capture the flag, he kept telling us to be careful of stepping on the flowers or breaking the branches of the shrubs. He was always polite when he spoke: "Please, Jimmy, take care of pretty flowers." One of my favorite memories as a seven year old child was a visit to Mr. Kubota's landscape garden near Seward Park in South Seattle. I can still recall the hidden ponds of water, paths winding past flowering bushes over small hills, and most of all the miniature bonsai trees that I had never seen before. We were welcomed by the whole Kubota family even though speaking English was difficult for some of them, and we felt at home in that garden of beauty and mystery.

Suddenly Mr. Kubota stopped coming to care for our yard and I missed him. I asked my Dad, "What happened to our friend, Mr. Kubota?" I was told about President Roosevelt's declaration that all Japanese people on the west coast would be interned in camps for the duration of the War. I could not understand why a nice man like Mr. Kubota and his family would be put in prison camps, and my Dad told me he thought it was wrong for our government to treat Japanese-American people this way. He said he would try to help Mr. Kubota and work with others to save the landscape garden in South Seattle if he could. I do not know exactly what Dad did, but there are two incidents that lead me to believe he followed through on helping his Japanese friend.

In 1942 the doorbell rang in our Laurelhurst home and my older brother Art opened the front door. An FBI agent flashed his identity card and asked to see Dad about Mr. Fujitaro Kubota. Dad was a reference for the Kubota family and was clearly working to protect them in any way he could. They were taken off to the camps, along with thousands of others, but Dad was part of a group of people who did their best to preserve the garden through the War years.

The second incident came shortly after the War ended and the Japanese families returned to their west coast homes. Mr. Kubota came to our house and invited our entire family to the wedding of his son, which would take place in the Kubota Garden. All six of us drove down to the garden in South Seattle, which was in the process of being restored. The wedding was beautiful with a large crowd of people in attendance. After the ceremony, Mr. Kubota took our family on one of the paths through the garden to a place where the earth rose up before us. We were amazed to see that the sign before us said, "Symons Hill". Not only that, but because my brother Tom had a birthday soon, Mr. Kubota brought out a carefully wrapped gift. Tom opened it to find a brand new fishing pole. When I think of what the Kubota family went through from 1941 to 1945 when they lost so much, their generosity in giving an expensive birthday gift to my brother is truly remarkable. It also said something about the esteem in which they held our Dad.

My Dad's frozen food business went through a difficult time after the war and we were never able to hire gardeners again. We kept the lawn mowed but the rest of the yard suffered. My parents sold their Laurelhurst home in the 1950s, and I lost track of the Kubota family until I saw that sign on August 10, 2008. When Corinne heard my story, she brought me the latest issue of The Kubota Garden Foundation Newsletter. What a delight to see that my childhood friend, Mr. Kubota, was remembered in such a beautiful way by so many people. I read about the plant sales, flower and garden shows, visits by Seattle dignitaries, public tours, and many volunteers working throughout the year. The family garden I visited in 1941 and at the wedding after the war has turned into the "most impressive and enjoyable Japanese garden in the Seattle area," to quote the foundation newsletter. The vision of the man who was a friend to a seven year old Laurelhurst child has become an inspiration to a whole city.

Once Is Enough
(A trip I wouldn't want to make again)
Gene Terpstra

The conference ended in early afternoon. Along with all the others attending, I quickly got my things together so I could check out. I had a 4:30 flight and there was no margin for delay. The woman who checked out just ahead of me left a leather portfolio on the counter. As I was checking out I noticed it. I picked it up and ran after her, hoping to find her before she disappeared into the crowd in the square. Fortunately, I did find her, but my spontaneous errand of mercy took precious minutes out of my own tight schedule.

When I checked out myself, I had to figure out how to get to the airport. The hotel where the conference was held was in a suburb near New York City. The area itself had no direct transportation to the airport. I thought I would take a bus or van to a nearby town or transportation hub that did have airport connections. Unfortunately, I didn't see any busses or vans, and I didn't know how to get any information quickly about them or their schedules.

Now what? Concerned with wasting time in indecision, I made a decision that was more desperate than thoughtful. I'd hitchhike to a nearby town or transportation hub where I could make connections to the airport. The last time I hitchhiked was during my senior year in college, 50 years before, but my thumb was still flexible enough to make the old appeal for a driver's compassion. A more important problem was that hitchhiking in this day and age is a very uncommon—and generally suspect—activity.

I hurried to a street where there was merging traffic. A pickup truck went by without so much as a glance from the driver. The next car actually did pull over and stop. It was full of young

Using All the Colors

kids, probably returning from school. When the woman driving heard my problem, she apologized and said she couldn't help me. Even if she had offered a ride, I don't know where she would have put me, other than letting me have one of the kids' seats. Of course, that would have meant having one of them sit on my lap.

Soon a van pulled over and stopped. Strangely, this, too, was full of kids, except for the front passenger seat. Even stranger was who was driving: Doug Martin, pastor of the church I attend back in Pasadena! In retrospect, I can't imagine a more bizarre coincidence! What was <u>he</u> doing here? Had he been at the conference and I just hadn't seen him? That's a situation too impossible even to imagine. And who were all these young children? Did Doug have another—clandestine—family on the east coast? Were these children of *friends* he was visiting? These questions are all second thoughts. At the time I didn't think them or ask them. I was fixated on getting to the airport, and Pastor Martin's appearance seemed a providential answer to my problem.

Pastor Martin drove quickly to a house in a neighborhood not far away and unloaded all the kids. The smallest child was the last one out of the van; I actually handed her to the pastor and he escorted them all into the house.

It seemed, finally, that I would get to the airport after all. But would I arrive in time to get on my 4:30 flight? And, if not, would I be able to arrange another flight sometime later that day? I didn't relish the prospect of spending the night in the airport.

Unfortunately, I cannot tell how this trip ended, or explain Pastor Martin's presence 2,500 miles from home, or account for the strange children with him—because it was at this point of my dream that I woke up!

Paulus

K. Roberta Woodberry

The compound was only a short distance away from our home at the Christian Study Centre. Dudley and I, along with our three sons, were living and working as Presbyterian Missionaries in Rawalpindi, Pakistan. I tired to visit once a month in the early 70's.

I turned my head to the side. My eyes dropped to the ground. My heart skipped a beat. I had never seen anyone like him before. As I steeled myself to look, his ears were gone. His nose was just an indentation with two holes. His eyes were opaque and glassed over. His skin was dark and patchy. Both his arms ended in stubs and he hobbled with crutches on toeless feet. His lower lip hung way out but there was a smile on his face.

"Salaam, Memsahib! Welcome to the Leprosy Hospital. We're so glad you've come. My name is Paulus." He went on to tell me how he loved my friend, Miss Audrey.

Audrey was a beautiful young woman from a wealthy family in Massachusetts. She had sensed God calling her and worked day and night as a Presbyterian missionary in the slums of Rawalpindi, Pakistan caring for the lepers.

They had a large compound surrounded by a high wall. Inside were gardens, fruit trees, a hospital compound, an orphanage, homes for the staff, workshops, sewing rooms, and a large kitchen.

Paulus proudly showed me his home. It was one room with a small garden out front, a water tap, and a place for building a fire for cooking. Inside was a charpai—a single rope bed with a rolled up mattress—some nails for clothes and a small dresser. Everything was very neat. He swept the mud-dung floor each day and rolled up his bedding. I don't know how, but with the help of neighbors he even worked in his garden. But Paulus was famous on that compound for something else, he was a singer.

Using All the Colors

I would often bring our three sons and worship with the lepers. When you entered the chapel—a simple room—you took off your shoes. The men sat on the right side and women on the left. Those of us who were "clean" (their word for those without leprosy) sat in chairs around the outside. There was a cross at one end, a mat on the floor, some windows and that was all.

Before the service began, everyone quieted down and Paulus began to sing. He had memorized many of the Psalms and set them to Pakistani melodies. His voice was pure and lyrical. I would close my eyes and imagine I was hearing an angel singing. He sang for about 20 minutes, unaccompanied except by the occasional voice that would join him. We all sang lustily during the service, but the prelude - that was for Paulus to sing. His voice was filled with joy.

As I got to know him better, I began to ask Paulus about his life and how he had come to the hospital. "Oh Memsahib," he'd say, "I thank God every day that I am a leper." I asked him how he could say that and he replied, "Memsahib, I was an awful man. I had a good wife and children, a home and a good business, but I beat them, I would cheat and steal. Then I got leprosy and I lost everything."

"You see, I began to lose my feeling and had no pain. I begged on the streets for food, but people didn't want to come near me. Before long I was blind and dying in the gutter, covered with sores. That's when some people brought me to Miss Audrey and the hospital here."

"They cleaned and bandaged my wounds, gave me a little home, fed me and just loved me. From them I learned about Jesus and how he could forgive the awful man I was and that He loved me too. So Memsahib, I thank God every day that I'm a leper. Otherwise, I wouldn't know Jesus."

My eyes filled with tears. This grotesque man had a heart filled with love, joy and thankfulness. He was beautiful! I just had to look at his heart.

One day Paulus was especially excited as he found me. "Memsahib, Memsahib! I'm going to Karachi. There is a special doctor there who can fix my lips so I can sing better. Won't that be wonderful?" I was happy for him and we prayed that the surgery would be successful.

I didn't hear anything for several days and then I got a call from Miss Audrey. "Paulus has a new body!" she said. It took me a moment to realize what she was saying and I asked what happened. The surgery had gone well. His lip had been repaired, but his tired body had just shut down.

As I hung up the phone, I closed my eyes and I could see Paulus running and dancing and seeing and singing! And thanking Jesus that he had been a leper who now was clean!

When I get to heaven, I want to find Paulus and thank him for blessing me.

Using All the Colors

WWII Memories

Using All the Colors

WWII Memories

Sayings

Thomas Bousman

As a child, Tom lived in the Philippines with his missionary parents. During the war, along with all Americans and other foreign nationals, they were interned for three long years. Their amazing rescue from Los Banos has been recounted on the History Chanel.

When I took my wife, Ellie, to the Philippines for her first visit, it was 1966. Her parents had volunteered to drive out to California from Indiana and hold down the fort for almost two months with our children ages 5 to 10. I had already been involved in the Filipino-American teams of testimony for six weeks when Ellie arrived.

Ellie noticed quite soon that Filipino friends spoke of and quoted Hugh and Nona Bousman often, even though they had died in Manila over a decade earlier. Those loyal, devoted members of the United Church of Christ in the Philippines recalled that my parents always had coffee on hand, and so were surprised to discover that we drank only tea. They often quoted my Dad's famous saying, *"Where the Lord leads me, I'll follow and what he feeds me, I'll swallow."* Faith and Humor!

I don't know if they even knew the saying that has never been forgotten by my brother and sister and me. It was a direct quote from Dad's father who used to say *"Don't believe anything you hear and only half of what you see"*

During our time of internment by the Japanese military, we heard rumors daily. Mac Arthur was returning from Australia and had landed on the southern islands. We kids were excited. We believed the news! U.S. help was arriving at last. We were coming to the beginning of the end. Hooray!

Dad walked into our cubicle and we fairly shouted the good news. Our father sat down wearily, looking much older than his 49

Using All the Colors

years and responded, "Remember what your grandpa Tom used to say? We three kids nodded in boredom and in unison chanted words we knew by heart, *"Don't believe anything you hear and only half of what you see."*

We had reached an impasse, but we knew Dad was right in being cautious about war rumors. How often our hopes had been dashed when we learned that our information was false. We continued to hear wild rumors almost daily. Some were so preposterous that we didn't believe them, but others raised our hopes, only to be dashed to pieces the thought that our deliverance was close at hand. Life dragged on as malnutrition and hunger became our constant companion.

It was at this stage in our incarceration that I, by then 16, gradually became aware of the fact that several times a week our Dad might disappear for over an hour in the evening. I never spoke about it. At first I assumed it might be a small group of missionary men getting together for prayer or theological discussions. That may have been the original plan, but it was even more than that. Diffcrent men in the camp would hide component parts of a simple radio. The Japanese had threatened severe punishment or even death if any internees were discovered with a radio so those with portions of such hid their particular segments and then when a secret message went out to the chosen few, they gathered quietly (with other Americans on guard keeping a careful watch) and reassembled their treasured portions of the radio. Only a handful would be able to listen to the Voice of America from San Francisco. It was their responsibility to share the news bulletins with trusted colleagues. No one in camp ever spoke openly.

This clandestine activity was never mentioned of in our family. Dad wanted to protect us so we would be safe from possible interrogation. Finally, however, we did receive accurate accounts of the US Forces landing at Leyte in October 1945, followed by reports that the Americans were moving north and had taken the island of Mindoro. Exhilaration zig-zagged through camp like lightning. The very thought of land-based planes soon being overhead set our pulses pounding.

Then, in a few days, it finally happened. We had heard of a new type of aircraft called a P-38 with a double fuselage. It was reported to be exceptionally versatile, with great speed and maneuverability. We did not need to wait long before one of these marvelous new aircraft was seen over our camp 50 miles south of Manila. We kids happened to be outside, but our parents were working indoors at the times. Flashing silver in the tropical sunlight, the plane was the most beautiful sight we had witnessed in nearly 3 years. Our physical response was goose pimples and moist eyes, plus a lump in the throat.

We three Bousman siblings dashed into our cubicle to share the good news. Our brother got the first chance to speak, fairly shouting, "Dad, Dad, remember what Grandpa Tom always said?" Our father nodded wearily. Our brother continued, "Dad we just saw *half* of a U.S. plane flying over our camp!" And we three began to giggle. Dad realized that the old saying had come back to haunt him. "You win," he admitted as we three joined our parents in a five way group hug. We all chanted together: *"Don't believe anything you hear, and only half of what you see."*

Aboard the Escambia
Kenneth Grant

"Esky Maru"—that was the name the crew gave our floating home on the war-torn Pacific during WWII. It was an interesting, if obvious, title. "Esky" meant the Escambia, our ship, her name coming from the name of an Indian river somewhere in the United States. "Maru", on the other hand, was the Japanese word for ship. The name was used with some degree of affection, I suppose, and the inclusion of a Japanese word in the title had no particular significance other than the fact that the Japanese were often on our minds.

But, of course, the people on the ship were the most important part and the most memorable. Arnie "Blackie" Blackburn, Gus "Tommy" Thompson, Alvin Tuckerman, "Stoney" Stonecypher, and "Arky" Glover became my closest friends during those long months aboard the ship.

When we were not busy with other duties, Blackie and I often got together to sing and pray and read the Bible. We'd find a spot somewhere on deck where we'd not be disturbed. Sometimes Gus or Tommy (isn't this the same person?) would join us. The songs we sang were not the ones I had learned from Sunday School or Church, but the country and "hillbilly" songs that Blackie knew (and I soon learned): "Life is Like a Mountain Railroad", "The Great Judgment Morning", "Will the Circle Be Unbroken", and others that have faded from memory now. I still remember Blackie saying to me with his deep, southern drawl, "I don't know how you city folks can worship God usin' them big organs and all." His experience, and clearly his own preference, was for country songs accompanied by the strum of a good guitar! I was learning about life and people and the wonderful variety offered in both!

"Arky" Glover (whose real first name I can't recall) was clearly from Arkansas, and had owned and operated a dairy. A soft-spoken and somewhat retiring man, he too was a professing Christian. While I never knew him well, what struck me was that he fit rather uncomfortably into the more rough-and-tumble crew.

"Arky" was a bit older and petrified by heights. Since one of our duties as deck hands was to stand watch in the "crows nest" perched high on the forward mast of the ship, it posed a problem for Arky. But, bless him, he tried! He made the attempt, and I remember seeing him frozen with fear halfway up the slim steel ladder that ran up the mast to the crows nest. Someone had to climb up behind him and ease him back down to the relative security of the deck. Thereafter, he was excused from that duty.

My only other remembrance of him was his statement, slowly drawled in the soft southern way he said everything, "Ah surely do miss my corn bread an' sweet milk." AND he informed us, "Real corn bread is white rather than that yellow stuff you northern folks eat!"

Gus Thompson and I, on the other hand, had many a good talk, mostly about our homes back "stateside" and our families there. His was a homey wisdom, and mature, for he was an older man to my young years. Between him and Blackie I got a considerably different perspective on love and life. Both men served as a kind of emotional anchor, I suppose, though I might not have called it that back then.

Al Tuckerman was not in our division, but was part of the crew that worked below decks in the ship's engine room. Al was known to be a Christian, and, while not a big man, had a rather admirable physique. We became acquainted in the course of things and I learned that he had a wife and children back home and he missed them terribly.

I don't really remember much specific about "Stoney" Stonecypher, though I can see his face and frame clearly in memory's eye. He was tall, raw boned, with a square jaw and ruggedly handsome face, topped with a head of curly grey hair. He smiled often and was friendly and I felt he was the sort a fellow could talk to if need be. That tall, friendly man with the wide grin lives in my memory still.

Freddie Smithers is another story. Possibly near my age, he too was from somewhere in the South, judging by his drawl. Short, curly headed, with a quick temper and often rather careless mouth, he nonetheless became a friend when we were both assigned to stand watch in the gun tub of the forward three-inch gun. I had been assigned to be first loader on that gun during General Quarters and gunnery practice, and so the spot was familiar!

Freddie and I had many a long talk, though I recall one in particular. It was a stormy night. The seas were running high and our bow plunged alternately down into a giant swell and then rose high, sending salt spray singing back across our gun tub on the plunging bow.

Freddie and I hunkered down in the tub, trying to talk over the noise of the ocean's furious sound. And we talked about God. We talked about life and fate and where Freddie stood. He didn't claim to be a Christian, at least so anyone could tell. I finally asked him if he would like to give his life to Christ, and he replied, "I would." We knelt together in that rain swept gun tub and Freddie Smithers gave his life to God.

The storm blew itself out, as such storms do, but more storms lay ahead for Freddie. He was a changed man and the crew was incredulous. "Hey Grant. What did you do to Smithers?" "Nothing," I replied, "God did!" And it was true.

There are other memories to be sure. Fueling at sea was a regular occurrence. We received our cargo of fuel oil for ships and 100 octane gasoline for aircraft from unarmed commercial tankers which carried it as far as was safe into the South Pacific, usually to Ulithi Atoll where cargos were exchanged. Our task then was to join the flotilla of other supply ships that formed the "Fleet Train", and follow the battle fleet at a distance of perhaps only a hundred miles or so. Thus, we would be ready to re-supply the fighting ships with fuel, ammunition, medicine, foodstuffs and other needed supplies without their having to return long distances to land bases. The Japanese, long unaware of this technique, were taken off guard when finding the American fleet back "on target" so soon.

Personnel were sometimes transferred from ship to ship as well, using a line strung between heaving ships, both "under way." A "Bosun's Chair" made of crossed straps of fabric that supported the passenger and, to some extent, surrounded him, was suspended from this line and he pulled himself, across the heaving grey waves that rose and fell, often not far beneath him. Since ships do roll from side to side, the lines were sometimes known to slack a bit and dip and an occasional and unintended "baptism" had been known to happen.

It was, however, a day at Ulithi Atoll that is most clearly etched in my mind. An atoll, as most old hands know, is a circle of usually small islands, frequently joined by underwater reefs, that oceanographers tell us were formed when an ancient volcano blew its top, leaving only portions of the "rim" above water. The result is a natural haven for resting ships. Ulithi, considerably south and west of Okinawa is such a place, and large enough to hold a sizable fleet. It was our frequent R & R spot as well as contact with commercial tankers. Frequently, major ships of the Third Fleet also anchored there.

Our men were usually relieved to return to Ulithi, not only for a brief respite but to have liberty ashore at "Mog Mog by the Sea". Mog Mog was one of the small islands forming the Atoll and, while offering little more than sand and a scattering of palm trees, became a place where the sailors could get their feet on dry land and drink beer! Being a "Tea Totaler" at the time, I never visited Mog Mog.

But there was drama awaiting us at Ulithi. I don't recall the date, but I remember the day clearly. I was in my bunk in the crews quarters, when suddenly I heard the loud squawk! squawk! of the general quarters signal... but no drill had been scheduled. I rolled out quickly, pulled on my dungarees and hurried topside to my station at the forward three-inch gun. The sun was shining brightly that morning and the sea was its usual incredible blue. But less than a quarter of a mile from us there was a navy tanker in flames! Little was showing but her stern. The rest was engulfed in a thick cloud of black smoke, shot through with tongues of flame that billowed skyward in a huge column. Awe struck, we watched as small boats headed toward the spot to rescue sailors who had, at the impact of the torpedo, jumped into the water and swam clear of the spreading pool of flaming oil. Shortly, our own launch joined the effort.

What had happened, we learned, was that a Japanese submarine had towed a number of "two man" mini subs to the gate or opening of the Atoll and turned them loose to attack the fleet anchored there, which that day included a carrier. The subs were soon discovered, however, and destroyers were dashing through the Atoll's smooth waters dropping depth charges. One destroyer raced by, not far off our stern, dropping a charge that, when it detonated, sounded like a giant hammer hitting our hull, though no harm was done. The little subs were not so lucky. To my knowledge, the only ship hit was the Misisinowa, the hapless tanker that lay just across the gate from where we were anchored. A desperate mini sub, realizing they had been discovered, simply fired his torpedo at the nearest ship and it struck. We were fortunate. We later learned that the pilot of a seaplane belonging to one of the cruisers was in the air at the time. Seeing what had happened, he landed on the bay, taxied as close to the burning ship as he could. Then allowing swimming sailors to grab his pontoons, he taxied them to nearby ships before returning for another load. He was later decorated for his heroism.

As for the hapless fleet tanker, she continued to burn. The sound of explosions could be heard from time to time as ammunition in her magazine detonated. At last, her stern raised skyward and she slid beneath the surface of the lagoon, leaving only the black pall of smoke drifting overhead. Many of the crew had survived, thanks to the heroes.

WWII Memories

Ulithi, Mog Mog, the Misisinowa, the Escambia, all wrapped in memories of bright sunshine, blue water and the vast endless sky of the South Pacific. The stories of war time experiences in the South Pacific are endless, to be sure, and this is but a glimpse of mine. The rest? They are a heritage from a long ago place and time. A time of crisis, heroism, tragedy and growth. I am grateful to my God for lessons learned and a war survived.

The Escambia

The War Years
Hedy Lodwick

We moved to University Park, Maryland around 1940—at that time Europe was already heavily at war. This was of special concern to my parents and my Grossmama, Dad's mother, who lived with us. Mother had immigrated from Switzerland and Dad and Grossmama from Germany in 1924. Now they had great concern for Mother's family in Basel and for Grossmama's brother and nephews in Germany.

As Mother was anxious for news from Switzerland, Dad bought her a wooden radio, the kind popular at the time, but this one had the added attraction of shortwave. I remember the sound of cowbells when broadcasts from Switzerland were announced. I remember also Dad's fury whenever he heard Hitler's ranting. (My son, Philip, has this radio today and when we passed it on to him a few years ago, it worked in spite of layers of dust on the tubes.)

Then came the shock of Pearl Harbor. I remember that day vividly! We were gathered around the table of Swiss friends who bred cocker spaniel puppies. Our Tootsie, who grew fat from the diet Grossmama fed him, came from them. After Tootsie died, we got Pal. Mother fed him and he stayed normal size. Anyway, that December 7th our chatter about puppies and such was cut short abruptly as an urgent announcement broke on the radio declaring that we were now officially at war because of this infamous attack. Up until that time, the U.S. had been trying to maintain neutrality. On the way home, my brother, Roland, and I worried that Dad might be drafted. He said, no way, he was too old, though at the time he was not yet 40. Besides, said he, he would refuse to bear arms, as he had become a pacifist. He would drive a Red Cross truck and serve in such a capacity, but he would not bear arms.

I was thirteen at the time, and so my high school years were constantly overshadowed with news and worry about the war.

WWII Memories

Neighbor boys would soon be drafted, and Johnny next door lost his life. Our own lives were affected by rationing. Sugar, butter, and shoes were the ones I remember. Mother managed pretty well on the sugar and butter score as she had boarders and their ration books, along with ours, provided enough for all of us. She managed even to make jam and jellies. As for shoes, we never could afford to buy as many as we were allowed. When I left for college in 1945, I had to bring along my ration books for the college kitchen. By the fall of 1946, these were no longer needed.

For college, I needed to buy new sheets and towels. This was difficult as such items were also scarce. After hunting in several stores and becoming tired and discouraged, I must have sounded quite distraught at the last store for I remember a sales person providing me with some sheets - from below the counter!

Tin cans and fat were things to be saved and delivered, I don't know where, for the war effort. I remember stamping on tin cans in the back yard, flattening them for the collection. We assumed they were to be turned into parts for airplanes. What they did with all the bacon fat and lard we saved I can't imagine, but save every drop we did. Televisions made an appearance only after the war. Instead, whenever we went to the movies, the feature attraction was preceded by newsreels showing the plight of people in England, or planes flying on bombing missions.

Women were dismayed that silk stockings were no longer available. Nylon had not yet been used for them. Instead, there were rayon stockings which tended to get baggy. And this was just the time when girls our age were beginning to abandon bobby socks for stockings when we dressed up. Some young women used leg make up instead of stockings and this tended to come off on chairs and church benches if their skirts were a bit short. I remember hearing some even tried to paint a seam line up the back of their legs. I was not one of them! I remember the excitement after the war when one could get used parachutes, which were nylon, to use in sewing blouses and such. Nylon stockings followed shortly thereafter.

Using All the Colors

Heating oil was another scarce commodity. I remember Grossmama helping us tear newspapers into long strips and rolling them one over the other after having been soaked in a watery flour solution. These large balls were allowed to dry in the sun and then were used as slow burning fuel in our fireplace. Our church did not use heat during the week so we went to our organist's home for choir practice. There we worked regularly on a piece to be sung as soon as the war ended. I believe most churches were prepared for special services the very day there was a declaration of victory over the Germans and again over the Japanese.

I remember feeling aghast when the first pictures came showing the liberation of the concentration camps. Then we learned about the horrors of those camps, the gas chambers, the ovens. How could humans treat each other this way? Along with all the sense of horror, there was also joy at the prospect of being connected with families again. Mother had not been able to send mail to her family in Switzerland, as no U.S. mail could cross enemy lines. Occasional letters made their way from them to us and were received with rejoicing. Mother would then send a telegram telling them the letter had been received and that we were all well. Grossmama had had no contact with her brother, Willie, and his family still in Germany. Willie and his son, Gotthart, and Gotthard's family had needed to flee their home in Guben, Germany (now part of Poland) and Grossmama did not know where they were until after the war when a letter made its way to us. Again there was rejoicing and Mother quickly began to assemble care packages to go to them. I remember helping her tie some of the packages shut by holding a finger on the cross cords so that the knot would be really tight. Some of the clothes my brother and I had outgrown were sent to Gotthard's wife, Amelia, for their two children. Their daughter, Ingeborg, who visited us here in Monte Vista Grove in 2005, was the recipient of some of my dresses. Amelia was French and had an extra difficult time in Germany because of that. Gotthard had to serve in the German military but Ingeborg told me he let himself be captured by the British because he could not fight in Hitler's war. It was some time after the war before he could return to his family. He and Amelia then took in "Uncle" Willie, then quite aged and weak. Of course, Mother sent packages to her Swiss family also—probably coffee, sugar, soap and such.

Just before graduation, I went to town with my friend, Vera, to apply for a social security card. Social Security was still in its infancy, but I needed one to apply for a job. My first job the summer after high school was at the Veterans' Administration in D.C. What use I was to them I do not know, for my typing skills were rather poor, but I think they needed summer help to fill in for those taking vacations. I remember taking fistfulls of pencils to sharpen for the others in the office and other such low level tasks. I did help proofread stencils and to put some kind of sealer over the mistakes so that someone else could go over them with the typewriter. These documents were then reproduced in quantity on a mimeograph machine. Then there was a lot of collating to do. I said that if the government was going to waste money paying me for what I did, it was at least helping support my college education.

On a steamy August 8th, as I was on my way to catch the trolley home, there were boys all over the streets, excitedly waving early editions of the newspapers shouting "EXTRA! EXTRA! READ ALL ABOUT IT!" The atom bomb had been dropped on Hiroshima and the war with Japan was over. Of course, we were relieved that the fighting was done, but it dawned on us more slowly about the horror of what an atom bomb did.

Our country switched from fighting to helping restore Europe with the Marshal Plan. Did the Marshal Plan include outreach to Japan? I'm not sure, but, because of my family, our outlook was to Europe. It was a time of high hope. With a rebuilt Europe, the world would surely become a peaceful place. Unfortunately, we must continue all these many years later to hope and pray that people the world over can learn to live securely, with enough to eat, and in harmony with each other.

The War Years: 1941-1945
Robert Lodwick

My wife, Hedy, and I had been glued to the TV each evening watching *The War*—A powerful and riveting film by Ken Burns and Lynn Novick on PBS. The daily viewing of this documentary by one of America's leading film producers took me back in memory to the events being portrayed on the screen.

My earliest memory of the beginning of World War II was Thursday, September 2, 1939, as news of the German Blitzkrieg into Poland the previous day was reported on the morning radio and in giant headlines in the Cincinnati Enquirer.

I was 11, riding my bicycle with a friend around the field of our elementary school. My friend was talking about "the future" and I interrupted to tell him what had just happened in Poland and the threat of war. Together, we wondered if we, in America, would become involved in this war. For some strange reason, I have always remembered that day and that conversation.

Then, two years later, on Sunday, December 7, 1941, shortly after Sunday dinner, we received the news of the devastating bombing of Pearl Harbor and were glued to the radio the rest of the afternoon. That night our family—uncle, aunts and grandparents—all gathered with other fearful families in a special Sunday evening gathering for prayer.

Seeing the video this week has jogged my memory of the years following that "day of infamy" as described by President Roosevelt. There was rationing and I remember my mother, active in PTA, being called to help distribute the Ration Cards. Every family in Bond Hill had to go to register at St. Agnes Catholic School, just across the street from my school. I have always remembered my mother returning home that evening saying "how nice the nuns were, how calm and how great to work with them." I think this was her first experience in knowing Catholic nuns. Those words were imprinted in my psyche and throughout my work with Catholic nuns, I have also found Mother's words to be true.

The war years were not difficult years for us until gold stars began to appear on windows in Bond Hill. My brother was 3 years older than I and his girlfriend's brother was in the service and killed. In 1943, my brother was conscripted into the army. Then the war was part of our family. Dick got through basic training with flying colors. He looked smart in his uniform and we were proud of him. Mother wrote to him several times a week and care packages were mailed to him monthly. We learned a lot of geography during the war, not only of nations but of tiny villages, as well as islands in the Pacific that we had never known and found difficult to spell or pronounce.

Saturday movies always had a newsreel of the latest advances or withdrawals of troops in Europe or the Pacific. Dick was sent on a troop ship to France and was in the Battle of the Bulge which began in December of 1944. This was a tense time for the family as we watched the Americans advance and retreat and advance again. The Battle of the Bulge was the bloodiest of the battles that U.S. forces experienced in World War II; the 19,000 American dead were unsurpassed by those of any other engagement. During those months we had just rare notes from Dick, but Mother kept all of them and later had them bound. They were cryptic notes that left everything to the imagination for good or evil. Dick was one of the fortunate survivors and after the defeat of the Nazis remained in Europe as part of the staff of General Eisenhower.

I have vivid memories of V-E day and the gathering in Fountain Square in downtown Cincinnati. There was dancing in the street and much confetti. It was an event clouded only by the continuing war in the Pacific.

The following Sunday evening we had a special service in our congregation in Bond Hill. We entered the dim sanctuary in silence. Then the names of countries in Europe that had been liberated were called out one by one, a candle was lit, and the room became much brighter I don't remember if we lit a candle for Germany or not? I think we did.

V-J Day was August 15 in Japan, August 14 in the USA. In the USA there were great celebrations but some were muted as many also prayed for the innocent victims in Japan from the nuclear bomb, code named "Little Boy", dropped on August 6 on Hiroshima and another, code named "Fat Man", on August 9 on Nagasaki. They effectively ended the war in the Pacific but these bombings caused the immediate deaths of around 120,000 innocent people and even more over time because of injuries sustained and long-term radiation.

Watching *The War* these past two weeks on PBS, we were reminded of how many things we had forgotten and how much we never knew because of war-time secrecy and facts not shared. Tom Bousman (another resident at Monte Vista Grove) has helped us know what had happened on the Philippine Islands when he was interned there as a teenager, but the fierce battles on Iwo Jima and Okinawa were ones I had forgotten and I found the number of deaths staggering for both the US and Japan in comparison to our current war in Afghanistan and Iraq. I didn't think I wanted to watch the Ken Burns film but am glad that we did.

A Rosie Reunion
Jacquie Terpstra

A few years ago, my two daughters, my granddaughter and I had a unique experience. We attended the first "Rosie the Riveter" Reunion held at the Rosie the Riveter/World War II Home Front National Historical Park in Richmond, California. I received an invitation because several years ago, I had submitted my mother's story to the Park collection. The park is located on the site of Henry Kaiser's shipyard and eventually, will include a museum in the Ford building, the restored childcare center, a monument to the Home Front workers and various exhibits as well as the shipyard.

Many of the "Rosies" attending had actually built ships at that location during WWII. They came, with their hair tied up in bandannas and wearing their plant identification badges. One woman was wearing her regulation coveralls. Most were accompanied by family members. A number of the women appeared to be quite frail.

The weekend included a variety of events but the most meaningful for us was the afternoon spent hearing the women tell their stories. Many spoke with trembling voices and some were weeping. We heard about women moving across country to work there and how difficult it was for them to find housing. One woman talked about having to descend several stories on a ladder to work at the bottom of the ship and then having to climb back up that ladder to the top at the end of the day. We learned how for every riveter there had to be a "bucker", someone to hold a metal shield behind the object being riveted. One woman recalled that because she was small, she was assigned to do welding in extremely tight quarters, but eventually had to ask for a transfer because of her advancing pregnancy. Another woman spoke of working her way up to journeyman welder. A black woman described how the blacks always had to order carry-out at a side window or back door of the local restaurants because they weren't allowed to be seated inside.

I shared some of my mother's experience in building bombers at Henry Ford's Willow Run plant in Michigan. According to Ken Burn's recent documentary, by the end of the war, Willow Run was producing a bomber every 63 minutes. Afterwards, another woman who had also worked at Willow Run talked about how the few men in those plants frequently gave the women workers a hard time. The women were often made the butt of a joke as when sent to find a handle for an Allen wrench.

Later, I talked with that woman. She was there with her daughter, granddaughter, and great granddaughter. I discovered that she had been a student at the University of Michigan at the time that the war broke out. She dropped out of college to go to work at Willow Run and then returned to the U of M after the war to finish her degree. We shared memories particular to Willow Run (mine from my mother) and laughed about some things such as how the plant guards were referred to as the "Gestapo" by the workers. After wishing each other well, we gave each other the high five and a "Go Blue" for our shared alma mater.

One of the speakers was Emily Yellin, author of Our Mothers' War. Her mother had served on Saipan with the Red Cross during the war. She prefaced one of her remarks by saying that she wasn't in the habit of quoting Nazis but thought it worth noting that Goebbels had said that the reason that the Americans won the war was because they put their women to work. I purchased a copy of Emily's book and while she was autographing it, she thanked me for sharing my mother's story. She wrote, "To Jacquie, I hope this re-connects you with your own mom."

Minnie's Story
Jacquie Terpstra

This story was originally presented at a celebration of Women's History Month held at the Bergen County Technical School' Workforce Center in Hackensack, New Jersey. March 2003.

While enjoying a sight-seeing cruise around Manhattan a few years ago, we passed the *Intrepid,* a decommissioned aircraft carrier which is now a museum. I was surprised when our guide made a special point of mentioning that the huge ship had been built by women. After a moment, I thought "Well of course it was built by women". It was built during WWII by hundreds of "Rosie the Riveters". This was the name given to the women who helped build the planes, tanks, ships and bombs that were needed in that great war. As I reflected on that, I thought of the "Rosie" in our family. Her name was Minnie.

Minnie was raised on a farm in Iowa, one of eleven children. She loved learning and excelled in school. When she had to leave school after 8th grade and go to work as a "hired girl", she was extremely disappointed. However, in spite of those circumstances, she didn't give up on her education. She took every correspondence course available to her through the teacher's college at Cedar Falls, Iowa, and eventually she was certified to teach in country schools. She taught there until she married.

Minnie and her husband had six children. Though the family suffered severe financial setbacks during the Depression, Minnie never lost her zeal for education, especially education for her children. When WWII broke out and people were being recruited for work in defense factories and shipyards, she saw it as an opportunity to aid the country, improve the family's finances and educate her children as well.

Almost everyone who left for defense work from the small Iowa town where she lived headed for the shipyards on the west coast, but not Minnie and her family. She and her husband chose the new aircraft factory, commonly called the "Bomber Plant", which was being built by Henry Ford at Willow Run, Michigan. There the B-24, the workhorse of the Air Corp's bomber fleet, would be built. Minnie realized that the University of Michigan at Ann Arbor was nearby. She decided that if the family moved there, she and her husband could get jobs building bombers and her children could get an education at the university.

Minnie

Her husband left in April 1942 to get settled in Michigan. He was the first man from that small Iowa town to leave for defense work. As it turned out, he arrived at Willow Run so early that he was hired to help complete the building of the factory. He reported that he had difficulty finding a place for the family to live because of the prejudice that he encountered against those moving into the area for defense work. (The Dollmaker by Harriet Arnow vividly describes this attitude.) Minnie's husband found that newcomers were classified as "ignorant hillbillies", a label applied to even those from the prairies of Iowa! Eventually, however, he found a house and Minnie and the children arrived later that summer. The younger children started school and Minnie soon began working at the Bomber Plant.

At first she helped build generators for the planes, but later she moved to the main plant and to what was referred to as the "dope" room. This was where a heavy, gummy, waterproof coating was applied to the canvas skin of the planes. She earned more money there because the flammable materials used made it a hazardous work environment. Minnie worked on the aileron, that part of the wing that enabled the plane to roll or bank. When she was in her 80's, she impressed a couple of her nephews, who were airplane enthusiasts, with her knowledge of airplane construction, even down to the grade of canvas and type of waterproofing used.

Working in a factory put Minnie and, no doubt, most women in the defense industry into a totally new environment. These were women who for the most part, had not worked outside their homes prior to the war. Suddenly they were wearing coveralls and carrying lunch pails along with the men. Women who were used to working alone at home or on their farms were now working with many others, including men who were too old for the draft. Minnie enjoyed the socializing, teasing and opportunity to make new friends, and she often regaled her family with stories of the day's happenings. However, she was very distressed and disappointed with those among her coworkers who were having extramarital affairs, especially when the wife of a serviceman was involved. Her commitment to her marriage, family and faith enabled her to draw very clear boundaries for herself, though she used to joke that she had her share of opportunities!

At home, a flag with two blue stars hung in her window. One was for a daughter in the Navy, a WAVE, stationed at a naval hospital in Oakland, California. The other was for a son in the Army Air Corps who flew B-26 bombers. She also had a brother and numerous nephews who were in the military service as well as another son, a merchant marine, ferrying supplies across the Pacific. She always kept up with the war news and had a special compassion for the suffering and starvation of innocent people, especially children, everywhere.

So how did it all turn out? Well, the war ended. Minnie, along with the other women, came home. I don't think they realized the magnitude of their contribution until the Women's Movement of the 1960's began to recognize them. Yes, Minnie's children all had an opportunity to get a college education and five of the six earned graduate degrees. When her youngest child started college, Minnie also went back to school and fulfilled her lifelong dream of becoming a nurse.

If you had known her, you would have thought her an exceptional woman. At the same time, she was representative of the group of women who were part of what Tom Brokaw has called *The Greatest Generation*. She and they are a hard act to follow. Personally, I salute her: my mentor, my friend, my mother.

Using All the Colors

Noteworthy Events

Using All the Colors

Noteworthy Events

The King's Visit
Don Hawthorne

I thoroughly enjoyed seeing the movie, "The King's Speech," and plan to see it again while it is still the focus of so much attention in the media. Because it has been talked about so steadily, it got me thinking about the story of King George VI, and that brought to my mind the time I was only about 30 yards from him (<u>ever</u> so briefly!) when he came to my hometown—Washington, D.C.

It was in the late 1930s, and the King and Queen were scheduled to make the first visit ever of a British Monarch to the United States. Washington was all atwitter about the visit. They would be staying at the British Embassy, dining at a White House State Dinner, and entertaining at a Garden Party at the Embassy. The newspapers carried detailed descriptions of every occasion during their visit, including menus at the various events. The big public event was to be a parade down Pennsylvania Avenue, and our family went for it...

Needless to say, we were not alone on the Avenue! The crowds were thick on both sides of the street, and it being in the 1930s, while some security was possibly there, it was not at all obvious. The sole focus was on two open touring cars (I was sufficiently concentrating on the people in the cars that I forgot to check whether they were riding in Cadillacs or Rolls Royces.) The first car was occupied by the King and President Roosevelt. The second car carried the Queen and First Lady, Eleanor. They moved by fairly quickly, but my mind made a recording of the moment that still remains vivid in my memory.

In the light of "The King's Speech," I realize that I have no recollection of him speaking publicly during that visit, but then, why should he have? We were just a former rebellious colony, and he was under no pressure to do more than just show up, which he graciously and regally did!

185

Unexpected: A Night I Will Not Forget
Robert Lodwick

As Area Secretary for Europe for the Presbyterian Church USA from 1978 to 1993, my interactions with sister churches and movements in Europe were exciting, sometimes difficult but also very fulfilling. While our Presbyterian office was located in the Ecumenical Center in Geneva, our work was with churches and movements on both sides of the East/West divide.

On November 9, 1989, I needed to fly to Berlin for a meeting with church officials on the 10th. My flight to Berlin was delayed for almost an hour waiting for a team of Japanese Press photographers to arrive and join our flight. The rumor was that the infamous BERLIN WALL had been breeched. Could this be true?

We arrived in Berlin at 11 p.m. My colleague, Jane Holslag, was at the airport and she said to me to hurry because all Berliners were celebrating the open gates between East and West Berlin. No one was sure how long they would be open. So we dashed to the WALL near to the Brandenburg Gate, known as "The Gate of Peace" since 1791. The gate was incorporated into the Berlin wall during the years of Communist government. That night traffic was at a standstill because hundreds of small East German Trabant cars were circling the area blowing their horns. People were drinking beer and placing lighted candles along the road leading to the Brandenburg Gate.

It was a night to behold. It was true that the crossings were open. There were East German soldiers with their guns still walking on the top of the wall even as West Germans were taking hammers to the wall itself, breaking off small hunks as souvenirs. One offered me a pick ax and I chipped away. It was hard to go to sleep that night for fear of what would happen the next day.

In the morning we headed to the church offices. The German bishop welcomed us and then told us that just ten days ago, the text for that Reformation Sunday was from Isaiah 62:10 "**Go through, go through the gates, prepare the way for the people, build up, build the highway, clear it of stones, lift up an ensign over the peoples**." Then he said, "That which we had been praying for these past 28 years, we were not prepared for when it happened." Thanks be to God that it did!

Euphoria lasted many days before the hard work could begin of reuniting the two governments and two churches into one Government and one Church.

The 500 Year Flood Plain
Hedy Lodwick

Son in law, Mark, grew up in Bismarck, N.D. and, so, it is not surprising that he loves fishing and hunting. Somehow he went to Whitworth College in Spokane, WA and that's where he and Margaret met. How she got there is a story for another time. Each of them after graduation did an internship at Dale House in Colorado Springs, Colorado. When these were completed and they needed to find permanent employment, Mark said to Margaret, "Do we need to live far from both our families?" Bob and I were in Geneva, Switzerland. Margaret thought this was a question to which she had no reasonable objection, and so she is one person who went TO North Dakota to live. And she soon joined Mark in loving the Missouri River, especially in summertime.

It was Mark's dream to live by the river and after 18 years in town, they managed to buy a piece of property right on the banks of the river where they then proceeded to build a home large enough for their family of 3 and a frequent invasion of family members, as well as other guests. We hoped they were safe from floods but they assured us they were in the 500 year flood plain and so were confident that it was safe to live there. I ventured that I hoped they were not in year 499. However, on seeing the property, I relaxed. After all, their front lawn sloped down a reasonable distant to the water's edge with what seemed to be a significant bank into the river. It looked like they were far enough inland to assure safety, but we had never experienced a real flood.

While winters are harsh, long, and dark, summers are lovely and our family began to plan a reunion over the 4th of July each year. They acquired an old, but usable pontoon boat that carried us all to a favorite sand bar, which became a private beach for us, and to a shallow pond sheltered by this sand bar where swimming was enjoyed, in addition to kayak rides and noodle jousts between the older grandchildren. Daughter Marion began to call Margaret and Mark's place, Camp LoMurray.

Also enjoyed were floats down the river. Mark would drive us up river, often with assistance from the youngest grandchildren (who thought *they* were driving the boat). Then he would turn off the motor so that we could drift back home enjoying the peace and beauty of the river. After supper floats were especially quiet and peaceful.

Another gathering was planned for this summer, July 2011, where we would also celebrate our 60th anniversary with all the family present. Margaret and Marion, however, decided they would *have* to come for THE day, which they did, and we had a lovely time on May 19th. Mark surprised us the day afterward, stopping off here on his way to Seattle where he was scheduled to do a training program on his suicide prevention curriculum. Margaret knew then that the Garrison Dam was releasing water from time to time because of abundant snow melt and rain in Montana and we knew the river would be higher than usual and covering all the sandbars. We did not expect the Dam to be overwhelmed for the first time since its construction 60 years ago. We had expected still to have a lovely time. However, this turned out to be year 500! Shortly after returning from Pasadena, Margaret and Mark began to receive phone calls from the neighbors with information that their home was in danger of being flooded and the access road to their home might not last 12 hours. Mark canceled his presentations and flew back home to help. With the help of friends, they moved the contents of their basement upstairs, while starting the process of gathering sandbags to build a dike. Soon it became clear that serious flooding would be in the picture and more major precautions were needed. As the situation became of greater concern, it was obvious that even more help was needed. Grandson, Justin, 20, and with no permanent employment yet, flew from Port Townsend, WA to lend his hand.

Then one day, they had a surprise phone call from

Using All the Colors

Margaret's cousin, Paul, who lives in South Dakota. Could he come and help? Communication in the past few years had been mostly via Christmas letters, but now they were delighted to accept his offer, and he came promptly with Debbie, his wife. Paul had been an engineer on oil rigs and has a lot of savvy. He, therefore, could do more than fill and pile up sand bags. He assisted with setting up pumps, generators, and other strategies to fight the imminent flood.

Also helping were their son Keith and his ballerina sweetheart, son Scot who came from Colorado and a local niece and her husband. Lisa, their daughter, found it difficult to leave her work but she plans to be there for sure when the arduous work of clean up begins.

Margaret reported that 20 – 30 persons were helping daily, some of whom were Native American young people who had come to their place for retreats in the past. Now they came to help with sandbags. When they had the house surrounded with bags, Justin said he believed 10,000 bags must have been piled into place. Justin also helped moving furniture, even appliances, out of the house. These were taken here and there to family and friends all over town. Some residents who had begun salvage work before Margaret did had called in moving vans to empty their homes. Everyone was trying to save what all they could. We believe Margaret may have a hard time remembering what went where. Many friends brought in enough food daily to feed this whole crew. From what we hear, all of Bismarck became mobilized to help those living along the river. Over 11 million sandbags were filled by the community in a weeks period of time.

When all the work was complete, a four foot high dike of sandbags surrounded the house and several pumps had been strategically placed. These were to function with a generator which would be fueled from the gas tank regularly kept for their fleet of cars, lawn mower, and pontoon boat. It, however, had to be anchored and tied to a tree! It is not known how many weeks of gas supply is left.

Paul, Justin, and the other helpers have gone now and the waiting has begun. The water becomes higher each time the dam releases more cubic feet of water but as I write it has not yet reached the sandbags. Hopefully it never will, but that is no doubt wishful thinking. The highest level should not be reached until well into the middle of June and then the water will remain high until the middle of August. The course of the river will surely change. The hope is still that the foundation of the house itself will be able to withstand the force of the ground water. It will be a tragic loss if it can not.

Boating on the 500 year flood plain

Many friends have offered lodging to Margaret and Mark. Fortunately, however, they have been able to move into the basement apartment of the home they still own in town. The downstairs renter was leaving in August anyway, so he has moved upstairs with the upstairs renter who is alone now that his teen aged son has moved on. Margaret is trying to collect enough of their scattered belongings to furnish this, they hope temporary, apartment for the duration. However, this is a happy solution because now their two labs can be with them and that had been a concern. The friends who offered lodging were not prepared to

Using All the Colors

have the dogs also.

Now we wait and pray that the river will be kind to them and to all those up and down the Missouri and the Mississippi, which is fed from the Missouri, and that the Garrison Dam will not be overwhelmed again. May the next 500 years at least bring no more floods!

Martin Luther King's "Finest Hour"
Jim Symons

On Sunday, March 5, 1965, Dr. Martin Luther King led 500 peaceful marchers from Selma to Montgomery, Alabama to demand equal voting rights for African-Americans. They were tear-gassed, beaten, shocked with cow prods and chased back to their churches by Governor George Wallace's state troopers. When Dr. King issued a call for another march two weeks later, I bought a plane ticket from San Francisco to Montgomery. Days later, a Boston minister and a Michigan housewife were murdered by white thugs in Selma, chilling evidence of the challenge faced by Dr. King and his supporters.

When I arrived in Selma I joined others from across the country in an orientation. "When you are attacked," we were told, "lie down in a fetal position and protect your head with your arms." He did not say "if" you are attacked, but "when". I was given a place to stay in the African-American community at the home of Mrs. Parker, a domestic worker in her 60s. That night, and every night that week, I joined the crowd that packed Brown's Chapel. What an inspiration—powerful preaching by Dr. King and his brilliant young associates, joyful and exhilarating gospel music, a pulsing spirit of hope that God was leading us to a better America and a conviction that "we shall overcome".

One day three of us walked into the white community to learn what people there were thinking. A pick-up truck came from nowhere attempting to run us down. We knew what that driver thought! We met Selma's Presbyterian minister, a pharmacist, and a Jewish small business owner who all sympathized with Dr. King but could not speak out directly for fear of their lives.

With such anger against the movement and Dr. King, I realized that Mrs. Parker's job was in jeopardy if her white employers learned that she was hosting me as an "outside agitator".

Using All the Colors

I told her I would move out so that she would not lose her job. She fixed me with her eyes. "Jim, don't you even think of moving out. I have been waiting all my life for this moment. Finally, I can look at you and other white people in the eye. I feel deep joy and acceptance I have never felt before. I don't care if I lose my job. You belong here!" I stayed.

Dr. Martin Luther King Jr.

The end of the march saw 25,000 people in the state capitol, and I sensed the power of God's Spirit blowing through us and through our country. Dr. King spoke from the Capitol steps like the prophets of old. The crowd joined in a chorus that proclaimed the day of fulfillment would not be long in coming. "How long? Not long, because the arm of the moral universe is long but it bends toward justice. How long? Not long, cause mine eyes have seen the glory of the coming of the Lord.... Glory, glory hallelujah!"

On August 6, 1965, with Dr. King standing behind him, President Johnson signed the Voting Rights Act. It was the "finest hour" of Dr. King's movement and ministry.

That September Day
Jacquie Terpstra

During the years that we lived in Northern New Jersey, I worked for an agency located in a building that overlooked both the Hackensack and Hudson rivers, and on a clear day, the Manhattan skyline. On this particular day, the view was unimpeded. In fact, it was a beautiful, cloudless, sunny day. Shortly after I had seated my first client of the day, our receptionist (who always had her radio on) came up to me and quietly told me that a plane had just crashed into the World Trade Center. My first thought was that it was an accident similar to the time that a plane had crashed into the Empire State Building years ago. I invited my client to come with me and we went over to the large windows that overlooked the river and the skyline. Sure enough, smoke was billowing out of one of the towers.

I knew that Gene, my pastor husband, hadn't left for the church yet so I phoned home to make sure that he turned on the TV. Our daughter-in-law was staying with us for a few days, and she immediately alerted our son in Sacramento who, in turn, phoned his sisters in Pasadena. Because of the three-hour time difference between the East and West coasts, they were all awakened by those phone calls.

I had just turned my attention back to my client when our receptionist rushed over to me again and announced that the other tower had been hit. At that news, it was apparent that this was no accident. I told my client that I didn't think that we could accomplish anything meaningful that morning and rescheduled her appointment. From then on, my attention was focused on what was happening down river. It is hard to recall the exact sequence of events but I know that as I watched out of the window and talked to my colleagues, my anxiety was building. I know that I made several calls home to Gene.

Using All the Colors

When word came that the Pentagon had also been hit by a plane, I assumed that our whole country was under attack. With a growing sense of panic, I phoned my children to tell them that I loved them. I didn't know if I would ever see them again. A number of people in the office were crying because they knew people who worked in the towers, and still others were frantically trying to call family members who worked in the city. Strangely, we discovered later, that some of the counselors were unaware of what was happening. They either worked on the far side of the building or were so engrossed in their work that they didn't hear or see what was taking place.

Just a short time later, the South tower collapsed. We watched the huge cloud of smoke rise into that perfect sky and couldn't believe that what we were seeing was true. The North tower collapsed and we got word that another plane had crashed in Pennsylvania. My mounting terror was matched by my conviction that we needed to get home. *I* needed to get home. A year later, when our agency held a memorial gathering, my friends recalled that I had kept saying that I had to get home to Gene. It wasn't just me; several of the counselors wanted to pick up their children from daycare or school. Apparently, it was the nature of witnessing such a tragedy that instinctively made us want to gather our loved ones around us. All that I remember is frantically approaching both our supervisor and director insisting that we had to be released to leave. Finally, I met our director in the stairwell. He told me to go back upstairs and inform the others that as soon as we were sure that all clients had left the building, we could leave. On my way out of the building, I stopped to say good-bye and hug my best friend and office soul-mate. We didn't know if we would ever see each other again.

The next challenge was getting home. All of the bridges and tunnels into the City had been closed. That meant that there might be a back-up on state routes 17 and 4 my fastest route to cover the 13 miles home, so I decided on a rather circuitous route using surface streets. As I finally approached our house, I saw Gene talking to our neighbor. I pulled the car to the curb and reached out to clasp his outstretched hand. I immediately recalled that we had done almost the same thing following President Kennedy's death. That time, I was the one at home and went out to meet him as he drove up and then we silently walked hand-in-hand, up to the house.

For a little while, I watched TV, catching up on what the rest of the world had been watching all morning. In the meantime, Gene was on the phone helping to organize a community worship service for that evening. The deacons were asked to phone every member on their lists, to tell them of the service. As a deacon, I found that phoning people turned out to be a blessing. It not only gave me something to do, it also provided opportunity to hear people's stories and concerns. I remember two in particular. One young woman was very distraught. Her husband happened to be out of town and she was having a difficult time because she, too, had witnessed the event live from her workplace. Having someone listen to her experience, and learning that we would be gathering that evening with our congregation and other residents of the town seemed to assure her that she was not alone. The other person was a man in his 80's who said that this event was bringing back a flood of wartime memories. He had been with the marines who landed on Iwo Jima. Later, his wife said that he never talked about his war experience, but that afternoon he needed to talk.

We also had to check on the well-being of the people who were working on or near the site. One young father in our congregation who worked in an office in one of the towers, had delayed going to work that morning because of a child-care conflict. A young lawyer, had scheduled an 8 a.m. breakfast meeting at the towers, but at the last minute, the meeting was cancelled. Another father of three worked on Wall Street. He happened to take a later train into work that morning. As he was approaching his office building, he saw the plane crash into the South tower. He turned around and caught what turned out to be the last ferry back to New Jersey.

My nephew was a surgeon on the staff of Sloan Kettering in New York. I discovered that he was in Washington D.C. that morning for meetings. He was on the Metro Line and his train had pulled out of the Pentagon station just minutes before the building was hit.

Most people who followed the news, heard about the Cantor Fitzgerald company tragedy. The floor housing its offices was the floor struck by of one of the planes. Our daughter's neighbor worked for the Los Angeles branch of that company. She reported that because the two offices were linked by open phone lines, the employees in the L.A. offices could hear terrified screams coming from the New York office. We later learned that the niece of one couple in our church worked for Cantor Fitzgerald and perished in the attack. Her husband of four months worked in an office building nearby and was unharmed except for his broken heart.

The evening worship service helped. I have no memory of what was said or sung but I do remember hugging a lot of people, hearing their stories, and gaining reassurance about their loved ones. It was so good to be with people of faith from the entire community and to mark this event that had brought us together in such a tragic way. We needed to know that we were not alone.

My first thought upon waking the following morning was of disbelief. Had the United States really been attacked? My second thought was that those behind the attack had certainly succeeded. Our offices were closed that day and I spent most of my time listening to the commentary about the event. On the following day, work started with a meeting where our director encouraged us to take time to talk with each other about our experience and to make use of the professional counseling that was being made available to us if we felt that we needed it. While we might have disagreed with him about a number of decisions, he certainly came through for his staff on this occasion. He, like Mayor Giuliani of New York, seemed to instinctively know what to do during this crisis.

For weeks after the attack, I could see the pillar of smoke and dust rising from the ruins as I drove to work. In the next few months I had occasion to view the site from several different locations. We walked along the Sinatra Memorial River Walk in Hoboken directly across the river from the smoldering ruins. We were saddened by the mass of memorials that lined the walk: the flowers, candles, pictures and messages, including one with a photo of a little girl of about two years of age with the message, "Has anyone seen my mommy?"

In early November, I had an appointment in Manhattan and decided to take a closer look at the site. I took the ferry from Weehawken, to the dock at the foot of the seven-building World Trade Center complex. Not all of the buildings had been destroyed, but as I got closer to those that had, I encountered the barriers that had been erected to keep the public away. However, I could see some things; the grid-like building façade that leaned precariously outward, the blasted-out windows of nearby buildings and the inch-thick grey dust that was everywhere. I walked the many blocks that took me around all four sides of the site so that I could view it from every angle. I stopped to read the innumerable messages and posters that lined the fence between Trinity Church and St. Paul's. Many of the messages and offerings of condolence were from visitors from all over the world as well as all over our own country. The crowd milling about was very solemn, but even so, strangers spoke to each other with the easy familiarity born of shared tragedy. The President and the Mayor had both urged the people of America to resume their normal lives after the attack but it was apparent that before we could do that, we needed to grieve. St. Paul's was closed to the public because it was being used as a rest center for the recovery crews. I learned later that it actually was kept open for Sunday worship during those days when bodies were being recovered. It was felt that having regular worship there at the site

Using All the Colors

was essential as a reminder that God was with us in the midst of our suffering.

Gene and I attended several photo exhibits. One was a collection of pictures taken by ordinary citizens and some of the shots were remarkable. Another was a collection of photos taken by the photographers working for Magnum. There is an interesting story behind that collection. Staff members of Magnum had traveled from their various assignments around the world to New York for their annual meeting, which was held on September 10th. At the conclusion of the meeting, they had all scattered around the city to stay with family or friends. When it was reported that the first tower had been hit, they tried to get as close to the site as possible to get photographs. The pictures that were the most memorable for me were not still photos but those shown on a video. One of the photographers who had been staying in a hotel near the towers had a camcorder with him. As soon as he got the news, he ran with his camera toward the towers. He reported that he happened to have the camera focused on the south tower when the second plane hit it. I know that I gasped out loud when I saw it because as that plane ripped into the building, it looked like the top was being sliced from a cake. He kept the camera going as he approached the buildings, catching pictures of people running toward him and away from the towers. When the south tower collapsed, the images recorded by his camera jiggled erratically as he ran away. Finally, everything went black as he dove for cover under a truck.

For weeks, there were obituaries in the papers. The New York *Times* had a crew of reporters who visited the families and wrote lengthy, moving obituaries about the victims, many of whom were policemen and firemen. The iconic photo of the firemen raising the flag over the rubble was done by Thomas E. Franklin, a staff photographer for our own *Bergen County Record*.

Perhaps the most poignant story of the firemen who sacrificed their lives was portrayed some time later in a TV documentary prepared by a group of French photographers and journalists. I will never forget the image of that long line of firemen, loaded down with their gear, walking purposefully into a building where they would soon meet their death.

At the office, we were counseling clients who had lost their jobs because their business was physically destroyed or because of the ripple effect of 9/11. Our agency received additional funds to train and support these individuals as they sought alternative employment. The counselors also attended workshops designed to help us meet the unique needs of this new group of clients. Much had been learned from the Oklahoma City disaster, so we were alerted to look for signs of substance abuse, as well as spousal or child abuse, that were apt to surface at the 3, 6 and 12 month anniversaries of the tragedy.

However, most of my clients were simply bewildered by what had happened to them. I remember one woman in particular who worked near the towers but was one of those fleeing from the site. When she finally was called back to work, she got off the train and simply wandered around, confused, unable to remember where she was going or why she was there. It was months before she was able to work again. When she did, she chose something closer to home on the Jersey side of the river. Another client simply couldn't get over her narrow escape. She had just started a new job in the north tower on Monday, September 10th. She took the commuter train intending to get off at the station under the tower. When they reached that stop, the doors of the train wouldn't open and they could see police on the station platform. Over the loudspeaker, they heard that because of a "police action", the train would move on to the next stop and they could disembark there. Only after she emerged did she learn that her train had actually traversed the lower level of the tower that had first been hit.

In the months that followed, I asked myself some hard questions. What would it have been like to be trapped on a floor above the fire? Would I have chosen to jump? Could I have stayed with someone confined to a wheelchair while others fled to safety down the stairs? One man did stay. However, the concern that persisted in my personal reflection was, why hadn't I called upon God during those first terror-filled hours? Why hadn't I even thought about God? I'm sure that unknowingly, like so many others, I uttered the words, "Oh, my God", over and over again, but I have no memory of consciously calling upon God for help. Some of my colleagues went to the church down the street to pray during that terrible morning, but I don't remember even considering that for myself. The question that persisted in my mind, was what kind of a Christian was I if I couldn't even be a fox-hole Christian? Thankfully, my pastor-husband helped me understand my response. "You're a problem-solver and there was a big problem to be solved", he said. "You called your family to assure them of your love and you petitioned management so that you and the others could get home to your families. Your relationship with God was not the problem."

My relationship with God was not the problem. That comforts me greatly. I can think that I came to that state only by ingesting the "meat and potatoes" of the faith that nourished me over a lifetime. The epistle to the Ephesians uses another metaphor by encouraging us to "Put on the whole armor of God" so that we can take our stand against evil. The experience of September 11th has shown me that our readiness to withstand tragic events or everyday occurrences in this age of violence depends upon our *every-day* devotion to God. Without that, we will not be ready. The time to listen to God's word for us and to be faithful in worship is *now* because we never know what the day, even a beautiful day, will bring.

Noteworthy Events

Family Matters

Using All the Colors

Dreams
Carole Hoffs Bos

I'm convinced that dreams are gifts from God sent for the healing of spirit. Our job is to discern their meanings in the situations which prompt their genesis.

Some dreams throughout my adult life reflect a feeling of being unprepared on my part. There are usually three settings. One finds me in a college English class about to take a final test. I'm in extreme angst because I have never read assignments or attended the required classes. The professor is one whom in reality I held in great esteem, and I would never have entered his classroom without preparing the day's assignment. The dream ends after I read the test, shaking in quiet panic.

The second setting centers around a wedding. I have been asked to sing and I realize I only have a few minutes to dress for the occasion. I have no idea what colors the bride has chosen so I could match her scheme, nor do I know what music she has selected. I have never practiced with the organist/ pianist and I can't seem to dress fast enough. The clock is moving quickly and I'm in slow motion, having trouble locating every article of clothing. Just recalling this dream throws me into an anxious state.

The third dream is a typical teacher dream, one which usually occurs a week or so before school opens in the fall. My students approach the door and as I look around, I discover my classroom is bare of any stimulating decorations which usually soften the appearance of a plain, box-like room. There is nothing which would welcome the students. I have no roll book and no lesson plans are in my head. What the next hours would bring is a mystery to me.

I tend to be a "detail person" who plans far in advance so perhaps these dreams reflect that need and if thwarted by time constraints, my mind goes into wild alarm. The moral of the dreams shadows the Boy Scout motto: Be Prepared.

The most perplexing dream I have had was when Steve, our son, was in Iraq awaiting return from Desert Storm to Germany. I saw him clearly in my dream. He was trudging ankle deep in sand, desperately searching for a road. He seemed tired and thirsty. There was no bounce in his step, his usual pace. Sand dunes surrounded him over which he could not see. As an observer to this scene, I had an omnipresent view like a bird would have. I could see the road ahead of him just over the next berm. I cried out in my dream, "Keep going. It's there in front of you!" He couldn't hear, of course, and kept stumbling on. Finally he fell in utter exhaustion with the road only a few feet from where he lay. I awoke in frustrated tears and it took all day for me to shake this nightmare.

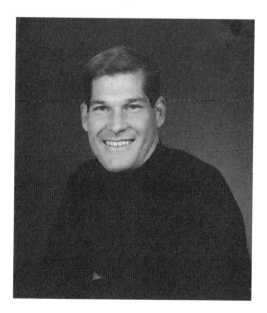

My son, Stephen

Two days later we received a call from Steve in Germany. He had been medivaced from Saudi Arabia where he had been taken after experiencing severe pain. After doing some figuring, we arrived at the conclusion that my dream took place during the time he had been in distress. His commanding officer had first taken Steve to Kuwait City where there was an x-ray machine. Because of sandstorms, the helicopter could not fly him to the fully equipped military hospital in Riyadh, Saudi Arabia so they took him by jeep to Kuwait City. He had nothing to ease his discomfort and the trip was extremely painful for him. This experience was the beginning of a long journey dealing with renal cell cancer which ended with Steve's death eight years later. Was this a dream of preparation for me? Was the dream a result of a strong connection between parent and child, an ESP experience? I will never know.

Two Family Reunions: A Gathering of Cousins
Bruce Calkins

Sixteen cousins were called together for the first reunion in Chehalis Washington. Fifteen came. We were all (well most of us) hoping that Dixie would come with her mother, our Aunt Mildred. Aunt Mildred was enough of a free thinker to create her own culture. She was raised in a strict family that considered card playing, dancing, going to the movies, and smoking to be grave sins. However, Mildred owned a bar in Fairbanks, Alaska.

Mildred's bar was profitable, so she drove a large Cadillac. She needed a smooth riding car so her drink wouldn't fall off the dash board. Several months before our first reunion of cousins, Mildred had driven down to Washington state. At one point, she turned too fast and rolled her Cadillac over. She was banged up, including a broken arm; and the front door on the drivers' side was ripped off. Mildred, who was in her 80's, and now with a broken arm and a broken caddy, with only three doors, drove several hundred miles to her nephew Leland; because he was the only one she would trust not to over charge her for repairing her car.

Oh, yes! We wanted to see Aunt Mildred!

We especially wanted to observe the greeting between Aunt Mildred and her sister, our Aunt Anna, the conservative Pentecostal preacher, who still considered card playing, dancing, going to the movies, smoking, and certainly drinking to be grave sins. Such encounters are what make a reunion of cousins memorable.

Even though Dixie and Aunt Mildred didn't make it to the first reunion, the sharing of old stories about our parents, uncles, and aunts was a rich rediscovery of our roots. I'll never forget the story about Uncle Abe that was told by his grandson Dan.

Family Matters

Abe was back in the mountains, and he met a badger trying to get back into its hole. Abe was standing between the badger and it's hole. As the badger scooted toward its hole, Ab kicked it hard enough to stun it. While the badger was unconscious, Abe put his lariat around him and cinched it up. When he did that, the badger came to. The badger started hissing and scratching and trying to bite. Abe had to hold the badger away from his body. Then, with the badger dangling from the rope, he tried to mount his horse. The horse was not pleased with the idea of being close to a hissing, twisting badger. But anyone determined enough—or crazy enough – to kick a badger and then tie it up had at least a chance of finding a way to get on his horse while holding a badger. Abe made it onto his horse, but the badger continued to twist around and make badger noises. With one hand on the reins trying to control a spooked horse and the other hand holding the badger so it couldn't scratch or bite his horse, Abe made it back to camp—horse, badger, and all. An amazed group of cowboys asked, "How'd you catch that badger?" he said as casually as he could, "I roped him." Folks had always figured that Abe would do things that others wouldn't do, even if they could. Now they knew for sure.

At that first reunion, some us met cousins we hadn't seen for 40 years. After hearing stories that made us laugh and cry, we decided we shouldn't wait 40 years for the next reunion.

Reunion number 2 took place about seven years later. None of our parents or aunts or uncles were still living. It was all cousins who shared a common grandmother and grandfather.

We met at the home of our cousin Ella. She lived a few miles outside of the small Idaho town of Jerome. She had about ten acres—plenty of room for a reunion of cousins and their children—plenty of room for her son Dan to train his horses.

Dan was about 30. He'd finished law school, passed the Idaho bar, and had served with a law firm; but he quit because he didn't like it when the firm won a case for a poverty stricken widow and then took 80% of the settlement and left only 20% for the

Using All the Colors

woman. He decided to quit law and become a cowboy—not a cattle herding, badger catching cowboy but a "<u>singing</u> cowboy"—a cowboy who did rope tricks, cracked bullwhips, trained his performing horse, twirled pistols, shot water balloons out of the air, and threw knives and tomahawks at targets. He goes by the handle "Rhinestone Roper." He hasn't roped any badgers yet; but, like his grandfather Abe, he does things that most folks couldn't even imagine themselves doing.

Dan tours with his horse Lucky Joe. He's performed in hundreds of county and state fairs, rodeos, theaters, and over a thousand schools in 46 states. I saw his performance at an elementary school in La Habra. He talks to the kids about how special each of them is and how each of them has a special purpose. Then he ropes them and teaches them how to twirl ropes. He shows them that they can do things that they never thought they could do.

At reunion number 2, there was more sharing of stories; and there was a simple memorial service for our parents, aunts, and uncles; but the highlight of the reunion was Dan. Just as he inspired school children by showing them new horizons of possibilities, Dan did the same for his older cousins. Any who wanted to ride one of his horses got to do that. Any who wanted to learn to twirl a lariat got a special lesson. Those who wished got lessons in how to throw knives and tomahawks at a target and occasionally hit some part of the target.

One of Dan's most memorable courses of instruction was the proper use of the bullwhip. I figured it might be handy to know that. Maybe I could work it into a children's sermon.

The bullwhip is made from kangaroo hide. The last three feet of the whip is another material that provides a loud crack—as loud as a gun shot. The whip can also cut. Dan gave us a loud demonstration of cracking the bullwhip. It included cutting long stocks of grass by snapping off an inch or two at a time as the grass was held by a trusting volunteer—like me.

Family Matters

It's hard to imagine anyone being able and willing to perform with the skill and precision that Dan does—but if anyone could, it would most likely be someone who had a badger-catching grandfather.

After Dan's lesson and some chances to practice, I decided I needed someone to trustingly hold a piece of grass so I could chop it down—inch by inch—always closer to the hand of the trusting volunteer. So, whom did I ask to hold a piece of grass so I could find out how much I'd learned in my *one* lesson? I was surprised when Lynda agreed. Lynda and I were both pleased that her trust did not result in blood and pain as I chopped little pieces off the end of the long stem of grass she was holding.

After our lessons and practice sessions with the ropes, knives, tomahawks, and whips, Dan had a special knife throwing demonstration for us. While his wife stood in front of a wooden target, Dan threw knives on both sides of her arms, legs, and head. Everyone was focused and silent as the knives went "plunk!" "plunk!" "plunk!" all around her. I was more impressed than worried. I knew how much he loved her, and Dan had already told me that he never comes closer than four inches.

After Dan finished we were all relieved and impressed. Knife throwing isn't what you expect at a family reunion. I decided that here was a unique opportunity. When else would I have the opportunity to stand in front of a target and have knives thrown within a few inches of my body? I reminded myself that Dan's wife was precious to him, and neither of them seemed to have any fear. Dan's only instruction to me was, "Stand still. Don't move." I heeded his advice. Now you know why my list of hobbies includes bullwhipping and tomahawk throwing.

We concluded our reunion with a worship service and the release of balloons—one for each of our parents and aunts and uncles. None of us will forget that reunion—certainly not me—certainly not Lynda.

The Lord Is My Sheep Herder?
Bruce Calkins

In my early years in Idaho, most of the sheep herders were Basque. The majority population looked down on them, and questioned their morals and their honesty. No one I knew liked or trusted the sheep herders. Perhaps that was because very few members of the majority culture actually knew any of the Basques; however, their lack of knowledge didn't reduce their confidence in the validity of their stereotypes.

As a child, I was impressed when I saw a large herd of sheep. Near by, there was often a man on horseback and a small covered wagon that was his home. Never in my wildest dreams did I associate these sheep herders with the loving, courageous shepherds of the New Testament.

Then I met Lynda's father, Ed Baird. He was part of a family whose survival depended on rigorous and dangerous child labor. When Ed was seven and his brother was nine, they were given responsibility for a herd of 400 goats. Their father had leased the goats in order to raise them to maturity, and then return them to their owner for a share of the profit from their sale.

Little Eddie and his brother had to do all care taking. That meant they had very little schooling—lots of life-education, but not schooling.

The herd was several miles away from their home. Ed said, "Once a week, our mother rode out on horseback, and brought us a bag of beans and a bag of flour. That was our food for the week." They had a pot and a pan, a lantern, and a six-shooter. In addition to the gun, they also had the shepherds weapon of a slingshot. (Note: One time I tried to use a sling to throw a stone into an orange grove. I aimed straight ahead. I was off by 90 degrees.) Ed said his brother was so accurate that he could knock the horn off a goat with his slingshot. He said their Dad came out there one time and was wondering why some of the goats had only one horn!

One night the goats started making a racket. The boys had to go out to see what was bothering them. Ed carried the lantern. His brother carried the six-shooter. As they walked through the herd, the goats moved back and then closed in behind them; they were always surrounded by a circle of goats. All at once the circle was larger. There was a mountain lion with the goats. Ed said, "I threw the lantern at it! My brother threw the gun! We ran one way, and the lion ran the other! It took us all the next day to find the lantern and the gun."

One other time, a bee stung Ed close to his eyes. His eyes swelled shut. He thought he might die if he stayed out there, so he decided to try to walk home. Neither of them questioned that his brother had to stay to take care of the goats. That's the way life was, and that's what goat herders did. Lynda's father was a true shepherd in the King David tradition. He said, "I was able to get to a canyon. I couldn't see anything, but I knew that if I kept going down that canyon, it would lead to the house." He said, "I was falling over boulders, walking into cactus, listening for rattle snakes! Sometimes I had to crawl. I was all scratched up. Finally, I heard my mother yell, 'Eddie!' Then I started to bawl!"

As I listened to Lynda's father, there was no longer a disconnect between sheep herders and New Testament shepherds. I knew that sheep herders and goat herders were true shepherds!

Hurdles of Pregnancy and Children in Alaska

Carolyn French

The pregnancy with our first child was greatly anticipated, and while that is not too unusual for a young married couple, the near loss of the father, the loss of an airline pilot and plane, a 120 mile trip for a prenatal visit, and a 4000 mile trip to deliver the baby was NOT usual. Art and I were living on St. Lawrence Island in the village of Gambell where he was pastor of a Yupik Eskimo congregation and I was an Itinerant Public Health Nurse for the Territorial Department of Health. We were both responsible for care in the two Island villages of Gambell and Savoonga—60 miles apart.

When I was in early pregnancy, we were returning from Savoonga. We were traveling by boat and the Bering Sea was stormy with high swells as we landed on the gravelly north beach. The Eskimos jumped out near the shore to pull the boat in and Art tried to jump out to help, also. However, he fell under the boat. I thought he was a goner because I was aware that the large supply ship NORTH STAR could bring their ship right up to that beach due to very deep water there. However, the Eskimos quickly grabbed Art when the next swell released the skinboat from on top of him—WHEW!

Since one of our Eskimo families was being transported on a chartered Wien Airlines plane by the Bureau of Indian Affairs for relocation to California and there was room for me on the plane to Nome, I was able to fly free to get my exam to verify pregnancy and receive an initial evaluation. I was all ready to go when Winnie, the airline contact in Gambell, came and said the plane had crashed soon after takeoff from Nome – at first I thought he was kidding but soon realized he wasn't. It was later learned that the one engine on the twin engine plane had failed so the pilot had turned back to

Nome, but as he was landing the plane hit wires, crashed and he was killed.

The next day we did get off and landed safely in Nome. I saw the doctor, the pregnancy was confirmed, and the blood tests turned out well. I was so excited I wanted to shout to all the world, but since I was in hotel room by myself until I could get the regular flight back to Gambell, I wrote volumes in letters to my mother and my mother-in-law sharing the excitement. When Art met me at the plane upon my return, I nearly flew out of the door yelling, "It's true! We are going to have a baby!"

I continued to work as the Public Health nurse for the Territorial Dept. of Health but notified the Dept. that in June, shortly before our baby's due date, I planned to resign from the position. I took vitamins and checked my hemoglobin regularly using the finger stick method. While I could stick myself accidentally with a sewing needle I'd have a dickens of a time pricking myself to get enough of a sample on the first try!! I intended to have the baby in Nome at the one doctor Methodist Hospital. However, in early April we were informed that the hospital would have no doctor available through the summer. What to do? After much prayer, and shortly before we were to leave the island (so Art could attend Presbytery and I could attend a Maternal and Infant Care Conference in Anchorage), I was sweeping the floor, and, in frustration about where to safely deliver this child, I said, "Oh, I might as well go home to mother." Art picked up on that and agreed this indeed was the answer, and that I should just plan to go on home to Harrisburg, Pa. following the attendance at the conference. Since this was Saturday, and we were due to leave the following Thursday, it meant sending a flurry of telegrams to my parents and to my supervisor at the Health Dept. (no way to phone at that time) and arrangements were made to go with this plan. My supervisor chastised me at the conference but the Chief of Nursing for the whole territory of Alaska took one look at me and said she was very happy I was leaving the Island now.

Using All the Colors

After the conference I boarded an Alaska Airlines plane—a DC-3—from Anchorage to Seattle and then boarded a Northwest flight to Minnesota where I literally ran from one plane to the next connecting flight to Pittsburgh. There I boarded a flight to Harrisburg—almost 24 hours of flying! I was glad to get home but I surely did miss Art being with me. He, meanwhile, worked it out with the mission board to let him have two months of furlough at the time the baby was due, in July. Our usual term was to be at the mission for three years followed by a six month furlough.

My first visit with the gynecologist in Harrisburg at now 7 months pregnancy had him quite concerned about my salt intake as I was quite puffy from the flights et al. He did multiple tests to make sure I wasn't becoming toxemic and ordered me to avoid any canned foods!! Now it hit me that if I'd stayed on the Island, the canned foods (which were our primary staples and with choices fast diminishing as we awaited the yearly supply boat due in July) could have been disastrous for me!

Well, our beautiful blue-eyed blond Cathy was born 2-3 weeks later than expected, but a very healthy 7lb. 15oz. and 20 inches long—born in the 90 degree (and equal humidity) temperature of summer in a NON-air-conditioned hospital! Thanks to our neighbor who is a doctor we got the use of a window fan in the 4 bed hospital room I was in, when the babies were NOT out to be fed.

When Cathy was three weeks of age, we drove to my brother's outside of Washington, D.C and he took us to the Baltimore airport where we caught our first jet flight on American Airlines which had a non-stop from there to LAX. They put us in a seat area that had a box-like bassinet for a baby, and Cathy did really well on the flight. We then went to stay with Art's parents in Rialto for a few weeks and there we had Grandfather French (Art's dad) baptize her in a Congregational Church that his newly organized Presbyterian church in Rialto was using for services at that time. In

Family Matters

Rialto we were adjusting to temperatures of 104-5 degrees Fahrenheit in the daytime and 54 degrees at night!

Then it was time to fly back to Alaska—this time flying from LAX to Seattle, Seattle to Anchorage, Anchorage to Nome and then Wien Airlines out to St. Lawrence Island and home at last!

The Eskimos loved Cathy and she was very sociable. We had to keep her pretty bundled up against the weather and she had two parkas made that she wore through the winter when outside—one was a sheep skin lined parka under a colorful snow shirt that could be taken off and washed easily. The other was a white with black rabbit fur jacket parka. She had multiple pairs of skin boots the Eskimos made for her.

One winter morning we woke up and it was really cold in the house. We realized there was ice in the oil line to the stove blocking the oil. I quickly changed her diaper and hurriedly dropped it on the floor while putting the other one on—and it froze! I took her over to the teachers' quarters and stayed there until Art and a couple of the Eskimos solved the stove problem and got heat going again. These teachers were like surrogate grandparents to Cathy—they were so loving and helpful to us all.

We moved to the more inland village of Savoonga just before Cathy turned 1 year old. We had gotten permission to ride on the freighter from Gambell to Savoonga—this was the famous North Star freighter that brought supplies to Alaska every summer and our two villages were their last stops before returning to Seattle. Soon after boarding the ship I was sick with vomiting and diarrhea. Art got Cathy to bed and finally things settled down for me and I slept. During the day we had a harness and a life preserver jacket on Cathy for walking out on the deck. The water was rough and the boat couldn't off load supplies to the skin boats so we were on the ship for 3 days. Other than feeling kind of dizzy often, I was able to eat and had no more sickness, but got some much needed rest during this time and Cathy was a love to all the crew.

Using All the Colors

On the fourth day we were able to get off the ship and our supplies were able to be off-loaded. We began to get settled in the manse part of the church building. There was just a small hallway type alcove at the top of the stairs before entering the only bedroom available. The other part of this attic-like area was full of storage shelves for the year's supply of groceries that had also been on the ship with us! We had Cathy's crib set up in the hallway area. We had gotten pretty well settled in and then Midge Stryker from the National Museum of History in New York arrived to spend 6 weeks with us gathering information and artifacts to set up a display at the museum. All through the process of settling in, I was tired and began to get more edgy and crabby at times and wondered what was getting into me!

Some weeks later a Coast Guard Cutter arrived and anchored off Savoonga. A doctor was aboard so I had him check me. What had gotten into me was a baby!!!

We were delighted but also realized many decisions lay ahead as this one's due date would be in February when dog team was the only travel available to the village of Gambell 60 miles away. Gambell had the only airstrip available for a flight off the Island.

Meanwhile, Cathy's first birthday was coming, and Art and I decided to have a village-wide party to get more acquainted with these villagers and show a movie to all. Midge and I baked 18 layer cakes and decorated the bases of them with the pretty purple flowers that were now in bloom this mid-July, and were like little violets in size. A great time was had by all and Cathy got all kinds of little mukluks the Eskimos had made, little pins made of the sealskin and embroidered with her name on them, beaded necklaces, and one a necklace from Siberia, as well as many other beautiful items.

Another couple, who were teachers in Savoonga, became quite close friends and we discovered that they had been married on the same evening, same time, same year as we. The year prior she had had to leave the island due to expecting their first child and had gotten out by skinboat to Gambell about the second week of November, so we thought this would work out for us, too, as we were scheduled to leave the first week of November. We had written Mother French to see if it was okay with her and dad to have me stay there from Nov-March and she had written that it was fine with them, and she looked forward to having her first and only at that time, grandchild around, namely 16-month old Cathy. So Art and I were all set to go out together to Fairbanks where he was going to attend the November meeting of Presbytery and be able to see Cathy and me off on the plane to California! As the time neared the Eskimos came and told Art there were very indicative signs that the sea ice was moving in and we would now only be able to get to Gambell by dogteam. When Art told me that I cried and said I couldn't do that but as I said it, I began to realize I had no other choice! I was five months pregnant, and knew at least this would be safer than at nine months!!!

The thoughtful Eskimos worked to build a frame over a sled and covered it with a zippered cover with the zipper opening over the frame so I could control opening and closing it as desired. They took the National Guard Armory's couch cushions with springs inside and put them the length of the sled and I had a sleeping bag I put around me in addition. There had been some snow but only a few inches of it around us—a little more outside the village, but this, being the first trip of the year when no trail had been forged, less snow and volatile temperatures the trip was inevitably going to be a difficult one. We started out at about 7 a.m. the day we left. I was bundled up in my parka with hood and wool blanket lining and wore sealskin pants over long underwear. 16-month old Cathy was in her parka that had the nice warm sheepskin lining and she had heavy duty long pants on. She sat between my legs on the sled and I sat inside the sleeping bag on the cushions which felt quite comfortable at that point, and we were off! Art was on another sled, the Christian Education Specialist that had visited us in Savoonga was on another sled, and all our baggage was on another. Each sled had an Eskimo driver and ten to twelve dogs pulled each sled. I cannot recall Cathy's being any problem on the trip—sometimes I'd shift her to beside my legs, and then back to sit between, etc, but I think she slept a lot being almost immobilized in the parka!

Eight hours later At 3 p.m. we had only made 20 miles to where a group of the village trappers were staying in an old Jamesway hut the army had left behind. This we learned was to be our motel for the night. It surely felt good to stretch and get inside where it was warm. In the middle of the hut the Eskimos had a pilot stove and when they would throw the driftwood pieces in it would heat up and get the whole place quite warm so that we peeled off our parkas. The front outer section of the hut was where they kept the bucket "toilet". We had brought along food and they had food and soon after we all ate, I climbed up and laid out our sleeping bags on the wide deck they used as a sleeping platform and Cathy and I bedded down. Later when everyone went to bed Art lay his sleeping bag next to Cathy's and that left the Christian Education person to set hers next to his, something I later learned had upset her sense of propriety!!!

The next morning we arose early, ate, and again left around 7 a.m. This day was a cloudy day with blowing wet snow, so I kept huddled under the zippered tarp, stretching out and changing position from sitting to lying with Cathy at my side or between my legs. The Island is pocked with numerous lakes—when frozen they are safe for the sleds—but at this time of year, many were not sufficiently frozen which meant the sleds had to detour around them, adding many miles to the travel. There were pit stops along the way, but no cabins, until about 9 p.m. that night when we got to a cabin before crossing the mountain into Gambell. There we stopped and had hot tea and snacks and I was so tired I could care less about any food. I saw Art eating what appeared to be twigs and I thought he'd flipped out on me! They were roots the Eskimos eat

Family Matters

at times and probably good for whatever, but I wish I'd had a movie camera on Art at that point. It's hilarious to me thinking about the scene and actually made me laugh some at the time!!!

At midnight, 17 hours after starting that day, we arrived in Gambell and were able to stay in the manse there as no other missionaries had yet come to the Island. Our hope had been that our moving to Savoonga would make it easier for the Board of National Missions (which it was called then) to find a couple to come to the Island since they could live in Gambell where the airstrip was. I ached all over and I thought of the women who traveled in covered wagons with wooden wheels and wondered how they did it because by now my very comfortable cushions had come to feel like rocks instead of pillows! The beds, which we got into as soon as possible, felt heavenly! Again, the grace of God working through the caring, helpful Eskimo friends got us through safely.

The next day the plane came to take us to Nome – this time via Kotzebue where the doctor I would contact by radio lived. On this flight with us was an official of KLM airlines who had been on the Island for some reason. In Kotzebue they said we had 45 minutes before the plane took off again. Art, Cathy and I went quickly into town to say goodbye to our doctor friend as he, too, was going to be leaving soon to complete a residency in pulmonary medicine in Pennsylvania. We got back to the plane within 35 minutes and saw plane already taxiing down the runway. Instant panic and then to our amazement, we saw it coming back! We never knew for sure why they turned back except it was to check something. We strongly suspected our KLM friend knew what to do to get them to turn back—bless this good Samaritan! He was on the flight to Anchorage with us, where Art attended Presbytery. I was headed on to Seattle and we learned our KLM friend would be on that flight, too. He told Art he'd keep an eye on Cathy and me! In Seattle where we arrived at 4 a.m. in the morning, I'd had to awaken Cathy from a sound sleep, which wasn't good news. Our friend Jeanne who had been with us on the Island as a volunteer in mission from the Presbyterian Church in Tulsa and now lived in Seattle met me to keep me company on the three hour layover I had before my flight to LA! What a true friend!

Cathy was back and forth between laying her head on my lap for about two minutes and then up and running in the airport – tired but too distracted to sleep. We ordered some food about 5:30 a.m. and of course Cathy fell sound asleep in the high chair before the food came. When it came time to board the plane and I had to wake her up again she screamed and screamed but as soon as she got into the little box bed they had on the floor in front of my seat, she fell asleep again and all was peaceful to LA. Although I had to awaken her again, she wasn't quite so upset, and getting off to see her grandparents thrilled her. As I recall she did okay on the ride in the car from LAX to Rialto where Art's parents lived.

What wonderfully different weather here in November. The folks had an orange tree and each morning I could take Cathy out to pick oranges for breakfast, which delighted her no end. I got a much needed appointment for pregnancy check and it was discovered I was somewhat anemic so onto iron pills plus mother French made liver about once a week during my stay with them. Art's sister was teaching school, was engaged to be married in June and still living at home. Being in this loving family was truly special but I really missed Art and of course we were apart that Christmas. To try to avoid Cathy's forgetting her dad we got her to call her grandfather "PAPA" instead of "DADA". Art again approached the Board of National Missions about getting the remainder of his furlough which entitled him to four months. It was later extended a bit so he could go to the Synod meeting in Seattle on our way back to Alaska.

Becky was born February 28th 1961, a dark haired bundle of joy. She was noted to be bluish when Art checked on her before leaving the hospital that night and he alerted the nurse. The doctor told me the next day that they had kept her on oxygen for an hour after that incident and she was fine. In April we flew east with both children to Harrisburg, Pa. to see my parents and have Becky baptized by my dad, a Lutheran pastor. After a couple weeks with the Venable parents and even Great-Grandma Venable, we returned to Rialto California for Art's sister's wedding.

Finally in late June we got back home to Savoonga, this time traveling by skin boat from Gambell. Well, now it was dealing with two girls in diapers, which we'd soak in a diaper container. No disposable diapers. We'd barely make it through the week with them and then it would be putting on rubber gloves and wringing out the very smelly ammonia aroma-filled diapers, getting the Kohler engine going, water hauled in and heated on the stove, and then washing and wringing clothes thru the wringer plus two tubs of clear water to rinse—twice! In the winter, it was hauling in snow and melting it in a large copper kettle on top of the stove—this had to be done a full day or so ahead as a container full of the snow would net only two inches of water! We used to merrily sing, "Safely through another week!" The diapers would then be hung over drying rack on top of oil heater stove in the church room—not the sanctuary—which adjoined our apartment.

Cathy and Becky

Using All the Colors

Becky enjoyed her playpen and when she would throw things out of it, she had Cathy to retrieve them for her! As Becky got on in age, I began to be concerned that she wasn't crawling let alone walking. A doctor visited the Island when she was about 14 months and tested her leg strength, etc., and felt all was normal, but instructed me to have her checked by a pediatrician in Anchorage if she wasn't walking at 18 months. I thought the amount of clothing the girls wore all year did hinder them in some of their easy mobility When we were visiting in Gambell with the Wycliffe translators' family I sat Becky on the other side of the room from where Cathy and the other children were playing, and lo and behold she crawled over to join them and that started her crawling at 15 months! And one day not long after turning 18 months, she walked on her own. Whew! She was the daughter who later did ballet and other types of dancing!

Cathy was only two months old when we went back to the Island. Therefore I was responsible for following up with many of her immunizations. These went well until it came to the Smallpox vaccination. She had the high fevers following it as expected, but there was no mark on her arm. I talked to the doctor on the school's short wave radio and he said she would undoubtedly need to have it done again later on, if no scar developed at the sight. She did have it done while we were staying with Mother French and oh, my what a reaction she got. Her upper arm was almost purple and she spiked 105 fever, so that mother and I were up a good part of the night getting that under control with baby aspirin, and cool baths.

The pediatrician in Anchorage gave me a supply of bicillin injections to use for the girls as well as Nembutal suppositories to prevent convulsions with very high fevers with any illness. One night Cathy was very congested with a cold she had and was feverish. At 4 a.m. I decided we'd better start the shots and before I gave her one I tried to explain that I was a nurse as well as her mother, and as a nurse I needed to give her the shot. Tired Art

Family Matters

thought I was crazy to be going through all this explanation with her, as he held her firmly for me to give her the long needle shot into her buttock. Well, at 4 p.m. the next afternoon when the next one was due I had it all ready, Art was holding her, and just as I was about to administer it, she decided to check my credentials by turning anxiously and saying quickly, "Mommy, mommy are you a nurse?"

The crisis we had the March before we were to return to California for Art's pastorate in Idyllwild in the mountains, was that Cathy had a bout of flu/cold, and then just as she was beginning to recover, Art and I got it at the exact same time. Little Becky was walking around wondering what was the matter with everyone. Art and I were running high fevers of between 102-104 degrees and unbelievably achy. One of us would drag ourselves to make meals and another would clean up and it all depended on which one of us had enough oomph at the time. I have never before or since ached so much. I did not want to expose any of the Eskimos to what we were experiencing even though I think some of them also had bouts of it, so didn't ask anyone to come in and help.

We had decided to leave the Island after the six years there and Art had preached before some committees that came to hear him at the Presbyterian Church in Rialto where his dad was pastor. He was called by the Idyllwild Church—a perfect place to go following Alaska. We then began packing up our things, to send the household items in our trunks via the North Star freighter due to reach our village in July. We were all done except for packing the books and our personal suitcases.

The next crisis that occurred was with Becky who was now two years old. She and Cathy were bouncing on a bed and Becky fell off and cut her lip on the edge of the wooden area through which the oil pipe to the stove passed. All my orders from the Health Dept. said never to attempt stitching on the face (and besides I never ever stitched anyone up, so I wasn't about to experiment on my child), but I was very concerned that she was going to be distorted around the mouth. I got the wound taken care of the best I could and then used the radio to talk to a doctor. He asked if I could get her into a hospital within two hours—"a total impossibility" I replied due to our location. He then told me not to worry too much as it could be repaired surgically if there was distortion after the swelling subsided. Thankfully, when all was healed, it hardly showed at all as it was more under the upper lip.

In the beginning of July, there was a doctor on the Island who checked on some of the kids that were ill. Just before he left to go to Gambell to catch a plane back to the army base Becky now age 2-1/2 seemed to be coming down with something and he checked her, too, and we decided to treat her symptomatically. Well, she kept getting more diarrhea—very thankfully no vomiting—and her fever kept climbing. We were praying what to do about Becky and then she ran a higher fever in the middle of the fourth night so we decided we'd need to get her off the Island. Art went to check with one of the Eskimos who had just returned from Gambell in his speedboat and asked if he'd be willing to go back to Gambell and take us all with him and then return Art and Cathy to Savoonga.

He agreed. Mind you it was light all night at this time of year. I got packed for Becky and me and just as the boat was ready to go I checked her temp once more and it was 105 so I had to tell them I couldn't leave until I got her temperature down which meant I had to cool her down with aspirin again and alcohol cool water sponging at which she cried and screamed. I also gave her one of the Nembutal suppositories to prevent a seizure. When it got down to 102, off we went. I hugged and cried and said quick goodbyes to the Eskimos that were up and outside as we left at about 6 a.m. A message had been sent to the airlines that we had an emergency and they were sending a plane to Gambell. We got to Gambell and the weather was clear, but as the plane attempted to land, the fog rolled in solidly and the pilot had to return to Nome. Art and Cathy returned to Savoonga. Becky and I stayed with the new

Family Matters

missionaries, the Galls, who had come to Gambell. They were in their 60's—he had trouble with asthma and she had chronic hepatitis. That night I felt Becky getting a bit warm again and checked her temperature and it was about 102. I carried her into the living room to get her some liquid and noticed as I got near the window that her lips and fingers looked bluish. Now I really was in a dither what to do. I woke up the Galls and asked Alvin to go get the doctor who was approximately half a mile or so away. Fortunately for us, the doctor had not gotten off the Island yet due to the foggy weather. He got dressed and went, and when the doctor came he asked for a temperature check again and now her temp had soared to 105.6 so it involved sponging her again with cold water and alcohol and another Nembutal suppository was given. He said her heart was okay, and her temperature did lower despite her screaming and crying. That day the plane tried again but didn't make it in due to the thick fog and the inability to find a clear hole to get down without hitting the mountain! I was so drained I asked if the doctor could come and stay at the manse that night also. He was willing and the Galls were willing even though it meant the doctor had to sleep on the couch in the living room.

Well, of course with the doctor no crisis arose. In the morning the plane came back and the weather was pretty clear until we started down toward the landing spot. The fog danced around, but this time the pilot was able to find enough of an opening to get down. Was I ever thankful as now she was swelling up all over and I feared something horrible like kidney failure developing. I asked the doctor if he would go with me to the Nome hospital before he went on to Anchorage because if we needed to go on to Anchorage I wanted to be on the plane with him.

As it turned out the doctor at Nome hospital said they could treat her symptomatically—that her puffiness was not due to kidney failure but to imbalance of protein. He stated that they wouldn't be able to find out what caused the illness as their lab didn't have some types of tests, but felt she would recover with getting her electrolytes balanced out. So, for the next three days in the hospital she was gradually fed more foods. There was no place for me to stay for the night at the hospital so I stayed with the Methodist missionary in Nome, whom we knew and had been with several times. The third day when I walked in to see Becky, she was all smiles and the doctor said she was ok to go home.

Would you believe? She ran a temp of 102 again that night and was looking a little rashy on the chest. So I took her to the hospital clinic the next day and they said they weren't sure it was really measles but if it was it was the German measles, not the regular measles. Nome and other communities were having outbreaks of measles but Alaska had not yet gotten the measles vaccine supply which was available in the "south 48," as we called the rest of the U.S. The rash actually subsided pretty fast and she steadily improved and her puffiness was soon all gone, too, as she excreted large amounts of urine over the next several days. Art and Cathy joined us in Nome a few days later, having gotten a ride on a Coast Guard Cutter from the Island to Nome.

We flew to LAX and took a helicopter shuttle ride to San Bernardino where Mother and Dad French picked us up. We got Becky an appointment for the measles vaccine but before she ever got in for it she broke out with the regular measles. I forgot to mention that Cathy had had the regular measles while we were staying at Mother and Dad French's before Becky was born! Thus, our departure from our dear Eskimo friends in both Savoonga and Gambell was terribly abrupt, but probably some verification that it was time for us to leave.

Chee Gah

Sherman Fung

Oldies like us love to see young children come onto the campus. They bring a breath of fresh air to our rather predictable environment. If the young ones happen to be grandchildren, so much the better—a blessing and a delight! A blessing because we see our own seed passed on and grow to be passers-on themselves. A delight because we often encounter surprises in their growth. Of course we sigh with relief that the wiggly bundle progresses from just "waaaaaaaaaaaa" to incomprehensible (that is to us adults) vocalization of a bilingual toddler to finally "cookie" or "apparik?" (meaning "Where's brother?"). We take their increasingly structured utterances as a sign of mental development.

Even when words do not accompany physical action, we gloat over the child's behavior—"How clever!" For example, Katya, our granddaughter of one year and ten months approached my wife, Alyse, with her plastic white frame sunglasses and offered them to her without saying anything, but her upturned eyes and outstretch hand meant that she, not only wanted Alyse to wear them but also to exchange them for the eyeglasses Alyse was wearing. Or take the time when I was seated with my quad cane next to me. Katya, obviously tired of her own toys, took hold of it and started walking with it, the top of her head barely reaching the curve of the handle bar. When her mother tells her that the cane is grandpa's, she turns around ten feet away and declares "Mine."

Young children's behavior reminds us oldies that nothing escapes them. This past Saturday we were invited to our son Ken's home in Tarzana. It was a get together of Alyse's nephew and his family from New York and two other visiting families from the Southland. Of course, there was a lot of catching-up conversations filling the air as well as less noisy appreciation over the snacks and big meal. Naturally moms swap stories with each other. Talin, our daughter-in-law, couldn't resist relating this recent story about Katya:

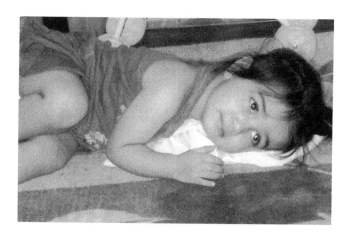

Katya

Talin and Ken had an engagement to attend and they got a babysitter to care for Katya and his brother Lucas. The babysitter, the daughter of one of Talin's cousins, had Kayta on her lap, facing her. Curiosity drove Katya to explore the young woman's upper garment. She had a low cut dress on. Katya was fiddling with the edge of the low collar and touched her breast. The babysitter, in the mood of a teacher, said, "Tzit-tzic," the Armenian equivalent of the English, "tiddies." Katya bent her head down and looked at herself and said, "Chee Gah," which meant in Armenian, "There's none."

As Talin was sharing this amusing story with the other moms around the table, she had Katya on her lap and Katya must have been taking everything in. Gennie, Ara's wife, was sitting next to Talin and Katya. Katya looked at her, pointed to her and said, "Tzit-tzic ure". Gennie, who was well aware of being thin on top, answered her, "Chee gah." Everybody burst into laughter.

Nothing escapes children. How the input comes out is another thing, sometimes in amusing ways and sometimes in amazing situations. As to their memory, you can't say "Chee Gah."

I wonder what's stored in her brain about gampa (sic).

Talking With Mom
Sherman Fung

Mom, even though you're not here as you once were, I think you can hear me, even see me. It's true that you left us more than 23 years ago, but I think some form of you is very present with me and at the same time you are existing in a dimension of reality that we earthly creatures don't understand. Our ignorance, of course, does not prelude this reality; it's real enough so that you can hear me talking to you.

Now that you are no longer confined by our physical world nor by the conventions of human society I like to ask you some questions about your world, if your existence can be called a world. Have you seen Grandfather and Grandmother? You used to talk to Grandfather as you stood facing his photo portrait that hung in our living room. You clasped your hands together in the manner of Asian gesture of respect or was it the Buddhist or Hindu bowing in prayer? Ever since I can remember, I've seen you in that posture mumbling softly. My childish mind thought that you were worshipping him. I was always curious as to what kind of existence Grandfather and other departed went to. They aren't in the heaven that my Sunday School taught me about. You burned paper money and paper clothes for them as well as offered special foods to them. I wondered whether or not they ever received those provisions. You must have had opportunity all these intervening years to find out. Tell me, did your offerings make any difference? Perhaps such a religious practice is not self-deception as some people claim. It seems to me it's an act of filial piety. I find that people in any culture do not wish any less for the welfare of the departed than for them when they were still living in this world.

Mom, me, Phyllis and Herbert

Mom, now that you're in the same existence as Grandfather and Grandmother, have you seen them? Like me you have never seen them personally. By the time Father brought you to America, your in-laws were long gone. What is it like to have a reunion with Father and my little sister Phyllis? How about Wellington? I've always wondered about him. His time on earth was so short. I don't really know how long. He must have joined our family when I was two or three. If he had survived whatever illness that killed him in infancy, I would have another brother, just a few years younger than I am.

You can see that I'm doing O.K. You don't have to worry about me. Of course, I've had to deal with the results of a stroke. I can't walk too well now. After my recent cataract surgery I've become far sighted. That means I have to change glasses again. Life is still good, Mom. I have a good wife, a comfortable home, good children who visit whenever they can, four grandchildren whose growth and development is intriguing to watch, and a lot of caring friends around. Like you I believe that spirits have some influence over nature and human life, but the spirits that surround me are ones who look after my welfare. Are the spirits that are around you looking after you? I hope so.

You know, Mom. I've always wanted to tell you about the Supreme Spirit I've come to know through the Bible and through followers of Jesus, but I never knew Chinese that well to be able to talk to you. The Chinese I knew did not equip me to conduct an adult conversation. I think now you really don't need me to tell what I want you to know. Where you are, you can't avoid the Supreme Spirit of the universe. I hope you find that Spirit to be good, as I have.

Family Matters

Coffee and Sympathy
Laura Berthold Monteros

There's a coffee place in Silverlake that serves doughnuts that are very similar to the beignets served in New Orleans. The coffee is much better than in New Orleans, which is bitter with chicory and needs a the fat and sugar in a beignet to dull the edge. My daughter, Ramona, and I went there on an April Wednesday to have a little mom and daughter time.

I hadn't planned on this, especially with my son Alessandro's college graduation and surrounding events coming up that weekend—picking my New York son up at LAX, driving out to Malibu, attending all the various ceremonies and receptions. But I knew I needed to set aside my to-do list for a few hours of time with her.

Ramona had been helping me with loose ends from my mother's estate and getting the house rented. We usually communicate by text or email, so I was concerned when she hadn't answered the last few communiqués. I finally asked her in a text how she was doing, and she replied, "Yucky".

"Would going out for a cuppa help?" I asked, and that's how we ended up in the café on Silverlake Boulevard.

Life had not been easy for my daughter in the previous year-and-a-half. She spent far too much time in hospitals with seriously ill relatives and far too much time in mourning. She has sat by her father's bed through one surgery or test after another, and kept vigil for her mother-in-law and grandmother as they died. Between her family and her husband's, there have been seven deaths and countless illnesses.

All this takes its toll, but true to our German stoicism and pioneer independence, she does not ask for sympathy. However, yesterday, I thought she needed a little with her tea.

After a full plate of doughnuts, we decided to walk around Silverlake. It's about three miles to make the circuit, and it was very hot. Even with sun block, my fair skin burned. But three miles at a slow pace is a lot of time to talk, and we were able to touch on many things—profound and trivial—as we strolled in the blazing sun. We found a beverage machine in the community center of the park and Ramona, concerned I was getting overheated, bought me a bottle of water.

I can't remember exactly what we talked about. It's not important. What matters is that we both put aside what we had planned for the day to spend some time together, to be there for each other.

I'm not usually good at that, at dropping everything to be with someone when it's not an emergency. Often I think about all the things I "should" be doing. How very self-centered and unChristlike that is! Jesus often stopped what he was doing to heal someone or answer the questions of his hopelessly dull disciples.

Isn't this what he meant when he told Martha that while she worried about accomplishing a list of tasks, her sister Mary had chosen the better part? Most of us are Martha people, but when we need someone to listen, it is a Mary person we seek out.

So yesterday, I was a Mary for a few hours. And in the end, my Martha list got done as well.

The Wild Side

Using All the Colors

… The Wild Side

Meeting a Bear on the Trail
A Tale of the Trail, with Metaphorical Implications
Bruce Calkins

Most of the wild creatures a hiker in the San Gabriel mountains meets are lizards, squirrels, and birds. There is an occasional deer, bobcat, or snake. There was one naked hiker. It was hard to tell whether he was wild or domesticated.

There are stories and occasional markings and droppings of bears and lions, but sightings are rare. Lynda reminds me that just because you don't see them doesn't mean they don't see you.

The most dangerous attack animal in the wilderness is the deer tick, which may be carrying lyme disease. I've encountered three of those nasty animals. There is also a breed of mosquito that seems particularly fond of "free range hikers."

Even though sightings of bears, lions, and big horn sheep are rare, they're exciting to see; so hikers are on the lookout. I have noticed that I tend to be especially vigilant when I'm hiking alone for the first time on a trail that is deep in the forest.

Such was the case one summer day a couple of years ago. I learned of a trail that started on top of Mt. Wilson, went down into a canyon on the back side, followed a stream for about two miles, then went up Mt. Wilson on another trail. It's what is called a "loop hike."

It is also a hike that is called "strenuous" in the book *100 Trails of the Angeles Forest*. "Strenuous" means it's strenuous for hikers. If you are not a hiker, other adjectives might be used. It is a 12 mile hike.

I didn't get an early start. I arrived at the top of Mt. Wilson in my car about 10:30 a.m., parked, found the trail head and started down the mountain. There is an exhilaration of the spirit when you're on a wilderness trail—even more so when it's your first time on a stunningly beautiful trail. No one except a workman was on

Using All the Colors

top of Mt. Wilson, and I didn't anticipate meeting anyone on the trail. Nor did I anticipate meeting an animal larger than I was.

The descent was wonderful. Every turn in the trail brought a new image of beauty. After about two and a half hours I reached a stream. There was even a rustic campsite there. I found where the trail continued by crossing the stream.

I have learned that the greatest risk of falling is in river and stream crossings, especially if you are trying "boulder hop" to keep your feet dry, as I was. In many places, one side of the stream would be a high cliff rising above the water. That meant the trail had to be on the "non-cliff" side. Since God had introduced a lot a variety in planning this part of the wilderness, the inaccessible side of the river kept changing. In the two mile section of the trail that followed the river, there were ten or twelve crossings. Most of them took some planning. You sort of needed to know whether your third and forth steps were going to be on a boulder or log that would keep you out of the water.

That stream is one of God's masterpieces, and I was not the first one God had help across a river. Still, it was a bit of a relief to come to the place where the trail began a steep ascent up Mt. Wilson.

There's more huffing and puffing on the way up. That's where you learn why this trail is called "strenuous." After about two and a half hours of climbing, the trail was cut into the side of a cliff. I estimated I was about two miles from the comfort of my car. There had been no wild life except for birds, squirrels, and lizards.

I looked ahead about 60 yards, and there was something black on the trail. Nothing in the woods would be that color – except a bear. Lying behind some large rocks on the trail was something large and black! I could see the ear. Almost as a reflex, I took out my can of bear-repellent-pepper-spray.

There were no detours from this trail. It was almost straight up on one side and almost straight down on the other. It was late in the afternoon. If I turned around, my 12 mile hike would be a 22 mile hike, and I'd have to cross that stream ten more times in the dark.

That wasn't going to happen. The bear would have to move, hopefully in the other direction.

I was equipped with a whistle. The bear hadn't seen me. I didn't want to surprise it. I blew the whistle rather tentatively. Nothing moved. I blew louder—nothing.

Is this a deaf bear?—or a dead bear? Am I going to have to step over it? I got rid of that thought.

I walked forward about ten yards and blew again. After repeating these steps several times, I was able to reach down on the trail behind those rock and pick up a black jacket lost by an earlier hiker. The ear was just a corner of the jacket sticking above the rocks.

I smiled the rest of the way up. I also realized that I was shaking a little. It was good that I had another two miles to go so I could use up all that adrenalin.

Noel

Charles Castles

Hearing the word "Noel," I think of Christmas carols. I remember a friend who was excited about printing his own Christmas cards with a stamp fashioned from a potato, and how crestfallen he looked when his card read, "LEON." But most of all, I recall my experience with Noel, our Christmas bunny.

Noel was a beautiful, white, lop-eared rabbit who was introduced to our daughter, Jhey, on Christmas morning. Noel was gentle and tolerant. She seldom touched the floor as our youngest loved her and carried her through our house. She became part of our family with the freedom to roam through our dwelling, for my wife, Shirley, had read that rabbits could be potty trained to use a litter box just like cats. Noel also enjoyed her quiet times in the lush grass of our well fenced back yard.

When I was growing up, my brother and I had a couple of rabbits that arrived for Easter, but they stayed outside in a special cage my father constructed. If they had names I don't remember them. Their enclosure featured eye-level viewing and a chicken-wire floor so they could be moved around to fertilize the whole yard. They weren't around long, though, after one got out and it took the whole neighborhood to find and retrieve it. During this adventure it's eye got scratched, so Dad had to take it to the vet.

Noel, unlike those rabbits from my youth, became a part of our family. So it was difficult when she developed a taste for chewing on our phone lines, indoor plants and furniture. Shirley had not read that bunnies liked to chew. Her unsupervised time outside her cage became shorter and shorter. It's not that we were just concerned about our plants and our ability to communicate with the outside world through our telephones. We worried that Noel might develop a taste for a 120 volt lamp cord. Shirley still tried to let Noel roam free in the girl's bedroom as much as she could...

...Until, Noel went too far. Killing living plants was something we had learned to live with. We had several phones and one was mounted high out of her reach. But when Noel amputated both of Barbie's legs, that was unacceptable!

Jhey and her big sister Claire were about to go to an ice skating competition, which would leave me alone with the suddenly destructive rabbit. Shirley, who really did love her plants more than the rabbit, decided to protect our house.

Fortunately, we had some good friends in the church with a daughter the same age as Jhey and a greenhouse which offered protection and a lot of space to roam. Everyone agreed the best place for Noel would be with Jhey's best friend Elena Walkup and her family. We made the transfer and the girls left town.

The next morning I got a call from Mary, Elena's mother, about a number of church concerns. She hadn't mentioned our loved one, so I inquired, "How's Noel?" "Oh, she's dead," Mary replied. That very first night in her new home, a raccoon broke into the greenhouse and killed Noel.

I conveyed the news of our departed family member to the rest of the family with greater pastoral sensitivity than the way I had received the shocking news.

Arctic Travel: St. Lawrence Island Dog Team Trips '57-'63

Art French

My wife, Carolyn, and I worked for the Board of National Missions of the Presbyterian Church (now PCUSA) from July 1957 to July 1963 in arctic Alaska. We served two Eskimo congregations on St. Lawrence Island off the northwest coast of Alaska in the Bering Sea. From the village of Gambell on the island's northwest tip, on a clear day, we could see the mountains of Siberia on the Chukotskiy Peninsula 35-40 miles to the northwest. The International Dateline, dividing today from tomorrow was approximately 15 miles west of St. Lawrence Island. Sometimes I kidded the Eskimo hunters that they went out to hunt today, really hunted tomorrow and ended up returning yesterday.

During our time on St. Lawrence Island, there were only two ways to travel between the two villages of Gambell and Savoonga. In the summer when the ice was gone from the Bering Sea we went by walrus skin boat. Then, in the winter, we traveled by dog team. Since leaving the Island a landing strip has been built on the tundra at Savoonga.

This was in the days before snowmobiles gained popularity in our part of the arctic. Dog team transportation was the only way for the men and their families to travel to their trapping cabins scattered around the island's million acres, and to service their fox trap lines. White fox pelts were a very substantial source of income when the fur buyers would come out to the island from Anchorage and Fairbanks. One year we bought one pelt from Gambell and one from Savoonga and had them made into a stole for Carolyn.

The last Dog Team Mail, a regular rural Star Route under contract with the US Postal Service, was on St. Lawrence Island between Gambell, where the planes from the Nome landed, and Savoonga. I particularly remember one beautifully bright, sunny day with a hard, fast trail. I was making one of my quarterly trips to Savoonga for pastoral visitation, preaching, communion, and weddings if needed. The plane had come in which meant there was mail to be delivered to Savoonga. Since it was such a gorgeous day several people decided to go to Savoonga also. My driver and I joined the procession as we headed out from the village skirting Gambell mountain. Such a day to travel in the arctic was thrilling. Even the dogs seemed to sense it and pulled eagerly at their harnesses. On this particularly beautiful day, at one point, we were going up a steep section of trail with the heavily loaded mail team behind. I stopped and took a picture, which I cherish as one of my most memorable dog team trips. After nearly fifty years I had the slide printed and the picture suitably framed.

I never had my own team. It would have consumed too much time providing for the dogs. I used my travel allowance to hire a team as needed, much as one would hire a town car for a trip here. I took turns driving the team as that was a very good way to keep warm. Part of the drivers job was to hop off the extended

Using All the Colors

runners at the back and help push the sled over rough places in the trail, through deep, wet snow or up inclines.

I was no expert dog team driver which was much in evidence on one occasion. We were heading out of the village of Savoonga on one occasion, going south to the DEW Line Air Force base at Northeast Cape. I forgot to stand on the runners before pulling the anchor out of the snow. Feeling the release the team took off immediately leaving one very embarrassed white guy standing there while every one laugh uproariously. Another team took off and soon brought the loose team back.

A sled has two ways of stopping and holding. One is an actual, small ship's anchor which would be jammed into the snow to hold the team in place. The other was a brake to slow the team and or hold them in place for a short time. The brake consisted of the largest, actual iron hinge I ever saw with big teeth cut into it. This was attached to the back of the sled by a heavy duty spring. All the driver had to do was to stand on the brake, pushing it into the snow which acted as a drag to slow the team to the walk or stop.

Dressing for a dog team trip was layering. I started out with full-body long johns, heavy wool pants and wool shirt. The feet were layered, also. First cotton socks, then wool socks (which I still have), followed by soft seal skin booties with the fur inside. The outer wear were seal skin boots: fur outside for dry snow travel and hair scrapped off for wet snow days. Into the bottom of each boot went a good fistful of dry tundra grass. We always planned ahead and put in a supply of grass before the first snow fall. On top of the grass went a very thick felt pad. With that kind of footwear my feet would stay warm in 40 below zero weather with no danger of frost bite. My mission predecessor was wearing regulation army cold weather boots when he suffered frost bite and lost some of his toes. Once I was thus garbed I put on my parka of heavy blanket material with an outer canvas cover. The hood was lined with dog fur plus an inner rim of wolverine fur closest to my face. The wolverine fur kept condensation from my breath from forming on the fur. It easily brushed away. On my hands I wore heavy wool mittens inside sealskin mittens. This completed my arctic traveling wardrobe and prepared me for any kind of weather out on the trail.

My longest trip was from Gambell to Northeast Cape approximately 100 miles the length of the Island. The US Air Force Distant Early Warning Site, or DEW Line for short, was there and I went to provide some pastoral service. My driver and I left alone in bitterly cold 40 below zero weather with a strong wind blowing. The positive factor was that cold weather made for a fast trail with very hard snow. At one point out in the midst of nowhere with the wind whipping the snow fiercely across the tundra, the brake line broke. No AAA out there on the treeless plateau high above the frozen Bering Sea. My driver began to make repairs on sight while I took some pictures nearly freezing my fingers in the process. I'm still amazed at that trip when I view those slides.

We came to the Toolie's trapping cabin and stopped for tea and food before pushing on. I took a picture of Mable Toolie sewing on a skin boot with a white fox pelt on the floor beside her. We made it to the DEW Line site. I conducted worship for some of the military personnel, spent the night and then returned the sixty miles to Savoonga.

We made a rather interesting family trip by dog team from Savoonga to Gambell. Carolyn was five months pregnant with our second child. Cathy was sixteen months old. We had planned to return to Gambell by boat, so that Carolyn could get off the Island by plane. However, the ice formed early that year which meant no boat travel until spring. That meant the only way to Gambell was by dog team. Being early in the fall the sea ice in the inlets would not be frozen solid enough for dog team crossing. Therefore, we would be forced farther inland making our trip that much longer. Also, there wasn't much snow yet making for a very slow trail.

At this time, the Christian Education trainer from Southeast Alaska was visiting and conducting workshops. It was obvious that she was none to happy about this turn of events. She had flown

Using All the Colors

into Gambell and come over to Savoonga by skin boat. She fully expected to leave the reverse way. However, it was dog team or wait until spring breakup!

Because of Carolyn's condition, beside having a 16-month old daughter along, too, the villagers outfitted a sled especially for them. A frame was built on the sled. The women sewed a canvas cover with a long central zipper which was then placed over the frame. Several padded cushions were brought from a couch in the National Guard Armory. The day of departure arrived. Carolyn climbed into her chariot with Cathy sitting between her legs. Then they were zippered in. I was on my sled. The C.E. lady had her sled. There was a baggage sled along with several others wanting to go to Gambell, also, including the mail.

With not much snow and even some tundra grass showing, progress was slow. That first day we only made it over the mountain to a trapping cabin on the other side. It was the same cabin where Carolyn and I had been let out years ago when we made our very first skin boat trip from Gambell to Savoonga. Our Eskimo friends soon had the fire going from conveniently stored drift wood. We refreshed ourselves with food and drink and climbed onto the sleeping shelf for the night. The C.E. lady was not amused. I thought it kind of hilarious myself!

The second day turned into a seventeen hour marathon on the trail. We did not reach Gambell until midnight, having left at 7 a.m. that morning. Those trusty sled dogs knew the trail and the closer we got to Gambell the harder they pulled.

Before making the last push around Gambell mountain, we stopped for a tea break at a convenient trapping cabin. These cabins are never locked, of course, and available for anyone to use anytime. I joined the others in an Eskimo delicacy eating the tender skin off certain roots. Local version of cucumber tea sandwiches. Carolyn thought the trip had been too much for me when she saw me eating twigs! We arrived in Gambell very thankful for a safe if somewhat strenuous journey.

The Wild Side

When the next plane arrived Carolyn and Cathy flew to Nome, then to Anchorage, from there on to Seattle and Los Angeles where they were met by my dad and mother. They stayed with my parents in Rialto until Becky was born in February.

I returned to Savoonga and my pastoral duties. That was a lonely Christmas, but later I was able to go to Southern California to greet our second daughter.

Lady of the Night or The Great Escape
Arthur French

Nobody warned me how strenuous and stressful life in retirement could be chasing old ladies at night! A particular one, in her mid-80's, is crotchety, of very determined mind and set in her ways—much like some others I know. She is very much given to her own odd notions, whims, and grouchiness.

I first noticed this grand dame, whom some have called a "princess" but I would call a harridan, when she moved on campus with her family. She moved sedately on her regular walks with her own destination in mind. What was so noticeable was her outlandish hair style—tinted black and very scraggly gray—typical of some ancient crones I've seen!

I really never gave her more than a passing glance, but one day I came home to discover we were entertaining company with the lady in question the center of conversation. I was cordial in my greeting but otherwise uninvolved until I thought I heard something which made me suspect this was more than a casual visit. I really do need to get some hearing aids. It became startlingly clear that we were going to have another boarder for ten days and ten nights!

I remained as calm as I could under the circumstances, while all kinds of wild scenarios were being formed in my thought patterns. Was I going to have to accompany her on her walks several times a day? Horrors! She was on a special diet of sirloin steak and rice. Eats better than I do, for goodness sake. What about the gentleman boarder already living with us with his own fixed routines, diet and queer eating habits?

And it came to pass, too soon as far as I was concerned, that we went from being a household of three to four.

The lady in question, Suki by name, is a twelve year old Pekingese belonging to our friend Mary who had urgent family business in Seattle. Mary would be gone for ten days—thus the arrangements for Suki to board with us. We already knew she was not partial to living at the Grove and was recovering from a mild upset.

Suki: The Lady of the Night

Thursday night after choir practice we picked her up and brought her home to our place. There was some adjustment to a strange new place, so she spent the night alone on her basket bed in the living room. Friday she evidently felt enough at home, or was it nerves, to relieve herself on the dining room carpet. Because her adopted "mommy" was gone all Friday morning, I played chef so our guest could eat. Her special diet had thoughtfully been prepared in advance and put up in individual baggies before being frozen. However, we had forgotten to thaw the first one soon enough. Therefore, I stood by the microwave thawing small portions, offering them to Suki, thawing some more, etc. You get the picture —I felt like a short order cook!

The GREAT ESCAPE came Friday night after we got home about 9:30 P.M.. We thought it would be a good idea for Suki to have another outdoor chance after the earlier accident inside.

Using All the Colors

Suki had other plans, however. As we were preparing to attach her leash, she bolted out the partially open door and vanished into the night.

Because she likes to go to the park, I got the car out of the garage again and we drove slowly over to our neighborhood park all the while scanning the sides of the street. She would have been almost impossible to see with her gray-black coloring and low profile—not unlike that of a skunk. There was no sighting, so we returned home filled with worry.

It was such a cold night! I turned on the porch light and put her basket bed outside under the light by the front door. We went to bed for a very restless rest, little sleep and growing concern! Thoughts and questions kept tumbling through our wakeful minds. Where could she be? Had she left the campus? Perhaps she had been hit by a car. With her coloring and at night she would not easily be seen.

At 3 A.M. Carolyn couldn't stand it, got dressed, and went our looking for her. She heard Suki crying, traced the sound and spotted her but could not get Suki to come near. Carolyn even opened the door of Mary's apartment but Suki would not go in. Suki disappeared again and Carolyn came home. However, before 5 A.M. she was up, dressed, and out looking again as light was returning. Around 6 A.M. she came home to get me up and dressed as Suki was sighted again—but no luck, and never even saw her!

Suki had disappeared again. Carolyn returned home but I continued walking the grounds in hopes of another sighting of the Lady of the Night. I was fearful that we were going to have to tell Mary, "We lost your dog."

About 7:30 A.M. Carole, who lives across the street from Mary's home, called and asked if we were keeping Mary's dog. "Yes, have you seen her?" "Yes, she's at Mary's now!" I put my heavy coat back on against the morning chill and slowly walked toward Mary's place. I didn't want to startle Suki and cause her to run away again. She must have thought, "Enough of this fun and games." She came down the walk toward me, so I laid down on the cement until she came up to me. I began to giving her my famous dog shoulder massage. None can resist it! While giving her the massage I eased her collar around until I could snap the leash to the ring. Then the test of wills. Suki did not want to accompany me back to our place. However, I prevailed and literally dragged Suki into our front door.

Suki ate and got up on her blanket on the couch and went to sleep!

You will understand when I say that the front door is guarded very, very carefully.

Oh yes, Mary called from Seattle!

Wildlife in Tucumcari

Mary Froede

Though we chase an occasional raccoon or possum from our garbage dumpster and periodically run across a coyote, skunk or bear here in the San Gabriel foothills, it cannot in anyway be compared to the wildlife in Tucumcari, New Mexico. When we arrived in town, about the only wild thing my kids had ever seen outside of the zoo were squirrels.

The elk were abundant and there was a hunting season for them each fall. The law said that no shots could be fired within a distance of five miles either side of the road during hunting season. Needless to say, those animals were smart. They must have gotten the memo because they would gather in large herds well within the five mile limit until hunting season was over allowing us to view the animals grazing peacefully with no fear of the hungry hunters.

My husband, Jim, was returning one night from a conference and was coming down off the mesa near Trementina. A car came racing past him and Jim was concerned because he knew that the cattle came onto the road at night. The road is open range which meant there were no fences to contain the livestock. The asphalt is still warm from the day's sunshine and a magnet for the animals to bed down. Sure enough, within minutes, Jim saw the brakes light come on and the car slammed to a stop. The driver waited until Jim came along to lead him slowly around all the cows until they got back into town. One unlucky driver we talked to had slammed into a cow and it had completely destroyed his car.

Mr. B. ranched here outside of Tucumcari, in Santa Rosa, New Mexico and also in Texas. His herds were sheep and cattle, some Santa Gertrudis cattle (an extremely sturdy cross breed of brahman and beef shorthorn cattle developed in the King Ranch in Texas). He always had the most exotic pets. One year his kids had a boa constrictor, long before snakes were considered popular pets.

The Wild Side

The poor thing made the mistake of crawling between the screen and the winter storm window. They missed him, but couldn't find him 'til springtime—he had frozen to death in the winter. Their dearest pet was a wild javelina (a type of wild boar) that they discovered on a trip across the hills. She was immediately named "Harriet, the Havelina" and grew from about one pound to 25-30 formidable pounds on the good food given her by the family. She was most affectionate, noisy, and playful. Her coat was anything but comforting: if you can imagine petting a Fuller brush—those are boar bristles, or at least, were in that day and age. When she got to a fairly good size and was knocking over the tables and people, she was sent to the San Antonio zoo where she may still be.

One of our unusual pets were my son Rick's tarantulas. He was fascinated by their docile nature and knew that they were different from the poisonous South American banana tarantulas. He was often seen with one of them perched on his shoulder and believe me, everyone kept clear of him at that time! Every fall, the tarantulas would migrate. They were about the size of a saucer in diameter and as they crossed the highways at their snails-pace, the cars would demolish them in no time flat (figuratively speaking!). One day, Ruth Ann invited her friend Clara over to play and wanted to show off Rick's collection of tarantulas. They went to the box Rick kept them in, opened the lid to show the full box and since I was standing there, I looked in, too. Image my shock to find her thumb clutching the lid just about two inches away from a walnut sized black widow spider! Some pet!

When we had been settled for just a short time, the front door flew open and Rick was shoving a prehistoric monster in front of my eyes. My first impression was *"If I pass out, he may reconsider his bold actions,"* but good old Mary kept her cool and calmly stated "What a lovely looking lizard." Rick immediately went into a biological diatribe letting me know that this was a horned toad and that when it got mad, it could "spit blood". He then turned this two inch long monster over on its back, stroked it's soft tummy and

Using All the Colors

literally hypnotized it. I often found myself over the years, picking them up lovingly, holding them upright and then turning them over to do the same thing!

The day Rick came home from school with a ghastly, skeletal stray dog on a rope, I knew the old story "She followed me home, can we keep her?" Route 66 (Gaynell Avenue) was the local dumping spot for unwanted pets. No SPCA there! People would just turn them out as they passed through, and if they could survive, many found homes in the community. This poor pup had lived on a very sturdy type of gourd that grew wild in the ditches alongside the roads. We took her in and because of her red coat and "questionable" background, we gave her a good biblical name, "Jezebel". That little pup grew to pony size!! I should have looked at her paws and would have guessed. Anyway, the manse, situated as it was, was so close to the church and education building with our back yard also the church's front yard. On a particular Sunday morning, I noticed a gathering of elders looking into the yard, counting the dog piles, which I am sure they took no time to report to the congregation. Jezzy's favorite spot for loitering was on Rick's bed, stretched out full length with her head placed comfortably on his pillow.

It was a lovely spring Saturday, so I had invited the elders and families to a picnic in our back yard (which had been scrupulously cleaned by then) and we had a lovely barbecue. That morning, I had made three of my special, scrumptious "soda cracker pies" with fresh picked peaches and real whipped cream. They were on the kitchen table, waiting until we had eaten to dig in. I was floored to walk into the kitchen to get the pies and make a grand entrance only to discover Jezebel, up on her hind legs, gleefully licking all the whipped cream off one of the pies. I had to really cut small slices in the remaining untouched pies in order for each of us to have "just a taste".

The older kids in the neighborhood often went hunting out on the sage covered prairie, mostly for rabbits. One day, here came

Rick with his shirt full of wriggling baby jackrabbits. Their ears were far longer than their whole body and it was a wonder that their size didn't cause them to topple over by sheer weight. He and his buddies had killed a rabbit, not knowing it was a "mama" but they soon found the hole with the three little bunnies. Rick was devastated so he built a lovely cage for them and they seemed very happy. In the meantime, he had been thoroughly scratched on his chest bringing them home and I, suspecting some kind of lethal rabbit fever, brought out the merthiolate to paint the scratch marks. Well, also having a slight artistic bent, I made a lovely merthiolate outline of a rabbit with big ears. A few hours later, Rick came moaning in to the me to show me that he was allergic to the merthiolate and had puffed up at least half an inch on each lovely stroke I had made. He went swimming at the community pool in a tee shirt for many weeks!

Our most exotic pet was a baby skunk. Given to us by a local farmer, the mother was the victim of a traffic accident. We called her "Fiorella", translated "Little flower" ala Walt Disney. She was so tiny, only a pound or so. She had been de-scented and had a big fluffy tail. She wandered all over the house and would climb into our laps when we sat down. She would go around and around in a circle and wrap her voluminous tail around herself to sleep. She was so dear, but we never were able to completely get rid of the smell and it *was* offensive. As per usual, we gave her to a local farmer who loved having her and apparently had no sense of smell!!

On summer evenings, all the neighbor kids gathered under the corner street light to watch and catch exotic bugs. We grown-ups would flake out on our front porch and watch. We were well entertained by the antics. Rick one night caught an emerald beetle, a little over one inch in length. He tied a string to one of its legs and it would fly around like a model airplane. Those bugs were startlingly beautiful, with a heavy scarab-like shell of a bright metallic green. What a treat to see.

As I am sitting in my car on a gridlocked "parking lot"

Using All the Colors

freeway, gazing off toward the blurred San Gabriel Mountains, all of which I have climbed, and enjoying a smog inspired sunset, I often find myself longing for the quiet, simple life I led in New Mexico. Then I remember going to the Music Center to see Baryshnikov dance, hear the music of the Philharmonic, play with my grown up daughter at Disneyland, see my grandchildren reveling in the pleasure they have had at Knott's Berry Farm and I don't feel so bad.

The Kindergartner
Bill Hansen

Mary Ellen was the lead teacher for the Sunday School Kindergarten Department of the Church of the Valley. At the same time she taught the kindergarten class at the Rancho Verde Public School nearby. She taught in both capacities for many years. And quite often she would have students who attended both her public school class on weekdays and then ALSO her church school kindergarten class on Sundays. One of those double-dipping students was a cute 5 year old little boy named Dustin. In fact Dustin happened to be the son of Dusty and Linda Rogers... and also the grandson of Dale Evans and Roy Rogers.

One morning in Sunday School the class was studying the Creation and the children were finding delight in describing the animals that God had created. That same morning, during the "show and tell" sharing time, the children took sheer delight in telling the class about their own pets and household animals of various kinds. But Dustin stole the show... no one could match him.

He couldn't wait to share the news that he had 5 new bunny rabbits at home. The children were thrilled! Not just one....but *Five Bunny Rabbits!*

The next day on Monday during class time at the Rancho Verde School Dustin asked if he could share his news with the public school class. Thinking how delighted the class would be, Mary Ellen allowed Dustin to share his good fortune... however- along with the good news of the five bunny rabbits, about which the class was understandably excited, Dustin then shared the bad news that overnight one of the bunnies had died.

The whole class gasped—they felt so bad for Dustin and his dead bunny. Again, the next day, Dustin sadly reported the death of a second bunny. The young students made helpful suggestions for saving the remaining bunnies, like putting a cold wash rag on their foreheads if they had a temperature. But nothing that they suggested worked. It seemed like a disease of some sort had stricken Dustin's bunnies. The sharing became sadder and sadder each day until on Friday young Dustin reported the death of the last bunny.

You can imagine that the class was stricken. Dustin's mother, Linda, was one of Mary Ellen's volunteer helpers on Friday. Mary Ellen ran into Linda in the hallway as Linda was coming into the school that afternoon to help with the class. Mary Ellen shook her head and said: "Linda, I'm so sorry for what's happened to Dustin's five bunnies... all five of them dying! The class is just SO upset"!

Linda looked puzzled and said, "Five bunnies?" and then her expression changed into a frown. "Oh, Mary Ellen," she exclaimed, "That dickens! You know last Sunday when Dustin came out of Sunday School he came up to his dad and he said 'DAD, I TOLD A LIE TO MRS. HANSEN THIS MORNING. I TOLD HER THAT I HAD FIVE BUNNY RABBITS AT HOME'. Dusty just said, 'NOW DUSTIN, YOU KNOW WHAT YOU HAVE TO DO... YOU'RE GOING TO HAVE TO MAKE THIS RIGHT WITH MRS. HANSEN."

Linda was quiet for a moment and then said, "But really Mary Ellen, I don't think THAT was what his father had in mind."

The Gift Horse
Kenneth Grant

"I've never heard of that before." Many have said it, but it is true none the less. The following is a short piece of personal history that has to do with horses and my involvement with them. It is, in a way, my response to the often asked question. "How in the world did you, a Presbyterian minister, get involved with horses?" Here, in brief, is how it happened.

Like most small boys (and girls as well) I was attracted to horses early on. Probably it was to ponies at this early stage since they were smaller and more my size and somehow less threatening. Growing up in early twentieth century Glendale, California, I had access to the pony ride concession on what was then the edge of town and my mother saw to it that my youthful fascination was not disappointed. I took riding lessons, with my docile little mount plodding along the brush-edged trails that once wondered over the mountains where Glendale College now stands.

Years passed. Busy, growing, school-filled years with interests blossoming in many directions and ponies and their larger relations largely forgotten. I say largely, but not altogether, for there was a brief attempt to learn to ride real horses, the "real thing" you might say. Since the nearest riding stable was "Pickwick Stables" in nearby Burbank, my ever supportive mother saw to it that I was enrolled in a riding class there. I'm not sure how long that lasted but my life moved on to other interests.

Many years passed with little or no contact with horses or riding. I graduated from Hoover High, spent two years at Occidental College with the V-12 Program and another nine months overseas with the Navy during World War II. Having made a decision for Christ during high school years, and deciding to become a minister, I returned from my Navy days and enrolled at USC. After graduating from USC in 1950, I entered seminary and

Using All the Colors

graduated in 1953. After a rather adventurous time serving churches in California, horses again entered my life and in a most unexpected way. It happened as I entered my Mid-West ministry.

I had become what is known as an "Intentional Interim Specialist" -- a challenging task I much enjoyed. Nevertheless, while I served churches in several mid-western states, one of the most memorable experiences was at St. Andrew Presbyterian Church in Iowa City, Iowa. It was a thriving congregation of friendly, energetic, and committed people. It was my first real experience of the Mid-West and I was immediately drawn to the rolling countryside, rural atmosphere, and the sight of Amish buggies along the highway. Since Amish/Mennonite Kalona was not far from Iowa City, I managed to attend the monthly horse auctions held there. Those auctions drew folks for miles around, including the Amish with their horses and quaint black buggies.

It was at one of those auctions that I spotted a handsome quarter horse that was to be part of the sale. "Golly," I thought, "Maybe I could find a place to stable that horse and do a bit of riding." I noted the number on its hip and sat quietly while the horse went unsold, its owner unwilling to accept any of the bids. I, with a sudden attack of good sense, realized I had no place or time for a young quarter horse, beautiful as she was. Nevertheless, I did tell the men at our next Men's Breakfast about my Kalona visit and the beautiful horse. The men understood, knowing my love of horses. They also remembered that I had occasionally invited an old cowboy named Cactus to share the pulpit and tell spiritually orientated Western tales. That cowboy was none other than Ken Grant in riding gear and mustache! Cactus was more popular than I will ever be.

Months went by and my interim drew to a close. One Sunday, as the last day drew near, one of the men from the breakfast made an announcement. On behalf of the congregation, he presented me with what was to be their parting gift, a beautiful quarter horse. It was the very one I had seen at the Kalona auction! It seems they knew the owner and, unknown to me, had purchased her and in appreciation both to me and to "Cactus" they made this amazing gift. It came with a generous check to buy hay as well.

Me with one of my horses

When the last Sunday rolled around, I arranged to have "Cactus" give the sermon. He entered the church not walking down the isle as usual but riding his new horse up to the clear windows of the sanctuary which looked out to the woods behind the Church. Swinging down, he entered by a side door and told the congregation; "Parson's out roundin' up strays an' asked me ta come an' talk with you folks." I told him, "Shucks, Parson, I caint preach no sermon." 'I didn't ask you to preach a sermon, Cactus,' he said. 'just tell them your stories.' And that's what I did. The memory of that day and those gifts from a loving congregation will remain with me as long as I live.

Racing Days

Kenneth Grant

Owning a horse for pleasure riding is one thing. Owning and racing a horse is quite something else. Of course, the question is one I was often asked. "We know you love horses but how in the world did you get involved in racing them?"

I have written elsewhere of my gift horse from a grateful congregation. The racing part, however, came later. I had served interim pastorates in Iowa, Arizona and Missouri. Following these it was back to Fort Dodge, Iowa, and another happy and productive interim. It was there that I entered a new chapter in my "horse history."

Unfortunately, it had been necessary to sell my lovely gift horse. She had been bred to race and my fantasy was to race her... a dream never fulfilled. In Missouri, however, I was able to purchase a couple of failed race horses hoping to train them to be jumpers. It did not work, but the dream of racing had been born.

I was definitely interested in the thoroughbred racing picture by now, though with little time and less money to do much about it, as my ministry was keeping me very busy and it did take first priority! I followed the reports in the papers, however, and thought, "If I could find an owner who wanted to get rid of a race horse that would never win the Derby but...." Then one day I spotted a likely prospect in the newspaper, drove to the track at Prairie Meadows, went to the Racing Office counter, and asked about this particular horse. A tall man with a clean Stetson who smelled of shaving lotion looked over at me. "I know that horse," he said. "He's not for sale. But I have one that is and might interest you." I followed trainer Mark Bader to his barn and there I met Dusty Dolly. I walked around her, just as though I was an expert sizing her up. She wasn't a show boat, but she didn't look bad either. She'd run a good deal, placed a lot of seconds, thirds, and fourths in claiming races, and her owners were willing to sell her at a very modest price. I bought her on the spot and was in the racing business!

My racing partner

Dusty Dolly did her best, always. She had heart. You just had to give her credit. Then too, her trainer didn't charge much, and in Iowa, in those days, a modest amount would keep you going. Furthermore, since the first four places in any race paid something, I managed to break even. Dusty was almost always somewhere "in the money" though not in the winner's circle. In short, she paid her keep. When her running days ended I bred her to her half brother, a notable winner, and her colt (we named Hustlin' Dusty) was sold and did what his mother never quite could. He won often for his owner. It just wasn't me. As "Breeder of Record," however, I received a small check now and then when he won.

I could tell many horse tales but want to tell you about "Key to Dixie", "High Tech Gal", and "Runder Bound", all horses I purchased from Bader Farms. It was the home farm from which Mark Bader, the man with the shaving lotion and clean white Stetson had come. His father, Jim, was a long time breeder and

Using All the Colors

highly respected in the Iowa racing community. He was also a wonderful human being and gave me much sage advice.

Key to Dixie was a beautiful, dapple gray filly that I bought when she was quite young. Bader trained, she ran quite well though she struggled in her early races. She, like Dusty Dolly, had heart and was often somewhere "in the money." When she began to show signs of wear we sold her to a family whose young daughter wanted a dapple grey for a show horse and was thrilled with Dixie. Yes, Dixie's stiffness vanished and she lived on to delight a young girl.

High Tech Gal was a gorgeous thoroughbred that looked like a picture. She had a beautiful, calm disposition as well. We had high hopes, but she didn't like to race. It was that simple. She could. She would run to the front and slow down. "Why bother" she seemed to say. Then she became very ill and I spent several thousand healing her before selling her to a dentist. They tell me he couldn't wait to get home to ride her! She too found her real place in life as a pleasure horse.

Runder Bound was my most successful horse. Purchased from the Baders after she had been savaged by a loose stallion and sent back to the farm to heal, she had posted some notable work outs. When healed, she ran well, once winning by about ten lengths! I have that photo and cherish it.

Bev and I were at the track the night she ran over a sea of mud to win, going wire to wire. Unfortunately, the stewards claimed she had cut in front of the second place horse and thus was bumped to second. Other trainers felt this was a bad judgement on the part of the stewards, but it held. Runder Bound developed a chip in her knee which I had removed. However, another developed and I retired her, selling her to a young women who bred her to a fine stallion. I knew too that she loved and cared for all her horses. Runder Bound also had found a good home.

I've lost track in the years since, though I trust good fortune has followed all my equine "charges". They gave me much pleasure and cost me money I might well have saved or used otherwise. Still it provided a chapter in my life that introduced me to many dear friends and left me with a host of wonderful memories.

Now when Bev and I go to Santa Anita Race Track to watch the early morning workouts and eat our breakfast at Clocker's Corner, the memories come flooding back. Yes, and I have been known to say, "Bev, look at that dapple grey! Doesn't she look like Dixie?"

I am indeed thankful for this portion of life that introduced me to my horses and the many lessons I learned from them.

Using All the Colors

Remembrances and Musings

Using All the Colors

Early Morning Musings From the Porch of "The Odessa"

Carole Hoffs Bos

The Sun makes itself evident through cottonwood trees as I sit in contemplation; One lone figure walks along the water's edge, toes refreshed in cool, calm water; All is quiet but for a child's cheery voice across the way.

God surely blessed this sacred place, a cottage found along the
    shores of Lake Michigan.
Its surrounding beauty envelopes me as I remember the
    challenges, the joys, the tears, the adventures which have
    occurred here.
Family members have invested their dreams and talents in
    making this a real home:
    sewing, reconstructing, decorating, painting—
    imagining what could be from what has been.
Although surrounded by neighboring cottages, there is a sense of
    solitude and refreshment found in the comforting arms of
    this cottage.

Our family's history is visible through pictures: some hung, some
    saved in shelved albums:
    children on the white sandy beach,
    sailors on kayaks or a sailfish, watching for a dancing wind or
    breaking wave,
    people around an abundant table,
    cousins, aunts and uncles enmeshed in conversation,
    a trio of sisters singing around the old pump organ,
    a foursome engaged in a game or puzzle,
    Mother perched on her favorite porch swing,

parents and children enjoying the playful waves of our Great Lake,
neighbors and family seated on benches, thrilled by the oranges and golds of sunset.

How you have blessed us, O God, with comfort and peace.
The nostalgia within these walls gives us assurance of Your ever faithful presence.
For it was You who led us to this place; You who have given us the resources to share with friends the bounty of this retreat.

Mine is a grateful heart, giving thanks for a family grounded in Your precepts, for this "home away from home," and for every family member and friend who shares in its wonder and comfort.

"PRAISE THE LORD, FOR THE LORD IS GOOD."

The Odessa

Traffic Tickets
Robert Bos

In my rearview mirror, the flashing red lights of a patrol car quickly caught my attention. "Oh no," I gasped. "Is he after me?" My heart raced. Yes, I was the object of his chase. I pulled over to the side of the road. While I tried to reconcile myself to the situation, the officer walked up to my side window and asked for my driver's license. This kind of happening was not a one time occasion. Over the years, I've had such experiences. What were some of my reactions? This is what my writing is about.

My cousin and his wife were visiting us from Louisville, KY. It was a nice afternoon so Carole and I decided to take them on a scenic drive from our home in Westlake Village to the beach in Malibu. We would get there by traveling through the Santa Monica Mountains, about a forty minute drive. Malibu Canyon Road was well maintained with its curves and mountain passes. As we started down a rather steep grade I saw a Highway Patrol car parked at the bottom. He was parked so that he could quickly pull out in either direction. My car had already picked up speed so that I knew that I was in danger of exceeding the speed limit. It was too late. After I passed him, I saw in my rear view mirror that he had already started his pursuit in my direction with lights flashing. This shouldn't happen to a carload of respected citizens. After all, both my cousin and I were Presbyterian ministers, his wife was a professor of Old Testament at Louisville Seminary, and my wife was a highly respected and honored teacher in the local school district. Would it help if I told this to the arresting officer? No, I couldn't do that. It was my mistake. He would only be doing what was his job. That's what he was trained and paid to do, to maintain safety on the highway. When he came to my window and informed me of my speed, I could only say, "I'm sorry about that." After he issued me

Using All the Colors

a ticket I could say no more than "Thank You." For the record, what was my reaction? Gratitude for a job rightly done.

There was another time when I did voice an alibi, an excuse, a cop-out you might say. It was on a Sunday evening when Carole and I were driving to Santa Cruz to visit our daughter and her family. We were hoping to arrive before our two young grandchildren went to bed. It had already grown dark and we still had about an hour to go. We were on a single lane road with traffic moving in both directions. The speed limit was 55 but I was driving at least 65. Before I knew it, I saw the flashing red lights behind me. The policeman had been coming from the other direction, saw me, turned around and made his catch. I had done it again. Excessive speed. This time I explained the reason for my haste. The story about the grandchildren didn't arouse any warm, homey feelings in the trooper. He may have thought, "That's a likely story." What did I expect? For him to tear up the ticket, an apology for delaying us, a police escort? No, of course not. He only said "Be careful" and gave me the citation. What was my reflection on it? Deserves you right.

In the collection of tickets that I received over the years, I remember the time I was driving down a street in Thousand Oaks on my way to the dentist. I thought that I was in a 45 mph zone when the limit was 35. This time I was apprehended by a motorcycle police officer. He dismounted and walked toward my car wearing his mirrored shades. I explained to him that I thought the limit was 45. He again clarified it for me. While I was telling him that I was on my way to the dentist, he was filling out a page in his book. His only sympathetic comment was that he had followed me for some distance before stopping me. I couldn't get myself to say, "How considerate of you." My opinion? Inconsideration.

A family member found some humor in this one. Carole and I were helping to move our daughter home following her graduation from Cal Poly University in San Luis Obispo. Our car was packed with her things, so much so that I couldn't see out the back window of our station wagon. We were on 101 just north of Santa Barbara when I saw in my side view mirror the familiar red flashing lights. You guessed it. Speeding again. While the officer was tending to his business with us, our son Steve and daughter Karen sped by. I didn't know that until we arrived home, and Steve couldn't stop laughing having seen dad stopped for getting a ticket. I tried to see the humor in it. Response? Not funny!

No doubt I deserved all of my penalties but there was one time when I wasn't going to take it anymore. It was about 10:00 p.m. late one Sunday night when I was driving through the neighborhood, a short distance between my church and home. It had been a long day and I was tired and couldn't get home fast enough. A misty rain was falling and suddenly between the back and forth sweeping of the windshield wipers, my headlights fell upon the back of an unlighted car parked along the curb. I was quickly alarmed when I saw the words "Ventura County Sheriff" printed on the trunk. As I passed, the patrol car suddenly came alive as it picked up speed behind me with red lights flashing. I was almost home so I turned the corner and parked along the curb across from my house. This was the last straw. I had more that enough for one day. I was ready to confront the deputy. No sooner had he approached my open window when I told him that I was not going to get a ticket. I informed him who I was and that I had had a long day, and that I lived right across the street. He calmly asked me for my driver's license. He studied it for a moment and said, "Oh, I see that you just had a birthday. "Happy Birthday!" That was the end of it. No ticket. My reaction? Thank you, God.

One summer when I was in seminary, I interned at a church in Chicago. At that time I drove a black 1942 Plymouth with painted white sidewall tires. On the back bumper I had placed a small, metal sign that read Clergy. Driving along one day I was stopped by the police. Expecting the worst, to my surprise, I didn't get a ticket. I didn't have to say anything. Approaching my car, the officer had noticed the clergy sign on the bumper. He then

Using All the Colors

informed me that he didn't give tickets to priests, rabbis, or reverends. My reflection? Saved again.

You may wonder if I ever had to go to court. Yes, one time. I was instructed to appear at the Malibu Court House at a certain time and date. It was kind of a tense feeling but some relief came. It must have been a busy day in court. Those with violations for speeding under 60 mph were to stand before the bench and plea: "Guilty your honor." They were then to go to a certain window and pay the fine. My opinion? It could have been worse.

After one ticket, I decided to go to Traffic School so that my offense wouldn't appear on my record. I attended an all-day class and received such intense schooling on traffic rules, that I was continually after Carole for the slightest infraction that I observed whenever she took the wheel. At noontime, the class dismissed for a lunch break. In the class there was a member of my congregation. When he went home for lunch he said to his fourteen year old daughter, "Oh, Rev. Bos is in the class." Her reply was, "What's he in for?" My take on it? Nobody's perfect.

In conclusion, I have to say that I have always been considered to be a good driver. Occasionally people will even comment on it. I am not reckless. I try to be especially careful approaching intersections with traffic-light cameras. I try to be responsible, obey the laws, and pay attention to what I am doing, and not have my mind off in the clouds somewhere as preachers sometime may be accused of doing. Oh, Carole might call to my attention something that I missed like, "Do you know that you just went through that red light?" Or, sometimes on the freeway, Carole may remind me to drive faster. Maybe having been stopped six times and having received only four tickets for minor infractions in over fifty years of driving isn't too bad. Generally speaking, I know that good driving is every driver's responsibility to be alert and obey the laws. If we are ticketed, it's for the good. We learn from our mistakes and in so doing we make the roads a safer place for all.

Walking with My Shadow
or How to Choose a Hiking Partner
Bruce Calkins

"Who hikes with you?"
"You're not going to hike alone are you?"
I hear those questions a lot.

A hiking club would be nice – one that schedules hikes every week at times I can go. The Sierra Club does that, mostly for weekend hikes. There's a group from San Diego that hikes on Mondays. I met some of them one day. They left home at 5 a.m. and started up Ice House Canyon trail at 9. I met them at noon. They'd climbed 3,000 feet in 4½ miles. They had another 1,000 ft. and 1½ miles to go to reach Ontario Peak. It'd be 5:00 p.m. by the time they got back to their cars. That's a dedicated and crazy group – eight hours on the trail plus six hours of driving. You don't find many who do that regularly.

But, at least when someone asks, "Do you hike alone?" they have a good answer. I don't.

If you're hiking to get in shape in addition to other reasons—mystical, esthetic, childish, and macho reasons—then, you have to hike regularly and plan ahead. You'll need a companion who is just as organized and crazy as you and who has the same schedule. Otherwise, you'll be hiking alone most of the time.

When someone asks, "You don't hike by yourself do you?" it's nice to be able to say, "Not always."

So, how do you find a hiking companion?

There are wonderful trails that can be enjoyed by folks of almost all ages. And there are many people ready to go on these trails, <u>occasionally</u>. However, if you want someone to accompany you every week on a six to nine hour hike of ten or fifteen miles on steep trails at a pace that is neither too fast or too slow, good luck.

Using All the Colors

The first potential hiking companion is the one who is <u>dearest</u> to you. Hiking with a loved one can provide an ideal opportunity to spend time together and strengthen the bond—or not. It can work when the hike is moderate and when both parties enjoy hiking and each other.

If you go on a <u>strenuous</u> hike together, it's better for the female partner to have more endurance and speed than the male and for the male not to be bothered by this. When the man is urging his wife or girlfriend to come on a strenuous hike so she can discover how much fun it is, there are risks!

I've met happy couples on the trail; however, one sunny day, on the way down from a steep climb, I met a man on the way up—probably in his early 60's. We exchanged a friendly greeting. Around a curve, 50 yards behind was a woman about the same age. I said, "Great day for a hike." She spoke slowly and firmly, one word at a time. "So-I've-been-told."

There was another couple, probably mid 20's. I'd stopped for water and some trail mix on the saddle between Jones' Peak and Hasting's Peak. That's where they caught up with me. We'd climbed about 2,000 feet in three miles to reach this point. The last section was the steepest—900 ft. in 9/10^{ths} of a mile.

By his backpack and shoes, the young man appeared to be experienced in the ways of the trail—if not in the ways of love. He had a dog, and the <u>dog</u> had a backpack! The dog wasn't tired from the climb. The dog was well trained. He kept his eye on his owner-trainer, ready to follow. The young man knew how to train a dog to be an unquestioning follower. Why shouldn't it be just as easy to train the girl of his dreams? He started up a rough trail with an almost 45% incline. The dog followed. His girlfriend said, "Up <u>there</u>?!" Without looking back, he said, "It's only 100 yards." He has a lot to learn about relating to creatures who walk on two legs. It'll take more than a 100 yards to do that.

Well, if you can't find someone who can hike on your schedule, and your loved one can't be trained like your dog, I suggest <u>another</u>

Remembrances and Musings

hiking companion—one you can always <u>count</u> on on sunny days and moonlit nights. This companion is always silent—and sometimes out of sight. When I walk toward the sun or moon, I don't see him. (A Jungian therapist might be able to help me with that.)

When hiking up hill, I don't pay much attention to my shadow; because my <u>uphill</u> shadow looks like a tired old man. But my <u>downhill</u> shadow is <u>strong</u>! He strides with a sense of purpose! As the trail grows steeper, the shadow grows longer, showing the power of my hiking companion.

As I swing around a switchback, the shadow leaps from my left to my right and then back, never stumbling (unless I do). It's a graceful dance. Taller and stronger, then shorter with greater intimacy, gliding from one side to the other.

No, I'm not alone.

   I have a companion who is ready when I'm ready,
      hikes at the same pace,
         goes the same distance.

And my companion <u>never</u> says, "Up <u>there</u>?!"

Recipes Through Time
Annabelle Dirks

Visiting relatives in Southern Illinois was part of my summer ritual as a young child. One special memory was sitting on a stool in the kitchen of my cousin's grandmother watching her make pies. No recipes or measuring equipment—just a wooden table top and rolling pin. She took a lump of lard and worked flour into it as needed, rolled out the pastry crust, filled it with whatever fruit was in season, and added a handful of sugar and spices. The finished products were always perfect and delicious.

One summer, we visited an aunt, Viola Bell, a professor at what was then Iowa State College in Ames. She and her colleague were developing standardized measurements for recipe ingredients. She invited our family of 5 to a chicken dinner at the college, prepared by her students. The only request they made was for each of us to carefully save all the bones, skin, or inedible parts of the fowl so they could be weighed—to figure out how much of the chicken was waste. My father was intrigued by the event and pleased to hear the results—that half the chicken was waste.

My aunt's students were also busy compiling a recipe file using exact measures for each ingredient. I was given the "Bell recipe file" (as it was called) as a wedding present and I used it for years. As I look back, I think my mother had only one recipe book, the *Fannie Farmer Cookbook*. She rarely used it except for cakes and an occasional odd recipe.

Cookbooks reflect the time period in which they became popular. During my years at *Good Housekeeping Magazine*, right after WWII, I did a lot of work on a new cookbook, which was written to appeal to the housewives who were preparing evening meals, often from scratch, for their entire families. For example, when my family was growing up, I often used *The Joy of Cooking*, *Better Homes and Gardens*, and *Betty Crocker* recipe books.

It seems to me every women's church or social group has published favorite recipes in book form and sold them for fundraisers. Many of the church recipes featured covered dishes, casseroles, and remarkable layered gelatin salads—great items for church potlucks—often humorously referred to by Garrison Keillor in his *Prairie Home Companion* monologues.

Later, there were also all the ethnic and gourmet recipe books. When I left India, some of my friends put together pages and pages of handwritten Indian favorites. Alas, they neglected to send along a cook to do all the chopping and grinding required for those Indian delicacies.

As I've been whittling down my collection of books, I've come across many scrawled notes of recipes I've enjoyed. The days are long gone when, as prescribed in my old Mennonite cookbooks, recipes called for enormous amounts of butter, cream, sugar, and salt. Old cookbooks show how our eating habits have been transformed. Today, pre-packaged dinners and prepared salads and entrees are numerous—some healthy alternatives and some not so healthy—but I applaud the changes that have come with our emphasis on organically grown foods, buying at Farmer's Markets, and having low-fat, low-carb, and low-salt diets.

However, I do remember Grandma's cherry pie—made with lard—with guilty nostalgia.

The Chinese Rugs
Annabelle Dirks

I was only three, but a vivid picture is still with me; the day the Chinese rugs arrived at our Chicago home. My father's older brother had been on a trip to China and at my father's request had ordered rugs for the entire downstairs of our large Victorian house. The picture in my head is the sight of the shipment, carefully wrapped, lying in a huge pile on the parlor floor and the excitement in the air. I loved those rugs.

A few years after my father's death, my mother downsized the house and decided to part with the rugs. I was thrilled to receive the very large rug that had been in the dining room, another 9x12 from the library, and two smaller ones. My own children loved them too. When we were called to India, I decided to sell the largest rug although with a heavy heart.

Years later, we returned to Connecticut. One evening, we attended a theater production at the Long Wharf Theater near New Haven. The play was Eugene O'Neill's *Long Day's Journey into Night*. When the stage curtain opened, I stared at the setting. There was my Chinese rug. I actually sprang to my feet and, rather too loudly, proclaimed "That's my rug!"

Needless to say, I bought my rug back for considerably more money than I had received when I sold it. All of the rugs were happily on our floors—from Connecticut to St. Louis to Santa Cruz, California. Now they reside at my son's apartment in New York City and a third generation enjoys them. There are a few spots that look rather worn but that just adds luster to their endurance and beauty.

Laundry in the Arctic
Art French

My wife, Carolyn, and I began our ministry in Alaska working for the Board of National Missions of the Presbyterian Church. We lived on Saint Lawrence Island which is located in the Bering Sea, 800 miles north of the Aleutian Islands. Vitus Bering, the Danish navigator, discovered it while exploring the north Pacific in the 18th Century. The island was approximately 190 miles over open water due west of Nome on the Seward Peninsula of mainland Alaska.

During our second three-year term, we lived in the Eskimo village of Savoonga, population 250. The Frenches and the Bureau of Indian Affairs government school teachers were the only two non-Eskimo families. At that time there was no plane service to Savoonga from the mainland. Travel from Savoonga to Gambell, an island village with airplane service, was by outboard motor powered, walrus-hide covered boat in the summer, and dog team in the winter. For the U.S. Postal Service, Savoonga was the last dog team mail rural route in the entire country.

Our home in Savoonga was a small apartment attached to the church building. The first floor had an office, bathroom, large storage room, kitchen and living room. Upstairs was a small bedroom and a half-bedroom. The rest was a large attic which extended over the multipurpose room and sanctuary. There was no running water or 24-hour electricity.

So, what was laundry day like in the arctic? Two part story. Two seasons.

Let's start with a summertime specialized wash day. The woolen clothes took a cold water Woolite wash. Out our back door and across the tundra for a short distance was a rushing creek fed by snow melt from the mountains inland from the village. Perfect for doing a large Woolite cold water washing. We gathered up all

Using All the Colors

our wool socks, long johns, pants and shirts and trudged across the tundra to the creek. We took a large tub in which to do the laundry. The temperature on a warm, sunny day would be in the 50's. After everything had been washed we lugged it home to hang and dry.

What was it like doing the laundry in the winter? The process would begin several days before the actual wash day with getting the water. I would put our large copper kettle, with the wide top, on the cast iron stove in the kitchen. The entire stove top surface was hot. Then I would put on my winter gear and go out for snow. If I had used up stored snow blocks, I would go away from the buildings to find clean snow and begin hauling in buckets of snow to fill up the copper container on the stove. You would be surprised how little water a tub full of dry snow makes or how many times it had to be jammed packed with snow before we had a tub full of water!

At this time in our family, we had two children in diapers; real cloth diapers, remember? We had a large enamel diaper pail with a lid. Even so, a week's worth of dirty diapers for two kids got pretty ripe before wash day.

Wash day began with a prayer to the god of all mechanical things as I started to wrestle with our 1500 watt Kohler engine. Was there enough oil in it? Did the spark plugs need cleaning? Was the fan belt good enough for another run? What if the radiator started to leak? My seminary training was sorely lacking in "Electrical Engines 101"!

When the engine was finally running and we had electricity, we rolled the washing machine into the kitchen and actually began washing the clothes. Nice whites first, then light colors, and finally, dark colors. We rinsed in the galvanized tub and kept filling the large copper kettle with snow so we could have enough clean water for all the wash. Second cycle, diapers: Two kids sure can use a lot of diapers in a week!

Then the drying. The diapers got the hottest place in the room because they needed to get dry the fastest. Other clothes were taken up to the little half-bedroom because the stove pipe went up through that space and was exposed. Finally, heavier clothes were hung in the attic where they froze until there was room for them where there was heat for them to finish drying.

So, as the winter sun begins to set around 2:00pm, the faithful little engine that could is stilled, and we light the evening lamps, our rest comes with the satisfaction of another day's work well done.

The words of a hymn of long ago remembered from Sunday evening Christian Endeavor meetings comes to mind:

> *Now the day is over,*
> *Night is drawing nigh,*
> *Shadows of the evening*
> *Steal across the sky.*
> *Jesus give the weary*
> *Calm and sweet repose;*
> *With thy tenderest blessing*
> *May mine eyelids close.*

Operating on Autopilot is Highly Unpredictable

Don Hawthorne

Some years ago now, but since we came to Monte Vista, my doctor at USC asked me to get an MRI in the USC Imaging Center. Because it was a closed-type of machine, and being a bit claustrophobic, I asked the doctor for <u>a</u> pill to keep me calm in the tube. For no known reason <u>he gave me TWO</u>! And thereby hangs this tale. On the morning of the appointment I took one pill, and my wife, Lee, drove me down Huntington Drive to the USC Medical Campus.

When I got there, I expressed my concern to the technician that I had 35 surgical staples in my abdomen and wondered if that would create any problems in the MRI. To be cautious, they opted to call the hospital in Santa Barbara where I had picked up the staples during surgery a few years before. It took them well over 45 minutes to get the answer, and I became concerned whether my calming pill would still be working effectively after waiting for over two hours, so I decided to take the <u>second</u> pill just to be safe.

Needless to say, I had <u>no problem at all</u> during the MRI! After it had finished, Lee observed that I was weaving, and seemed to be spaced out, so she undertook to guide me back to the car in the parking lot. We came to a stairway with a ramp beside it. I opted for the stairway, but Lee took charge and we used the ramp. She got me into the car and we headed home. Presently, for no known reason, I started to recite the Christmas Story from Luke 2: "And there were in the same country, shepherds, abiding in the field, keeping watch over their flocks—by night. And lo, the angel of the Lord came upon them..." Well, you know how it goes. I completed the quote with the shepherds eventually coming with haste and finding Mary and Joseph... and the babe, lying in a manger.

Lee indulged me and let me work my way to the end. But I then began to whole thing over again. After the second round, Lee says she suggested that that was enough, but she tells me that I proceeded to go through it all for the third time, and she gave up trying to slow me down.

Eventually we arrived back at the Grove and she parked the car by the long walk that goes by our house between A Street and B Street. She came around and opened the door for me to get out, but I sat and looked up at her and said, "My bottom is heavy!" (Translation: "I can't move on my own.") With some effort she got me up and into the house, guided me to the bedroom where I fell like a log across the bed and did not stir. In alarm she called the pharmacist and told the medical facts. He told her I would likely sleep the rest of the day and night.

A week before all of this took place, I had set up an appointment with a Fuller Seminary student for his <u>first</u> session with me for Spiritual Direction on the afternoon of my MRI. He arrived at the appointed time and rang the bell. Lee met him and explained the situation and said I would not be able to see him that day. From the bedroom a raised voice said, "No, I'm O.K., and I'll see him!!"

The next morning, I was troubled by a vague sense that I had seen someone with a beard the day before, and I asked Lee if there had been anybody fitting that description at the house. When she told me that I had indeed seen such a person and had gone through with the appointment, I was horrified. I called the man and apologized profusely, and asked if I had said anything. His gracious reply was, "Yes... but I did sense that you were operating on automatic pilot." We proceeded to set up another appointment.

Do You Journal?
Laura Berthold Monteros

Last week, when Anna, our facilitator, presented this as one of the questions we could write about, I thought about my own journaling habits and how they had changed in the past six months.

I've been journaling pretty regularly for the past twenty years. "Regularly" means a few times a week, with an occasional week or two of blank pages. This doesn't mean my mind was a blank or I had nothing to write about; sometimes I was just overly busy or too tired to put words on paper. Other times…well, I'll get to that later.

First I wrote by hand in 6" x 9" spiral-bound notebooks. Writing by hand has always been tedious for me—I hold my pen too tight and my hand cramps—but there is something very direct about holding a pen and pulling it across lined paper, watching the ink lay down swirls and lines and dots.

I often found it difficult to read what I wrote, however, because my handwriting is such a bird's nest. I write too big, I swoop too much, I use abbreviations and initials that I just *know* I will remember and then forget. It's also difficult to run through handwritten journals to find an entry to pinpoint the date of an event or dig up an idea for a story that I sketched out.

I started writing on the computer in 2003. This was a much faster way to get my thoughts down, much easier to read, and happily searchable. Sometimes I write about things I did that day, usually nothing momentous, and sometimes about my children or other people. I'm afraid most of my entries are rants about the unfairness of life or complaints about things I can't control. They're nothing my children will find helpful or interesting or even revealing when I die, no beautiful poetry or elegant philosophy and very little incisive theology. Nothing that will give any insight into any of my finer qualities, which I assume I have.

Remembrances and Musings

But what is odd about my journaling, something I'm trying to figure out and can't quite touch, is why I write so little when so much is going on in my life. When I most need to let the words flow like tears, I stiffen my upper lip instead. When my mind is racing and thoughts are scattering like buckshot and writing them down one-by-one would bring order, I can't get the words on paper. When so much is happening or has happened that the only way I will remember what I am thinking or feeling, or what in order things occurred, or who said what—then I can't even make it to the keyboard.

This has happened often enough that I don't worry about it. I write down notes or maybe make a list on the computer of what I need to write about, and in a week or two I get to it.

But for the past five months, I have barely opened the folder on my computer labeled "Journals". Since December 1, I have written only five entries. One was the day after my mother died and was more factual than thoughtful. Three of the others were nothing—a few paragraphs about how I hadn't written and needed to. One was a quote from a daily calendar. The last entry was February 25.

This is so puzzling to me. If there was ever a time to unload, debrief, cogitate, philosophize, weep, record, it's been the past four months. My mother died. I had to make all the arrangements for her care before she passed and all the arrangements for the removal of her body when she went. I handled almost all the memorial arrangements, all the cemetery arrangements, all the legal paperwork, everything that must be done when a person dies. Though my daughter kept my mother's books, I was the one responsible for her finances and medical bills, and I was the one responsible for having her final tax returns done and writing the checks to the government.

My inheritance was her home, and just getting that in shape to rent was an undertaking of much more labor, time, and money

Using All the Colors

than I could have imagined. The entire process gave me plenty to write about.

Yet I haven't written in my journal for two months. Not one word.

When my life is the most stressful or complicated, I close myself off from other people. I was raised to be independent, emotionally as well as financially, not to depend on others. I don't think this is very successful, because I end up complaining a lot, rather than sharing the inner turmoil that's at the root of the complaints.

In this case, perhaps I have shut myself off from myself.

Everything has changed since my mother's death. I don't know why or what, I just know it has. Dynamics of some sort, the kind that are deep in the guts of the machine, have changed. The changes are both imperceptible and inescapable.

Perhaps I'm not yet ready to explore the inner workings of my psyche in the aftermath, I'm not ready to organize my thoughts and feelings and put them on the proper shelves and in the proper drawers. Perhaps, being swept up in the tidal wave of things to do, I haven't been able to swim to shore. And maybe, maybe, I just need to tell myself to sit down at the computer, open up a document, and begin.

Are You a Swooper or a Basher?
Laura Berthold Monteros

Kurt Vonnegut put writers into two categories: swoopers and bashers. In his semi-serious, semi-truthful semi-memoir *Timequake*, Vonnegut spends a semi-chapter describing swoopers and bashers.

"Swoopers write a story quickly, higgledy-piggledy, crinkum-crankum, any which way," he explains. "Then they go over it again painstakingly, fixing everything that is just plain awful or doesn't work."

Most women are swoopers, he says. Most men are bashers.

"Bashers go one sentence at a time, getting it exactly right before they go on to the next one. When they're done, they're done."

Kurt Vonnegut is a basher. This may surprise anyone who's read *Slaughterhouse-Five*, which jumps around in time. It seems to me it would have needed a rather extensive outline or maybe a graph of the places his protagonist, Billy Pilgrim, unexpectedly found himself in.

I used to be a swooper. I am now a basher. I don't want to be a basher anymore. I want to get back on that free flight where words and ideas just pour out without concern for misspellings, typos, or exact grammar. I was a swooper when I was writing for a newspaper long time ago.

We had these long rolls of yellow paper, two or three sheets wrapped together with carbon in between. I pulled the cut end through the typewriter and stared at the yellow paper for a few seconds or minutes, forming the story in my mind, trying out various wordings, setting up a mental outline.

Then I would go at it, getting down every single thing I wanted to report every word someone had said in an interview, every fact or observation. Essentially what I did was transcribe all

Using All the Colors

the notes in my steno pad and interweave them with my own words to make a readable story. I had to get everything down quickly, before I forgot and before my deadline.

When I was done, I typed -30-, took a pica pole and tore off the paper at the end. I would read what I had written and then slash and burn. I took out whole sentences or even paragraphs, changed the word order, used a better word here or fewer words there, tightened up the writing, corrected typos, circled paragraphs and drew an arrow to where I wanted them to be or marked insertion points with numbers.

I would retype the whole thing, proof it for errors and mark them, and give it to my editor. I rarely had to do more than a second draft. The typesetters made the minor corrections my editor and I indicated and a night editor read the copy once more when it was pasted onto the cardboard pages before being prepared for print.

There was another reason I was a swooper.

Typing was a lot of work, and the keys stuck frequently because I don't have an even rhythm. If I made a mistake that I wanted to correct at the time, I had to stop and erase it with one of those roller erasers with a tiny whisk broom or a gritty grey eraser stick, and brush off the dust, making sure it didn't get in the ribbon or keys. If there was a carbon, that had to be corrected, too. White out wasn't any faster, but it looked better and didn't tear a hole in the paper.

Both methods were very effective at interrupting the flow of writing and required a few moments to get the juices going again, so swooping was much more efficient than bashing.

What turned me into a basher was the computer.

With a computer, backing up and making corrections is easy. I am doing it right now. I don't try to improve my typing, because I can correct as I write or go back and easily change the mistakes. I can move the paragraphs around while I'm putting them together, just like a mason building a river rock wall tries out different stones to get the right fit as he lays the wall.

The problem with bashing—at least for me—is that I'm concentrating so much on getting everything *just right* as I type that sometimes I lose a word or an idea or my train of thought derails entirely. I spend too much time forming a sentence before I'm exactly sure what the paragraph is going to say. I'm moving around paragraphs before I am sure what I want the page to convey.

I find myself asking the same questions more frequently instead of establishing the answers before I hit the first keys: What is the overall arc of this story? What do I really want to communicate? Do I want to put in this quote, leave it out, or use it elsewhere?

All those questions are answered in one fell *swoop* when I swoop and make the adjustments later. There's the satisfaction of holding the first draft in my hand and manually penciling in the changes I want, *seeing* the words and phrases as they will appear to a reader.

Bashing takes longer than swooping, I think. It also robs posterity of those valued first, second, third, and fourth drafts that literati love to pore over, because I can make the corrections in the original document and save them as though the whole thing came from my keyboard in one fell *swoop*.

I want to be a swooper again. I want to let the words pour out unhindered, unworried about mistakes. I need to discipline myself to be lazy about typos, grammar, and spelling. I want to forgo backspacing and *swoop* once again. Instead of it being a point of pride when the spell check doesn't find any mistakes, I should be dismayed that I was such a perfectionist.

Well, maybe next week.

Lured of the Rings
Gene Terpstra

From my earliest days, rings held a fascination for me. This was not because rings were prominent in our family, but probably because they were virtually absent. The only ring I remember in our family of 7 is my mother's diamond ring. I don't think my dad even had a wedding band, although I don't know why not. He was not posing as an unattached man for any woman who might be interested, and there was never a question for anyone about my dad's marital status or his faithfulness to my mother. Not having a wedding band probably had more to do with my parents' financial circumstances when they were married than with any disinclination my father had to wearing one.

The scarcity of money was an unspoken factor in the dearth of rings—and of any extraneous items—in the family. Supporting five children as a barber during the depression left no money to spend on anything that couldn't be eaten or worn on our bodies. My dad wouldn't have known the word "bauble," but its meaning would certainly have expressed his view about rings.

Rings, and anything other than the most modest jewelry, also had a worldly connotation. They suggested vanity and indulgence. Good Christian women didn't exhibit such attachments or attitudes. Rather, "women should dress themselves modestly and decently in suitable clothing, not with their hair braided, or with gold, pearls, or expensive clothes, but with good works, as is proper for women who profess reverence for God." This was not advice from a "Dear Abby" of the day, but from the Apostle Paul writing to Timothy about proper Christian behavior in the churches. This would have been an appropriate description of my sisters and my mother. They didn't even wear lipstick or nail polish. Apparently, jewelry and fancy clothes weren't an indulgence among men in Paul's time, but *they* weren't off the hook, either. Holiness was to be their adornment. Paul writes in the same passage to Timothy, "in every place men should pray, lifting up holy hands without anger or argument." (I Tim. 2:9-10, 8) But it was precisely the connotation of prosperity and worldly status that made rings so fascinating to me as a boy, although I couldn't have expressed that at the time. (Besides, Paul didn't say that the "holy hands" men lifted up couldn't have rings on them.)

My mother rarely went shopping. One reason was scarcity of money, but another was her genuine commitment to frugality and to simplicity regarding possessions. A refrain that followed her occasional shopping trips downtown was, "I never saw so many things I didn't need." Most of my mother's shopping was done through the Sears and the Montgomery-Ward catalogues, both of which we received at home. I loved to look at the catalogues. I wasn't interested in clothes. In those late depression days clothes were simply a necessity, not a fashion statement or a status symbol. Anyone attempting to market a "designer label" would quickly have become another failed business of the times. Clothing styles ranged from practical to practical, so choice was simply a matter of size and color.

But I *was* interested in men's rings. I was fascinated by the substantial, expensive-looking gold rings shown in living color on the catalogue pages. What captured my attention were not those with stones (which didn't seem manly), but those with a kind of diamond-shaped emblem on their face. My age and lack of money left these rings in a dream world, but I imagined a day when I would actually wear one. It wasn't until much later that I learned my dream ring bore the Masonic symbol, an irony in our household where secret societies like the masons were viewed with suspicion.

Among several other firsts of my ninth summer, I got my first ring. That was the middle of U.S. involvement in World War II. Our family spent the summer camping at Lake Michigan in Muskegon, where my father worked in a factory that made engines for army tanks. Life was spartan, with no indulgences and even fewer material possessions than we had at home. My ring was the

Using All the Colors

exception for me, though it had a decidedly subdued glory. I probably bought my ring in the dime store, a merchant that matched my meager money. The ring was made of very light-weight metal that before long turned my finger green underneath the ring. The band was not an unbroken circle, but two strips that came together at the bottom without joining. This allowed the band to be made smaller or larger, a genuinely one-size-fits-all design.

My brother Dave, two years younger, didn't have a ring and he wanted one. He began importuning me to give mine to him. I don't know what he offered in exchange for mine, if anything, but I was not about to part with my ring. He tells the story that I said I would give him my ring if he ate a handful of beach sand. I have no memory of such a proposal, but I can imagine saying that, thinking my ring safe against such so unlikely an event. Dave says he did eat a handful of sand (he must have shared my ring lust!), but that I refused to give him my ring anyway. I don't think my ring survived the summer, but Dave's story did. He still tells it occasionally at family gatherings, a bit of sinister history of his minister older brother.

I got my second ring the following year. I was an avid listener to Tom Mix, a late-afternoon cowboy radio show. In one of Tom's adventures he used a whistling ring. I don't know what use Tom could have for a whistling ring out on the lone prairie, but he probably used it somehow to capture bad guys. When he offered it to his listeners for a quarter and a box top from Shredded Ralston, I didn't waste any time. I waited eagerly for my ring, looking at the mail every day for that special package from Tom. One day at lunch my older brother, a high school student, stood up, blew on something in his hand, and I heard a little siren-like sound. It rose and fell with each breath he blew into the little pinwheel. My whistling ring! Vern was laughing, but I felt betrayed. He was making a joke of my secret bond with Tom Mix. I jumped up and demanded my ring, but he kept out of reach, laughing and continuing to blow that tiny siren. He finally relinquished it, probably out of breath from blowing and laughing. The whistling ring had worked for Tom Mix, but he never warned his youthful listeners what might happen if a bad guy got hold of it.

I was a high school senior when I got my next ring, a class ring. This was a real ring, gold, with onyx on the face flanked by 2 narrow strips of pearl and surmounted by a tiny gold Indian head, our school emblem. I loved it. It was worth the wait, but I didn't wear it very long. I was in love with Alice and we were soon going steady. We exchanged rings. Hers was a much smaller version of mine and I wore it on my little finger. She wore mine on her hand, too, with the help of a lot of tape to keep it from falling off. It didn't fall off, but it did disappear. Sometime during our freshman year in college she left it in the woman's rest room. She returned as soon as she realized she didn't have it, but it was gone. She was as remorseful as I was sad at the loss, but I still had Alice. I didn't realize the prophetic symbolism of the lost ring. I lost Alice before long, too. Not in a woman's rest room, but in a rooming house in Raleigh, North Carolina, the following summer. I was staying there while on a work crew when I received Alice's Dear John letter.

My next, and last, ring came five years later. It was the simplest and most enduring of all the rings of my real and fantasy life; I still wear it. This ring, too, has a mysterious symbol, but it is visible only inside the band: "14K Artcarved." The mysterious sigma means gold, so the skin underneath doesn't turn green. The band isn't adjustable; the ring is for me, not just anyone. It can't produce a little siren noise. The only sound it makes is when it is dropped. It bears no letters or emblems. It is a narrow band, remarkable only in its simplicity. It has been companion to the past 53 years of my life in all settings and circumstances, bearing mute witness to those years by transforming the original unblemished shine to a soft luster.

It is my wedding band.

News of the Day

Jacquie Terpstra

She sits on the front porch steps in the late afternoon sun. Out of boredom she waits. Finally he comes, cutting across the lawn on his bike, (a good thing that her father doesn't see that). He is so cute and today, he says, "Hi" before handing her the newspaper. She will have to tell her friend, Martha, that he actually spoke to her. Still smiling, she watches him ride off, then opens the paper and starts to read the inside back page, the funnies. The funnies are always first, then she turns to other sections of interest. She learned to read with the funnies, picking out the simple words first, and guessing other words aided by the drawings themselves.

On July 23, 2009 the headline read, *Farewell, Ann Arbor*. It was the last edition of the Ann Arbor *News*. Yes, there would be a reduced edition of the Sunday paper, but the paper's daily provision of the news would now be accessed only online. It was the end of a hundred-and-seventy-four year history of providing a newspaper to people living in Southeastern Michigan.

It began in 1835 as the Michigan *Argus* which later became the *Courier*. Other names followed: *True Democrat, Daily Times, Daily Argus, Daily Times News*, and finally, in 1937, The Ann Arbor *News*. Now it is found as www.AnnArbor.com. In all of those years and under all of these names, the paper missed printing only twice. The first was during the newspaper strike of 1958 and the second was due to the blizzard of 1978.

As the years passed, she would learn to rely on this paper for news of high school events, including articles where her own name or picture appeared. Later, she would search the society pages for news of friends' and classmates' engagements and marriages. The April 3, 1958 edition announced her own engagement and six months later, her wedding. After her class had graduated from high school and everyone had gone their separate ways, it was a good way to keep track of some of the major events in their lives. The announcement of the birth of her three children appeared there, and many years later, the death of her parents. Many more years later, the deaths of classmates would begin to appear.

This was the paper where she periodically saw photos of her handsome older brother in his white-scarfed aviator's uniform as World War II progressed, the photos of the lethal mushroom clouds hovering over the cities of Hiroshima and Nagasaki, and in an extra edition, the headline that announced the end of World War II. She followed the progress north of our forces in Korea on a little map that regularly appeared in the paper, read of the breakthrough development of the Salk polio vaccine, election results, sports' scores, and the comparatively mundane ads for the Sears Roebuck, Montgomery Ward, Kresge and Woolworth stores. It was the sports page or garden section that carried the specials at the locally-owned Schlenker's Hardware and Hertler Bros. Feed and Garden Store, the latter two having been founded by members of German immigrant families who settled in the town in the latter half of the 1800s. Even after she moved away, the paper continued to be a source of information to her through the articles sent by her family and friends.

Wherever she lived, the sight of the daily paper waiting on her doorstep brought a sense of peaked interest and anticipation, and if it wasn't there, the day wouldn't be complete until the problem of the missing paper had been solved. Over the years she would get her news from the Armed Forces' *Stars and Stripes*, The Detroit *News*, the St. Louis *Post Dispatch*, the Los Angeles *Times*, the Sacramento *Bee*, the Bergen *Record*, and the New York *Times*. It was in the *Post Dispatch* that she read of the first space flight circling the earth. During the late '60's she once again followed the progress of a war on a map, this one appearing in the Los Angles *Times*. This time her interest was largely driven by another brother on active duty. This one serving as an army surgeon in Viet Nam.

Using All the Colors

Across the country and many years later, it was the New York *Times* where she read the carefully-researched obituaries of those who lost their lives on 9/11. On September 12th, the day after the trade towers collapsed, she first saw Thomas E. Franklin's iconic photo of the firemen raising the American flag over the rubble of the World Trade Center. It appeared first in his employer's paper, the Bergen *Record*. The following day, it was printed worldwide, and became a symbol of our nation's resolve to recover and rebuild.

Over the centuries, newspapers have often had intriguing or puzzling names. *Enquirer* seems appropriate, but what about *Plain Dealer*, *Bee*, *Blade*, *Constitution*, or *Times Picayune*? Picayune? One can only wonder at the intent of giving a newspaper a name meaning, "of little importance or paltry". Taken literally, it wouldn't bring in much revenue. Perhaps one of the most interesting is the name given to the Lubbock, Texas paper, the *Avalanche Journal*. Whoever settled upon that name had to be longing for distant climates and snow-capped mountain vistas.

Once again, she steps out onto her porch savoring the Southern California morning. She lifts the paper off of the step, grateful for its tactile presence in her hand, and returns to her kitchen. No longer needing to hurry to work, she has the pleasure of enjoying her morning coffee while catching up on the morning's news, but first she turns to the funnies.

The Art of the Pie
Jacquie Terpstra

The other morning, in preparation for my husband, Gene's, 75th birthday celebration, Kaitlin, our granddaughter, and I baked a lemon meringue pie together. Kaitlin did most of the preparation with an occasional word of instruction from me. We would have to confess that we taste-tested the lemon filling and pronounced it delicious. It was made from freshly picked lemons that Kaitlin had brought from home. There were a few scraps of pastry dough left over after the pie was made, so we made them into little jam turnovers as a cook's treat. That was a trick that I learned from my mother. This wasn't Kaitlin's and my first cooking venture together, and I hope that it won't be the last as it is a pleasant experience for both of us.

My Grandma Whitecotton was known for her wonderful and plentiful pies. As the mother of ten children living in the area, she spent Saturdays baking in preparation for their visit on Sundays. My mother said that Grandma always baked eleven pies at a time: eight fruit pies and three with cream filling. On Sunday, she rested and enjoyed her family. Was all of this pie-baking done in a state-of-the-art kitchen? Oh no, Grandma worked in a kitchen that had a sink with a pump, an iron range that burned either wood or coal, a large table covered with oilcloth, and something that is commonly known as a *Hoosier Hutch*. It was a green one-piece cupboard unit that had a white porcelain work surface with storage above and below. It also had a pull-down shutter, much like those on a roll-top desk. I suppose the shutter was meant to hide any evidence of food preparation. In addition it had a really unique feature, a built-in flour bin with a sifter attached. I've seen Hoosier Hutches a couple of times in antique shops and always thought that it would be fun to own one. However, I have a perfect picture of Grandma's in my mind's eye. It somehow seems appropriate that when Grandma

Using All the Colors

suffered the stroke that preceded her death, she was reaching into her flour bin to make pancakes for Grandpa's breakfast.

Cooking or baking with someone seems to provide an opportunity for storytelling as well as for creating something good to eat. While we were working, I told Kaitlin about my first experience baking a pie. It happened before I was three years old. I don't remember it, but I remember my mother telling the story. I was at my Grandma's and she was baking pies. She let me stand on a chair beside her while she rolled out the pie dough. Apparently, she had given me a little piece of dough to work with also. After pounding my dough to grubby flatness, she said that I suddenly got down from my chair and, without saying a word, ran out into the back yard. After a bit, I came back with three green concord grapes and plunked them down on my dough. I don't know what Grandma did to sweeten that truly tart creation of mine, but I've heard that my independent search for an just the right pie filling gave her a chuckle.

Working and reminiscing with Kaitlin prompted me to recall other pie-baking experiences. My mother made wonderful pies, often apple or pumpkin. If we enjoyed this treat in the evening, my father always asked for a piece with his breakfast the following morning. He didn't seem to think that there was anything unusual about having dessert with his breakfast. My mother may have used lard for the crust when my parents lived on their farm, but by the time that I came along, she used a canned shortening called "Spry". She made a lot of good things with Spry. Of course this was before the era of differentiating good fats from bad fats. I have a feeling that Spry was in the latter category. While going through a box of keepsakes years after my mother's death, I found a tattered and food-stained copy of her Spry cookbook. Looking through it, I experienced an intense moment of overwhelming grief and longing for a time, now past; for that warm kitchen and that woman at the helm of her stove.

I don't know how it happened that I learned to bake pies while still a teenager, because I wasn't particularly interested in learning to cook at that time. On one occasion when my mother was in Chicago visiting my sister, my father went to the farmers' market and brought home some of our favorite apples, Northern Spies. He suggested that I make some apple sauce. I had no idea how to make apple sauce so I made an apple pie instead. I'm sure that my father was more than happy with the substitution. On another occasion, I made a pie for a friend and took it to his dorm for his birthday. As I recall, he seemed quite surprised and a little at a loss as to how to respond. Later he told me that he and his roommate ate the whole thing and every bite was delicious. That was response enough for me.

By the time I married, Crisco was the leading canned shortening, and I switched to making pie crusts using the recipe on the Crisco label. I've used that recipe all of my married life, but lately I've noticed that the crust is not quite as flakey as it used to be. After pondering the problem for a while, I decided that the change was due to Crisco itself. Gone are the palm oil and other bad fats, and in their place are vegetable oils that render Crisco a more healthy food. Whatever made the crust flakey and light went out with the bad fats. I detect the difference, but thankfully, most people enjoying one of my pies don't seem to notice.

When our children were young, I tried to make holidays special for them and that usually involved special food. They loved the month of February because it began with a chocolate-cake-and-whipped-cream Lincoln log on the 12th of the month. That was quickly followed on the 14th with chocolate cupcakes decorated with frosting and red cinnamon hearts for Valentine's Day. Of course the winner of this "triple crown" was the cherry pie in honor of our first president. That still is a favorite of both my husband and son.

I've worked with my daughters baking pies for holidays and other special occasions. The last time was a year ago when Karen and I baked apple and pumpkin pies together for Thanksgiving. I have even been asked for advice long distance when my daughters were in the middle of a pie-baking project on their own. When Wendy was a teenager, she and her friend Susan went through a phase of making cherry pies with a lattice crust. On one summer day, they decided to take their mothers on a picnic and made one of their cherry pies for dessert. We drove to Woodland, California from Sacramento, carefully protecting the pie and its fragile crust from damage. I don't remember the rest of the menu but the pie was delicious, and for the moms, the tender memory of that picnic was to be savored most.

Now, working with Kaitlin, pie-baking is a time for passing on tradition and for storytelling. It has also been a time for questions and the best answers that I could come up with at the moment. In times past, it had been such things as, "How much flour do I use?" or, "How do I keep the dough from sticking to the rolling pin?" or, "How do I fix this tear in the dough?" On this occasion the questions had advanced to, "How do we make the meringue?" Then, out of the depths of casual conversation, "How come you and Papa have stayed married when so many other people have gotten divorced?" How to answer truthfully when the reasons are complex and perhaps not even completely understood by me? I may have said something like commitment or covenant, loving each other, sometimes loving even in the absence of liking, caring about the unity of our family, or the understanding gained from experience that things can change. But I guess that what was foremost on my mind that particular day was that a lasting and loving marriage is full of second chances. In our experience; with prayer, the will for reconciliation and forgiveness will come, and will bring hope for the best outcome. The tear in that crust can be mended.

Pasin
Dot Turnbull

After fifteen years in Egypt, Bob and I and our five children were assigned to Thailand where we served for 20 years. We had many new things to learn. One of them was the pasin.

The pasin is a very important item of women's clothing in Thailand. It is a length of cloth, about two meters, which comes in many colors and patterns. It is sewn together along one edge to form a tube. It is worn by putting it over your head and dropping it down to cover your body. It is held in place by folding and wrapping it tightly around and twisting and tucking the top edge to keep it in place. It is very versatile and can be used as a skirt worn with a blouse or it can serve as a bathrobe, bath washcloth, and a dressing room.

Many Thai homes in the villages do not have the luxury of separate rooms for sleeping, dressing, or bathing. The pasin provides privacy for all these activities. By tying the pasin just under your arm pits you are covered. When taking a bath (which sometimes takes place in front of the house or wherever there is a jar of water or a river) you take your dipper, a small plastic bowl with which you can dip the water and splash it over your body which gets your pasin wet and allows you to use it as a wash cloth. You can soap up with the soap you brought in your bowl and then scrub using the pasin. You rinse off by dipping and splashing more water over your body. Then you slip on a dry pasin by dropping it quickly over your head and letting the wet one drop to the ground. If done properly you are never exposed naked. Then holding the pasin in your teeth you can get dressed in your private dressing room which may or may not become your skirt.

In 1969 I was planning to attend my first National Women's Conference. A number of women from the Farm and from Chiang Rai Presbytery were planning to go. A few days before we went,

Subin, the village girl who helped me in the house, told me that I needed to learn how to get out of a wet pasin and into a dry one. We practiced until she thought I could do it and I was very thankful that we had.

At the Conference we were staying at a Christian school, sleeping in the classrooms on mattresses on the floor and under mosquito nets tied to the wall and to strings stretched down the length of the room. There were 10 to 20 in the room. Our bathing place was the pig pen that had a cement floor and had been scrubbed clean. Two rows of large jars were lined up and filled with water by hose. Thai custom demanded bathing before dinner so with about 200 women at the conference the pig pen was a busy place. Two or three women were using the same jar, dipping and splashing to say nothing of those in the second row that might overthrow when wetting their backs and help you with yours.

It was a great experience and I was very thankful for Subin's instruction.

Using All the Colors

The Next Step

Using All the Colors

An Old Fiddle
Robert Bos

"What? I can't believe it." I'm too young for this." Such was my reaction when I received a phone call informing me that I had received the 2001 Older American award presented by both the City of Westlake Village and the County of Los Angeles. The plaques stated that these awards were in recognition of volunteer services rendered to the community by sharing my ability, knowledge and experience and giving freely of my time and energy to enrich the entire community. The fact is that I didn't think of myself as being in the "older" age bracket. I was only 72. When Carole told her mother, who was then 99, of my award she said, "You can still get some good tunes out of an old fiddle." Thanks much, I thought. Thanks for the encouragement.

Now 81, and recalling this, I have pursued thinking further about age groups. The dictionary defined age as "no longer vigorous", "aged", "elderly", "past one's prime", "far advanced in years", "decrepit". Such is the concept that a friend has of Carole and me. I really shouldn't include Carole as a partner in this because she is five years younger than I. Well anyway, a close friend in the Westlake Church laughingly phoned us recently to say that a former member of our church inquired about us. She and her husband had moved away and were now back living in the area. I had performed their wedding some years earlier. She was told that we were now living in Pasadena in a retirement community for Presbyterian pastors, missionaries, and church educators. "How wonderful," she said, "perhaps we can have lunch with them sometime. Oh," she went on to ask, "Do you think they will let them out?" So much for preconceived ideas of retirement communities that include nursing care.

On the internet I received this definition of *Old*. It pictured an elderly lady sitting in a straight back chair. She was well groomed,

Using All the Colors

attired in her prettiest dress, looking straight ahead with a somewhat bewildered look on her face. The caption under it read, "Very quietly I confided to my husband on the eve of our 50th Anniversary, that I was having an affair. He turned to me and asked…'Are you having it catered'" And THAT, my friends IS the definition of 'OLD'!!!

After old comes older. With the awards, I was placed in the category of an Older American. The dictionary defines older as "elder", "senior", "more aged", "more ancient". When do we know we are getting older? The following may sound familiar to you.

- You're startled the first time you are called "old timer."
- Your children begin to look middle-aged.
- Dialing long distance wears you out.
- You get winded playing bridge.
- You sit in a rocking chair and can't get it going.
- You know all the answers but nobody asks you the questions.
- Your back goes out more than you do.
- The names in your little black book are all followed by M.D.
- You find that your mind makes promises that your body can't keep.
- You burn the midnight oil after 9:00 p.m.
- You walk with your head held high trying to get used to your bifocals.

The last superlative of old is oldest. This is defined as "most aged." That was Methusalah. He lived 969 years. Carole's mother is now 108. What the heck. At that rate I'm still a kid. Whatever, age is not only chronological. It's also a state of mind. It is true that as one becomes older, one is more limited physically and socially. A person's world becomes smaller. His/her space becomes more confined. Some people become depressed and wonder "What good am I?" They lose their sense of self-worth. They may say, "I'm not going to worry about it. I've put in my time. I've lived a good, full life. I'm content with things as they are." Such people resign themselves to a quiet, less active life. Others say, "I want to do more. However, I have my limitations, yes, but there are still things that I can do to stimulate my mind and body, things that will help me to feel better about myself, to be a more interesting person, and even be helpful to others."

Most of us who live at Monte Vista Grove are aware that there is a plaque above the doorway near the entrance to the Commons. It reads, "This building is dedicated to those men and women who preached the Gospel of Jesus Christ at home and abroad and have come here to rest." Although we are retired, many of us are still involved in a variety of ways such as:

Off campus:
- Serving as interim pastors in local churches
- Volunteering services at a local elementary school
- Singing in local church choirs and providing other leadership

On campus:
- Attending music, writing, memory, exercise, and art classes.
- Conducting worship services
- Visiting those in Assisted Living and Skilled Nursing Care
- Serving on various committees
- Volunteering to do service in a variety of ways; receptionist, librarian, night security, etc.

Presently, designs are being drawn for a new, more inviting main entrance to our beautiful grounds. The committee is suggesting that the sign not include the word "Homes" so that the name will read Monte Vista Grove. This change will better describe the mind and spirit of residents who reside here. Yes, MVG residents need rest, too, but it comes after doing satisfying, rewarding work. It all adds up to the joy and fun of living in this very special place we really do call "home."

Using All the Colors

The final superlative is oldest. Being the oldest of children in a family, oldest in a group, community, or world brings with it such things as greater responsibility, wisdom, notoriety, and even problems. The end of the matter is that whether being old, older, or oldest, you can still get some good tunes out of an old fiddle.

Never Give Up!
Aging with Enthusiasm, Hope, and a Spirit of Adventure
Jim Symons

"Jimmy boy, never give up!" Dad said these words to me as I faced boyhood challenges at school or in sports. Now that I am in the middle of my eighth decade, I still hear Dad's voice echoing in my ears as I confront the process of aging or the problems of the world.

I remembered Dad's words as I watched a Bill Moyers TV interview with retired Harvard Professor Sarah Lawrence-Lightfoot. They talked about her book *The Third Chapter: Passion, Risk and Adventure in the 25 Years After 50*. Lightfoot described the second chapter of life (age 25 to 50) as a time for fulfilling responsibilities such as child-rearing, defining career goals, and becoming productive for the good of society. She saw more freedom in the third chapter where we can discover and express our inner strengths with creativity, joy and risk. Building her thesis on classic formulations of life-stage development, particularly those of Erik Erikson, the author described a wide variety of models for people who feel burned out or dissatisfied. Lightfoot urged all of us to look forward to this time of emergence, entering into it with enthusiasm and hope instead of seeing ourselves as "over the hill" or "giving up" because we are so old.

Despite the helpful insights of Lawrence-Lightfoot's book, what is missing are remarkable stories of faith development pioneered by James Fowler and carried forward by Sharon Parks and Sam Keen. Here we find a focus on faith as trust that carries us through life stages, and there is a freedom from social norms and restraints as we continue to grow no matter what our age.

I just had my 76th birthday, and I believe we need to add a fourth chapter for all of us who are moving forward from 75 to

Using All the Colors

100. While we face declining physical energy and health, this can be the most fulfilling and significant time of our lives, IF WE SEE IT THIS WAY.

Each of our lives is a unique, unfolding story. Still there are common tasks and challenges that face us in each of these four chapters of life. In an individualistic society, the dynamic of authentic community can provide the setting where we can help each other move through them if we share our stories. Here is mine, starting with an early memory from my chapter one.

It was H. O. T. hot!! I felt stuffed into a sardine can as my family drove across the endless and boring spaces of eastern Montana. I was five years old, the youngest of four kids, and we were going from Seattle, where we lived, to Michigan to see Dad's relatives. It was early summer in 1939 on a boiling day. From the jump seat in our seven passenger 1936 Buick I could see the speedometer pointing to 60 miles per hour. "C'mon Dad, you can go faster than that," I said. Dad smiled, and I saw the needle climb to 70. "Faster, faster," all four of us kids shouted. I saw a worried look on Mom's face as the needle slowly wiggled its way to 80. "Faster, Dad, faster," we yelled. Dad's smile became a little grim, but we saw the speedometer reach 90. Clouds of dust billowed up from that Montana dirt road. Then, without any encouragement, Dad pushed it to 93. Suddenly, we heard a loud POP. Then we felt the car start to bounce. FLAT TIRE. It took forever to slow that massive Buick down. When we stopped, I said, "Pee–uuu. That stinks!" The smell of burning rubber is my clearest memory of that boiling day in the middle of nowhere. The first chapter of my life story was being on the road, pushing my Dad's buttons, and exploring new experiences.

When I was ten, I was Christopher Columbus in a radio play on Seattle's station K.I.R.O. It was called *The Boy with the Bright Red Hair*. In the story, the other kids ridiculed my hair and would not play with me because I was different. I became an explorer, making the most of being different. Columbus was on the road of discovery from the time he was a child—that's the road I wanted to be on.

But sometimes we have flat tires. At eighteen, I went from Seattle to Williams College, 3000 miles away in Massachusetts. In high school I won lots of glory with top grades, basketball captain, and editor of the school newspaper. In my first weeks at Williams I failed at everything I tried—classes, football team, fraternities and I could not even make it as a cub reporter for the college paper. Psssst. I felt the air rushing out of me—flat tire. But after a couple months I fixed the tire, figured out what I really wanted to do, and enjoyed four of the best years of my life. Going from inflation to deflation was the best thing that could happen to the cocky kid from Seattle who thought he knew everything.

In 1955 between my junior and senior years at college, I was struck by a moment of inspiration at Chartres Cathedral in France. I was curious about where inspiration comes from, not only in me but in others. What causes us to do what we do or to be who we are? My road trip took me to theological seminaries at Yale in Connecticut; St. Andrews University in Scotland; and San Francisco Theological Seminary in California. Suddenly, I was twenty-five and the first chapter of learning and preparation were over. It was time to start the second chapter of my life.

In one month in the summer of 1960, I celebrated my 26th birthday; graduated from seminary in Marin County, California; flew to Seattle for my exams for ordination as a Presbyterian minister; then flew to San Diego to marry a beautiful and intelligent seminary classmate, Marilyn Sperry. Our road trip took us across the country to Warren Wilson College in North Carolina for a teaching/ministry position. I discovered that no longer was I pushing Dad to go faster across Montana, but I was pushing myself to be productive... responsible... to make a difference.

That included being a husband and father, with two beautiful daughters followed by the adoption of two Korean sisters. Our family adventures included road trips all over the western

Using All the Colors

United States, and one epic journey in 1982 of over 6000 miles going east—north—west—and south to cover the country. All six of us were crammed like sardines in a VW campervan (sound familiar?) with no flat tires but three engine breakdowns along the way. We were checking out colleges for our teen age daughters, and I was reminded many times of my first cross country drive in 1939. Only now it was our four girls who were saying to me, "Faster, Dad, faster."

Our ministries in the Presbyterian Church took us from teaching in the mountains of North Carolina to an inter-racial congregation in Marin City, California; to starting an alternative church in Olympia, Washington; and to an urban ministry in Tucson, Arizona. In each of these situations, I felt a concern for people left out in our prosperous and powerful country. So my road trip took me to Selma, Alabama, to support Dr. Martin Luther King and voting rights for African-Americans; to help the Nisqually Native-Americans claim their treaty fishing rights in western Washington; and to the Mexican border to provide sanctuary for refugees from Central American wars in the 1980s.

The third chapter, age 50 to 75, was a time of passing the baton on to those who would follow on their road trips. That meant seeing our daughters through their education, first jobs, marriages, and having children of their own. Now we could watch our grandchildren push the buttons of their parents, just like Marilyn and I were pushed, just like I said to my Dad, "Faster, Dad, faster." And Marilyn and I could be there to encourage our grandchildren without having to take all the responsibility. We found more time to pay attention to our road trip. Like our 30th wedding anniversary—a white water raft trip on the Salmon River, riding a two person raft over a stage four rapids that dumped us in the drink and left us bruised and smiling. More fun!!!

At age 58 I began my last ministry before retirement. Instead of being the head of staff for a large congregation in Littleton, Colorado, I was asked to be a mentor for a bright and capable young minister twenty-five years younger than me. It turned out to be a great opportunity to use my experience in support of him, while at the same time I was free from the responsibilities of running a large organization so I could branch out to do new things I had always wanted to do. I organized an ecumenical and interfaith learning center, initiated a series of work projects in Europe and Central America, and created a corporation to address the challenges of the 21st Century called *Toward a Millennium of Compassion*. Marilyn and I invited others to join us in global discoveries, leading mission study trips to Hungary, China, Israel, Egypt, Jordan, New Zealand, western Europe, Canada, and Mexico. Sarah Lawrence-Lightfoot was right—the third chapter can be freeing and fun, creative and covering new ground.

Now my fourth chapter begins. Where will the ongoing road trip take me? In my dreams I want to:
1) climb Mt. Rainier in Washington State (I climbed the Matterhorn back in chapter one, so why not another major climb in chapter four?);
2) see the U.S. Tennis Open in New York; and
3) travel with Marilyn to new lands I have not seen—South America, Africa, and beyond.

As I face this chapter, I feel released from the need to make a name for myself, to live up to any prescribed expectations. There is time to reflect, to connect the dots for not only my own life, but for the people of the world. Faith development research defines a process of growing that leads to a deepening and broadening in every chapter and stage of life. We can become more "universalizing" (Fowler), seeking "knowing through trusting" (Berryman), becoming the "lover/fool" (Keen). Jimmy Carter is a good fourth chapter model for me, faithfully continuing to act and write with courage and compassion on behalf of needy people throughout the world.

Talking about the fourth chapter with friends in their seventies, eighties and nineties I notice several responses.

Using All the Colors

First, there is the attitude, "I have lived my life, made my contribution to my family and the world—it is time to let younger people step forward." Yes, it is time to pass the baton, but does that mean we should be content to sit in our rocking chairs on the front porch? There are always personal risks and adventures we can take wherever we are on our journey.

Second, I am met all the time by questions of health. "Jim, this is all fine for you to say because you still have your health." While recognizing the challenges we all face as we age, I am most encouraged by friends who struggle with cancer, stroke, heart disease, diabetes and who still find ways to see their lives as an adventure. A new friend in the retirement community where I live had a stroke shortly after moving here fifteen years ago. While severely limited in his physical mobility, he has blossomed as a nature photographer, internet blogger, and organizer of a writing class. This year he has begun a new avocation as an artist. He inspires me to be expectant and hopeful.

Jim and Marilyn on Mokoia Island, Lake Rotorua, New Zealand—January 2011

The Next Step

Here are three things I am going to do in my fourth chapter.
- Follow, as closely as I can, the route of Lewis and Clarke and the Corps of Discovery from St. Louis to Astoria, Oregon.
- Write a memoir that includes themes of compassion and faith development.
- Drive with my wife and grandchildren along the most famous road in America, Route 66, from Chicago to Santa Monica. This is about as close as I can come to zooming across eastern Montana on a boiling summer day in 1939.

So never give up, keep driving and enjoy the ride through every chapter of your life, including the flat tires.

Using All the Colors

About the Authors

Robert and Carole Bos:
　　We were raised in Michigan and met at Hope College. Bob has served five churches in Chicago and Southern California. Carole taught English and social studies in middle schools. We have been formulating a personal history book for our daughter and are pleased for the opportunity to add our six life stories to the kaleidoscope of colors for this book.

Thomas Bousman:
　　As a son of missionaries to the Philippines, Thomas Bousman and his family and entire community were interned by the Japanese in World War II, enduring excruciating deprivation as documented in a BBC documentary. They were finally liberated when he was just 16. He became a Presbyterian minister and served more than 40 years in Santa Paula, California.

Bruce Calkins:
　　<u>Then</u>: Inner-city Pastor in the Bronx, NYC.
Consultant to church institutions, boards, and Catholic religious communities.
Interim Pastor in PA, NJ, and CA.
　　<u>Now</u>: Looking for the next open door (and trying not to walk into the door.) Father of four, husband of one.
　　<u>Sometime</u>: Wondering, whether I can help start some new churches or other ministry units? Wondering if I can and will climb Mt. Wilson on my 90th birthday.
　　<u>Hobbies</u> (and things I did a few times and like to think of as hobbies. This is relevant to some of my stories.) Hiking, cracking a bull whip, tomahawk throwing, and knife throwing.
　　<u>Whenever</u>: Once when I was traveling, I went to bed with many thoughts and questions going through my mind. I gave the questions to God and went to sleep. As I awoke, before opening my eyes, these words were going through my head"
"Before there were any yesterdays, I knew you."

Using All the Colors

I repeated the words over and over with my eyes closed so I would not forget them. Then I thought, "That's about the back half of eternity; what about the eternity of the future?" As I lay still with my eyes closed, these words came:

"After there are no more tomorrows, I will hold you."

I repeated the words over and over, then opened my eyes and wrote them down. That was a gift given to me. Now I give it to you.

Charles Castles:

Charles and Shirley Castles recently moved to Monte Vista Grove after serving churches in Union Star, MO, Oklahoma City, OK, and Woodlake, CA. Their daughters Claire and Jhey now live in Los Angeles. A graduate of Rice University (Mechanical Engineering) and Fuller Theological Seminary, Charles served two years in the army (Korea) and ten years as a manager with Procter & Gamble (Ivory Soap) before seminary and his life in the Presbyterian Church(USA). He's playing his trumpet in three community bands, playing tennis with Jim Symons, hiking with Bruce Calkins and Gene Terpstra, and trying to catch up with the writing class.

Jessie Coates:

Jessie was born in Yorkshire, England. She and her husband David, served 10 years with another denomination as missionaries to Japan. David came to the States on a preaching tour in 1969 and shortly after that received an invitation to be the pastor/administrator of Teen Challenge, a church sponsored residential program for young people who had been severely addicted to drug abuse but turned to God for rescue. Jessie and David preached several times a week and taught Bible classes every week-day. Eventually Jessie met Presbyterian friends and she and David went to Seminary in order to qualify for consideration for ordained ministry. After Ordination, David and Jessie served separate pastorates in Missouri, Iowa & Chicago. David died in 2003 and Jessie enjoys life at Monte Vista Grove Homes.

About the Authors

Howard Den Hartog:

My wife, Esther, and I both graduated from Central College located in Pella, Iowa. Esther's father married us in the Pella Reformed Church near Panama, Nebraska in 1958. In 1971 I received a Master of Science degree from Forth Hays State University in Hays, Kansas. I have taught school in Iowa, Arizona, New Mexico, and Alabama. In 1964 we went as missionaries under the Board of Domestic Missions of the Presbyterian Church (USA) to Wasatch Academy in Mt. Pleasant, Utah where we served for twenty five years. We have four grown children who live in California, Utah, Oregon, and Washington.

Annabelle Dirks:

I grew up in Chicago, Illinois. My father was a lawyer and an aspiring politician, so I was introduced early on to the world of politics. I received my bachelor's degree from Millikin, a small Presbyterian college in southern Illinois. I taught school for a year in the small Illinois town where I met my future husband, J. Edward Dirks, a student pastor in the local church who was studying at McCormick Seminary. While he planned to transfer to Yale Divinity School, I was interested in nutrition and spent a year in a Philadelphia hospital internship to become a registered dietician. At the end of our training, we were married in NYC and lived there as we both pursued advanced degrees at Columbia University. During our New York years, I had the pleasure of working on the editorial staff of *Good Housekeeping* magazine. My husband was called to return to YDS as a Professor in Religion and Higher Education, and we went on to have a family of four children. In Connecticut, I returned to high school and community college teaching, and also spent some time working with a Christian college in India.

We eventually ended up at the University of California (Santa Cruz) where I had the opportunity to work in the field of nutrition in the local hospital. Fortunately, I've been able to travel to many parts of the world, which has broadened my horizons. After my husband's premature death, I continued working with senior outreach and church programs in Santa Cruz, before retiring and moving to Monte Vista in Pasadena.

Dick Dosker:

Dick Dosker was born in Rockville Centre, Long Island, New York in 1929. He graduated from Maryville College in Tennessee with a degree in history in 1951. Afterward, he attended Princeton Theological Seminary in New Jersey, graduating in 1955. He married Barbara Jensen Dosker and parented three children, Deanne (dec.), David, and Sandra. Dick served as Director of the Redwood Camp for children and youth at the Mount Hermon Camp & Conference Center in California from 1956-1989 and was the Parish Associate at the Felton Presbyterian Church from 1990-2001. He and Barbara moved to Monte Vista Grove Homes in Pasadena in 2001.

Art & Carolyn French:

Art French was born in China of Presbyterian missionary parents and lived there 10 years, receiving home-schooling until fifth grade. He graduated from Wooster college in 1953, then attended Princeton Seminary. At the end of two years he went to Kings Lake Camp in Alaska and then spent a year providing spiritual care to the Presbyterian Church in Wasilla and other communities along the Alaska railroad. Then he returned to finish his last year of seminary.

Carolyn was born in Ohio and raised in Oak Park, Illinois, the daughter of a Lutheran Pastor. She attended two years at Wooster College and then went into a nursing program at the University of Pennsylvania and received her Bachelor of Science in Nursing (BSN). She then worked for the Denver Colorado Public Health Nursing Service for five months, returning to Pennsylvania where she & Art married in June 1957, two weeks following his ordination.

Two weeks later they were on their way to the mission field on St. Lawrence Island, Alaska about 40 miles from Siberia where one could see the Siberian Mountains on a clear day. Carolyn was hired by the Alaskan Territorial Department of Health as the only medical person on the Island of two villages 60 miles apart. They remained 6 years and had two of their 3 children during that time. They were there "at the end of an era" during which travel was by dog team in winter and skin boat in summer along with plane service twice monthly (weather permitting, pilot willing), to only the western most village with a metal matting airstrip on which to land.

From there they went to Idyllwild, California Community Presbyterian Church in a mountain community for six years and then to the First Presbyterian Church of Gardena for 30 years prior to retirement at MVG.

Mary Froede:

I lived my young life and had my schooling in Wisconsin. Married, had two children and went off to seminary with my husband who ended up being a Presbyterian minister for 42 years until his death. Jim's first job was Assistant Pastor in Beverly Hills. Our 3rd child joined the family while we were there. I still operate a full time business manufacturing vinyl aprons and tablecloths for restaurants in the entire USA (Taco Bell for one).

I have written a book telling of my family's experiences serving a church in Tucumcari, New Mexico in the '50s. Had great fun singing the music of the 40's with big bands (one of which was the Stan Kenton revival band). I am 83 years old, have seven grandchildren and six great grandbabies. I have loved being here at Monte Vista Grove for my final years.

Sherman Fung:

A native of San Francisco, I was born in 1925. I was educated by the Chinatown public grade school, junior high school in the Italian district, Commerce High School near Automobile Row, University of California at Berkeley, Dubuque Theological Seminary (Iowa), Wheaton Graduate School of Theology (Illinois), Educational Media Department of Bowling Green State University (Ohio). I worked for San Francisco City and County Department of

Social Service; served overseas in Presbyterian Church, USA related projects as well as those of the Evangelical Church of Iran. Before retirement, I did audio visual services work at two higher education institutions in California. I've seen, heard, read, thought a lot, and talked about a lot of things over the decades. There are still a lot of gaps in knowledge, in understanding, and in opportunities and challenges to be filled. I'm hoping the next decade provides the time and space to do so.

Kenneth Grant:

Kenneth E. Grant (Ken) was born in Los Angeles, California and raised in nearby Glendale. After attending Occidental College and serving a stint in the U.S. Navy in WWII, Ken graduated from USC. He attended both Princeton and San Francisco seminaries and has served churches in California and the Mid West. He and his wife, Beverly, became residents of Monte Vista Homes in 1994. He continues to preach and teach in his retirement and enjoys writing and oil painting.

Ken is perhaps best known for his portrayal of an old "cow poke" named Cactus who has been "guest preacher" in churches where he has served and for various organizations.

Bill Hansen:

Bill is a native Californian who grew up on the beaches of Southern California. He was educated at Occidental College and San Francisco Theological Seminary. Bill is the husband of Mary Ellen to whom he has been married 60 years. He is a father, a grandfather, and a great grandfather. He served his first pastorate in Kansas and served the remainder of his ministry for 40 years with the Church of the Valley, Presbyterian in Apple Valley, California.

Don Hawthorne:

A native of Washington, D.C., Don graduated from Wheaton College and Princeton Seminary. He married a seminary classmate, Lee, and they have three married children. Don served a rural Iowa National Missions church, then organized a congregation in La Mirada, CA, followed by pastorates in Ontario and Goleta,

CA. He developed two seminars ("Prayer and the Healing of Memories," and "Learning the Way of Forgiveness") which he offered in numerous churches over 25 years. He and his wife moved to Monte Vista Grove in 1993.

Robert and Hedwig Lodwick:

Robert (Bob) and Hedwig (Hedy) were employed by the Presbyterian Church (USA) in their overseas missions. They were Fraternal Workers with the French Reformed Church (1953-1958) and Mission Co-Workers in Egypt with the Coptic Evangelical Church (1961 - 1964). From 1964 - 1978, they lived in New Jersey while Bob was Program Director for Education, responsible for the church's schools and colleges on 6 continents. During this time, Hedy taught pre-school. From 1978 - 1993 they represented the Presbyterian Church (USA) in Europe, with headquarters in Geneva, Switzerland. Bob was the Presbyterian Area Representative and Hedy worked extensively with Swiss and European Christian Women.

Laura Berthold Monteros:

I am a writer. I once read that if one really wants to become a professional writer, she should not say things like, "I want to be a writer" or "I'm trying to write." So I am a writer and have been since I was a child. I've been a student, a journalist, a stay-at-home mother, and an administrative assistant. I'm currently an unemployed worker. I've authored about a dozen (unpublished) picture books and countless stories for online publications that pay very little.

My most satisfying writing, though, is for the class at Monte Vista Grove. There I can write essays, reminiscences, rants. I can share what I write with people who have been all over the world or stayed in Southern California, who have spent decade upon decade serving others, who have had experiences that I would never imagine. They inspire me to write, and they bless me by sharing their lives in their writings.

Rosemary Pierson:

A native Californian, I grew up in beautiful San Luis Obispo. While a student at UC Berkley, I met Paul Pierson. After marriage we spent seventeen years as Presbyterian missionaries in Brazil and Portugal, followed by a pastorate in Fresno, Ca. In 1980 we moved to Pasadena where Paul served as Dean and professor at Fuller Theological Seminary. Our daughter, three sons, their spouses, and nine grandchildren bring us great joy.

Jim Symons:

Jim Symons grew up in Seattle, then went 3000 miles to Williams College in western Massachusetts. After attending seminary at Yale and St. Andrews, Scotland, he graduated from San Francisco Theological Seminary in 1960. That same year Jim married classmate Marilyn Sperry, and their ministries included Warren Wilson College (Swannanoa, NC), St. Andrews Presbyterian Church (Marin County, CA), Community for Christian Celebration (Olympia, WA), First Christian Church (Tucson, AZ), and Columbine United Church (Littleton, CO). After retirement in 1999, Jim and Marilyn led international study groups to Palestine, Egypt, Jordan, Western Europe, New Zealand, Canada and Mexico. They have done short term interims in Colorado, Texas, Australia, and nine ministries in what has become their second home in New Zealand. Jim and Marilyn have four daughters and eight grandchildren.

Gene Terpstra:

Writing has always intrigued me. First, it was others' writings. I was an English major. The great works of literature that were requirements quickly became revelatory. Then as an English teacher, it was teaching literature, and teaching students to write thoughtfully and coherently. Then as a pastor, I was occupied with the writings of scripture, along with the newspapers and books of contemporary life. Pastoral work also involved a lot of writing for me: weekly sermons, newsletter articles, pastoral letters and notes.

This writing was all focused on others. It needed to be caring, not only clear and coherent.

Now that I'm retired, writing has a new focus: my own life. Never having kept a diary or journal, I found the life-story writing class a new experience. It has been the occasion to recall, and record, persons and events that have done so much to enrich my "story" and to shape the person I have become.

Jacquie Terpstra:

I've been blessed with a good memory of events in my life, *as I remember them.* (There is a difference.) Now that I am retired and have time to reflect on my life, I have discovered that there is a certain sadness that comes with remembering even the happiest of times. This is the sadness of recalling the people and places of my childhood that can no longer be visited, touched or engaged. Writing my personal history has enabled me not only to honor and celebrate these experiences, but also to dispel the grief of knowing that even the best of times cannot be repeated. Even so, writing my memories has helped me recognize and embrace the loving people who nurtured my life. For this I am very grateful.

Norman E. Thomas

Norm joined the MVGH community in December 2006 after marriage to Grove resident Mae Gautier. A native of New Hampshire, he graduated from Yale University with A.B. and M. Div. degrees, and Boston University with a Ph.D. in Social Ethics and Sociology of Religion. An ordained United Methodist minister, Norm served as a pastor in Portland, Oregon, and as a missionary for fifteen years in Southern Africa (Rhodesia, now Zimbabwe, and Zambia). Later he taught missions, evangelism and church renewal, ecumenics, and world religions successively at Boston University and United Theological Seminary (Dayton, Ohio). Norm is the father of eight children (including four foster children from Zimbabwe), and grandfather of 26 with 3 great-grandchildren. He has authored and edited fourteen books and numerous articles on missions.

Using All the Colors

Dorothy Turnbull:

Dorothy Turnbull served as a missionary/wife/mother/teacher in Egypt for 15 years and then in Thailand for 20+ years. Having been raised on a working dairy farm, she used her abilities to help her husband establish agricultural improvements in each country. She is a Bell Choir enthusiast.

Roberta Woodberry:

Born and raised in the Midwest, our family finally settled in St. Paul, Minnesota where my Dad (Dr. Bob Smith) taught at Bethel College. I was the eldest of five children. We were privileged to spend our summers traveling all over the United States and then internationally accompanying my Dad, who was a well-known preacher and teacher.

My Mom. a teacher and musician, made a loving home for us all--even as we travelled and eventually spent time overseas. Mom taught me piano and voice from the time I could barely reach the keyboard and I intended to follow that path. But during my junior year in college, our family moved to Lebanon where my Dad was teaching. It was during that time that I sensed the Lord's calling to serve Him in the Middle East and I switched my major to elementary education, but have continued to use my music.

It was in Beirut that I met Dudley. After finishing graduate school we served together in Pakistan, Afghanistan, Saudi Arabia, Michigan and California.

We were blessed with three sons. As a stay-at-home Mom for 20 years, I was able to still teach, direct adult and children's choirs at church and school and provide a home for my family in some difficult places.

With two of our sons in college, I began teaching full-time again at Pasadena Christian School and then at Valentine School in San Marino. Subsequently I taught in Peshawar, Pakistan. (We were there on 9/11) and in Kabul, Afghanistan.

In 2011, Dudley and I moved from our home in Altadena to Monte Vista Grove Homes.

Made in the USA
Charleston, SC
08 November 2011